BLOWING THE WHISTLE

BLOWING THE WHISTLE

IAN BENT, RICHARD McILROY,
KEVIN MOUSLEY AND PETER WALSH

By the same authors
Football Confidential

First published 2001
© Ian Bent, Richard McIlroy, Kevin Mousley and Peter Walsh 2001
The moral right of the authors has been asserted

ISBN 0 563 53410 9

Published by BBC Worldwide Limited,
Woodlands, 80 Wood Lane, London W12 0TT

Commissioning Editor: Ben Dunn
Cover Artwork: Peacock design

Printed and bound in Great Britain by Mackays of Chatham
Cover printed by Belmont Press Limited, Northampton

CONTENTS

FOREWORD

Click-click.

Pause.

Groan.

The email icon has popped up simultaneously in the bottom right-hand corner of every computer screen in the BBC's *On The Line* office. It's another sports trivia question hopping its way around the nation. You know the type: What cricket club, with 81 members, does every English player want to join, and then immediately want to leave? What, in sport, is a Condor? Which is the only football league club in England and Scotland not to contain any of the letters MACKEREL in its name?

Take it for granted that no licence-fee money is ever frittered away as publicly-funded journalists put their feet up and discuss these hoary conundrums. Nor do we ever use BBC computers to forward these gems to our friends. Perish the thought.

Enough of this frippery: *On The Line* exists to ask difficult questions. As BBC Radio 5 Live's long-running investigative sports programme, our aim is to discover who the people are that run the sports we play and watch. Do they wear blazers, lab coats, tracksuits or city suits? What are their methods and motives? Why do so many of them (with a few notably wonderful exceptions) make such a mess of the job? Who do they answer to? Above all, where does the money go?

In this book you will find 18 stories which answer those questions. Each chapter stems from the detailed research that underpins an edition of *On The Line*. Every report has been updated and revised for this collection, each chosen from more than a hundred programmes. Within these pages are tales of corruption, prostitution, violence, murder, bribery, wire-tapping, arson, ignorance, arrogance and incompetence. Whereas our previous book, *Football Confidential*, found many of these vices in soccer, the chapters of this book reveal the confidential side of golf, athletics, rugby league, rugby union, horse racing, boxing, cricket, hockey, greyhound racing and even bowls and chess.

All these sports are, of course, blessed with virtues like bravery, dedication, glory and skill. Such qualities are rightly celebrated with vigour, and nowhere more so than on Radio 5 Live, but it is the job of *On The Line* to look beyond the heroes and call to account the puppet masters who skulk within the corridors of power.

Increasingly, these people are taking control of the media. No sports body is complete without a press officer to promote news stories favourable to the bosses and suppress any leaks which might cast the masters in a bad light. Sports clubs, companies and committees have their own flattering websites and magazines, as well as a coterie of tame reporters in the national media who eagerly churn out the information presented to them. As the rulers of the richer sports become more aware of their value in the broadcast market place they readily make it known that, as well as blanket coverage from their media partners, they expect a sympathetic tone from the reporters. All these developments mean that the people who control sports are increasingly able to conceal their embarrassments and massage their message.

But the spin doctors and propagandists are operating at a time when sport should be more accountable than ever. Sport England, the biggest of the sports councils in the UK, has put more than a billion pounds into the trust of sports administrators over the past four years. For every lottery ticket sold, nearly four pence goes to sport. Millions more are pumped into schemes such as the Commonwealth and Olympic Games, for which Manchester has received £147 million in grants just to make the bids; the rebuilding of Wembley at a cost of £640 million; the fiasco of a National Academy of Sport, the full cost of which is detailed in Chapter Three. Other sports are funded through council taxes at local level and still more get their money direct from the exchequer. Sport is generously bankrolled from the public purse and the people who pay the piper (through paying taxes and buying lottery tickets) have a right to call the tune and to know if the piper is up to the job.

A good example is the Football Trust. Set up to help pay for the changes to soccer grounds called for in the Taylor Report in order to prevent another Hillsborough, the trust gave around £400 million to clubs. Looked at one way, this is a laudable use of public funds to keep all of us safe at soccer. Looked at another way, it is pots full of public money given to a selection of companies so that they can boost the asset value of their stadiums and increase their takings on the gate.

This critical approach tends to split sportspeople into two clear camps: those who hate *On The Line* and those who love it. For every person who accuses us of 'lying through our rotting, rotten teeth,' (a north-east newspaper reporter) there's someone telling us, 'If it wasn't for your work we'd never have got rid of the corrupt men at the top of our sport,' (a senior official in one of our major sports). The vociferous contributions of each of these groups give equal satisfaction to those of us who work on the investigations. You can't rattle cages without frightening the exhibits into kicking up a stink.

By the end of this book you will decide for yourself which camp to join. You will also know the arsonist's favourite sport, the pharmacist's favourite cricketers, the place where sports fans cheer with glee as a man is choked unconscious and why two men called Fuzzy Wuzzy and the Fat Man have been giving turkey to a former homicide detective.

Ian Bent, Richard McIlroy, Kevin Mousley and Peter Walsh.
March, 2001

10

Trivia answers:

Every player wants to join, and then leave, the one-cap wonders club – living members are Joey Benjamin, Mark Benson, Dennis Brookes, Simon Brown, Alec Coxon, Gavin Hamilton, Ryan Sidebottom, Andy Lloyd, Charles Palmer, Ken Palmer, Paul Parker, Tony Pigott, Dick Richardson, Arnie Sidebottom, Mike Smith, John Stephenson, Alan Wells, James Whitaker and Neil Williams. (Correct at time of going to press.)

A Condor is the name given to a hole in one at a par five. Only ever performed once, by Shaun Lynch, who holed his tee shot on the 497-yard seventeenth at Teign Valley Golf Club in Devon in July 1995. His club was invited by the Royal & Ancient to come up with a name for the unprecedented feat.

You'll find no MACKERELs in Swindon Town.

Fuzzy Wuzzy, the Fat Man and the Christmas Turkey
Undercover Revelations of Corruption in World Championship Boxing

The boss of the International Boxing Federation, one of the three most powerful bodies in world boxing, had a rule. You don't bring the enemy into your house. Especially if you run an empire built on bribery, corruption and greed.

As 67-year-old Robert W. Lee sits in his New Jersey prison cell he knows in his heart that he got off lightly. That's if he has a heart. Twenty-two months in jail is not much for betraying a sport; not much to show for a four-year, multi-million-dollar investigation; not much considering the overwhelming weight of evidence against him. If there is one good thing to come out of the probe into the International Boxing Federation (IBF), it is that Lee, its former president, has agreed to a lifetime ban from boxing when he leaves prison.

In February 2001 Lee was jailed for just under two years and fined $25,000 for money laundering and tax evasion. He also agreed to pay the IBF $50,000 in compensation. Yet it could have been so much worse for the boss of one of the world's major sanctioning bodies. He had faced up to seven years in prison when charged with 33 offences including racketeering. Fellow defendants included his son, Robert Junior, and two IBF officials, Donald 'Bill' Brennan and Francisco Fernandez (Brennan would be excused from trial because of ill health, while Fernandez remains a fugitive in his native Colombia).

The evidence seemed insurmountable: covert videotapes showing cash pay-offs, recordings of telephone discussions about kickbacks and rigged ratings; first-person testimony from a string of witnesses attesting that promoters paid graft to boost their boxers; damning admissions from top promoters; incriminating cheque stubs and bank statements. Yet on the afternoon of 17 August 2000 jurors concluded that Lee, a balding man with wire-rimmed glasses, was not a racketeer. Besides acquitting him of the main charge, the jury found him not guilty of conspiracy, mail fraud and wire fraud. It convicted him of conspiracy to launder money, interstate travel in aid of racketeering and filing false tax returns. His son was acquitted on all charges. After weeks of testimony and 15 days of deliberations, the trial was over. Where, many are still asking, does this leave boxing?

As a black detective on the streets of New Jersey, Bob Lee saw plenty. He perfected the poker face of the city cop and developed a world-weary view of life. Nothing upset him, nothing excited him, nothing surprised him. His phlegmatic demeanour would serve him well in the venal world of professional boxing. Lee was born on 21 November 1933, in Scotch Plains, New Jersey. He boxed briefly as an amateur and served in the army before pursuing a career as a police officer. In 1977 Lee began regulating boxing full-time under the state athletic commissioner, Jersey Joe Walcott, the former world heavyweight champion.

It was good timing. The transformation of the faded seaside resort of Atlantic City into a Las Vegas-style gambling centre was fuelling a boom in New Jersey boxing.

In the 1950s the sport in America had undergone a government purge to root out the pervasive influence of *La Cosa Nostra* – the US mafia. Jail terms were dished out to such colourful characters as Frankie 'Mr Grey' Carbo and 'Blinky' Palermo. But while the domestic sport was left cleaner and healthier, the governance of world boxing remained open to abuse.

From the 1960s onwards it was run by two bodies, the World Boxing Council (WBC) and the World Boxing Association (WBA). Both were dominated by Latin Americans. They controlled the titles and determined who could challenge for them. It didn't matter how good you were, if you defied the so-called Alphabet Boys, you would never be champ. If you were not in their rankings, you could not compete for a title. The ratings became all-important. With such power came allegations of abuse.

Bob Lee became a senior official in the WBA, and in 1982 challenged its Venezuelan president, Gilberto Mendoza, in an election at a convention in Puerto Rico. Lee failed and decided to defect, 'Some of our members returned to the US and decided they wanted to form an international branch and be on the worldwide stage. We sought to try to offer more opportunities for some of the young fighters coming up,' he says. He formed the IBF, based in the US, and vowed to run a clean ship, free from corruption and with 'fair and above-board' ratings. The IBF gained credibility by crowning middleweight Marvin Hagler as its first champ, and giving a belt to Larry Holmes.

But with Lee came baggage. Throughout this formative period he was still working for the New Jersey Boxing Commission, and in August 1984 the state's ethics panel charged him with soliciting money from promoters and casinos. He was suspended for six months and fined $600. Lee resigned and turned his full attention to the IBF.

Despite Lee's dubious past, his new organization thrived, even as complaints about its methods began to mount. Charles Jay is a former fight manager and matchmaker who now runs TotalAction, a sports website. 'Back in about 1986 when I was working for a promoter in Tampa, Florida, we had put together a tournament that we were going to attach Muhammad Ali's name to,' recalls Jay. 'We sought a world rating for the winner of this tournament. The IBF was approached and it came out later in the wash that Bob Lee had asked that in return for granting a top-five rating to the winner of our tournament, a donation be made to the "educational fund". Up 'till then I guess I was a little bit naïve because the IBF had presented itself as being the alternative to the WBC and WBA. It was amusing to find they were just like everybody else.' Jay never did find out what the IBF educational fund was for.

In the early 1990s the US Senate began holding a new series of hearings into boxing. These came to focus on what one member called 'anti-competitive behaviour and monopolistic and exploitative practices which hurt boxers and undermine the sport'. They didn't have to look far, according to Paul Feeney, who was counsel on the US Senate commerce committee: 'The rating system is pretty much a bad joke. One of the best ways you can move into the top ten and get a title shot is not to be a very talented or outstanding boxer but to sign with the right promoter who then is able to manipulate the system in collusion with the sanctioning organization officials.'

The break investigators needed came in 1995. Heavyweight boxer Michael Moorer had lost his IBF world title to George Foreman by a shock knockout. Moorer had a right to expect an early rematch, but was furious when a relatively unthreatening South African, Francois Botha, was elevated above him in the rankings. On the advice of his lawyer, Patrick English, Moorer sued for commercial bribery, tortuous interference and breach of contract. 'There was evidence that other boxers were being elevated above him due to an "unholy alliance" between certain members of the IBF, certain officers of the IBF and [promoter] Don King,' said English. 'Allegations had reached us that money had changed hands.' The IBF caved in and settled out of court. Moorer was given the ranking he deserved and eventually regained the championship.

A possible reason for the favouritism shown to Botha – who was also let off lightly after testing positive for steroids and who would go on to challenge Lennox Lewis for the world title – emerged in a sworn statement made to investigators by his promoter, Ronald Weathers. He had, he said, been paying off the IBF: 'In October 1992 I agreed with Robert W. Lee Snr to pay $10,000 in order to get heavyweight boxer Francois Botha rated in the heavyweight division of the IBF. After reaching that agreement, $10,000 was withdrawn from one of my business accounts. My employee Elbert "Duke" Durden delivered the money in cash to Robert W. Lee Jnr. After the pay-off was made, the IBF rated Francois Botha ninth in the heavyweight division in November 1992.'

The IBF rankings were nominally under the control of Doug Beavers, its ratings chairman, a shambling bear of a man who had served with distinction in the US Navy. His job was to keep tabs on fight results around the world and to draft the rankings every month to reflect who had won and who had lost. According to the IBF's own constitution, it was a job governed by strict rules:

The International Ratings will be published every month and will reflect the latest activity of all the boxers therein ... All of the boxers in the ratings will be advanced or demoted according to wins and losses; at all times taking into account the calibre of the opponents and the method of winning or losing.

In fact, the final say rested not with Beavers but with Bob Lee, who would often make changes without reference to anyone else. Beavers would later testify that pay-offs were accepted from promoters and managers, while those who did not cough up would see their fighters demoted.

Often deals were done at the IBF convention, held each year in a different city. All of the major sanctioning bodies stage such conventions, where boxers, managers, promoters and TV executives mingle with officials in an atmosphere akin to a Turkish bazaar. Everyone has an eye for the main chance. Panos Eliades, the wealthy London accountant who, until their recent split, was the power behind heavyweight champion Lennox Lewis, says promoters are solicited for contributions towards the cost of the conventions.

'We always pay for conventions,' he admits. 'They get other promoters to pay for meals because everyone goes, there may be three or four hundred people there, and they fear if they don't do the right thing they may not be treated the right way. So we've all got in the back of our minds that if we don't do what we're supposed to do we could be punished. And these organizations are very powerful because they're the ones that hold the belts.'

The flamboyant American promoter Butch Lewis concurs with Eliades's view, though he sees little wrong with this system of horse-trading: 'We have special interest groups who lobby our government every day and I've said in terms of the conventions I will put ads in the books, sponsor a cocktail party and I'm lobbying for my boxers and myself to be in the mix and that's just a fact of life. That's the way our government works. But all of a sudden they say those rules should not apply in boxing, there's something wrong with that.'

Not surprisingly, Bob Lee sees no conflict of interest in promoters and managers shelling out for the conventions of the bodies that run the sport. 'Every one of the promoters that support us at the annual convention are members of the organization,' he says. 'The promoters have done well in supporting us with coffee mornings and cocktail parties and this has been done through their own approval. We haven't gone out and hit them over the head and said, "Please support us." They have asked, "Can I do anything for the convention?" Sure. They would like the opportunity to be seen and heard at the convention and that's the reason that they support us.'

The IBF was due to hold its 1997 jamboree in San Antonio, Texas. On the eve of the event, Doug Beavers was gardening at his house in Portsmouth, Virginia, when he received an unexpected visit. Two agents from the Federal Bureau of Investigation said they wanted to talk to him about corruption in boxing. 'What took you so long?' said Beavers. The agents said they had evidence that bribes had been paid for ratings. Beavers was prepared to talk but wanted immunity to avoid jail. Once this was granted, he sang like a jaybird, recounting a scarcely credible story of routine bribery and corruption. He also consented to secretly record his regular conversations with Lee and others and to wear a 'wire' strapped to his ample body. He would make more than 200 tapes over the next 18 months.

One of the earliest recordings revealed Lee telling Beavers how new recruits should be brought in. They discussed asking for $50,000.

> DB: But 50 sounds reasonable to you, right?
> RL: Yeah, except ... if you want in, we'll show you how to get in.
> DB: Yeah.
> RL: I mean you got to come up ... and you gotta run the game the way we tell you to run it ... But if you

don't wanna do like we're directing you to do, then maybe you oughta go deal with somebody else.

DB: Gotta be quiet.

RL: You cannot tell anybody that we helped you out. All you do is you deal with me direct, one on one. We do what we have to do and get it done but don't go to other people in boxing. Because news travels fast.

DB: Yeah.

RL: And if it travels and they find out that we're helping you, then that's gonna cut off our ability to help you.

One of the most active conduits for pay-offs was Pancho Fernandez, the IBF's South American representative. He brought money from the likes of Colombian promoter Billy Chams, on one occasion flying in with $10,000. Beavers and Fernandez discussed further payments and what Chams would want in return.

PF: Billy [Chams] wants to know what we can do, because you know we never have a chance to have our boxer at the top of the rating.

DB: Right. With Pineda [a Chams boxer]?

PF: Pineda.

DB: You talk to Bob Lee about it?

PF: Well, he said to talk to you.

DB: Well, did he say you to bring something?

PF: Yeah, I gonna take you something ... How much you think?

DB: I don't know. What do you think Billy Chams will give?

PF: Let me see. Ten.

DB: OK, for Pineda, we move Pineda ... I think we can put him right behind Whitaker if Billy Chams sends us something good.

PF: Yeah, yeah, something good.

DB: OK, you want me to talk to Bob Lee and ...

PF: Yeah, and talk with Bobby and call me.

>DB: And say ten thousand?
>PF: Ten thousand?
>DB: OK, for Pineda.

The man who was most influential with the IBF was Don King, the world's biggest promoter and a controversial figure who many believe was the true target of the FBI probe, though he would escape without charge. Lee and Beavers codenamed him 'Fuzz', 'Fuzzy Wuzzy' or 'Cuzz' and referred to his pay-offs as 'turkey', 'stuffing' and 'ginseng'.

>DB: Well, how about Fuzzy Wuzzy? Is he gonna pass out some turkeys?
>RL: Well, he was, ah, the day before Thanksgiving so I have to talk to him.
>DB: Alright.
>RL: See what?
>DB: Yeah, Christmas turkey be nice.
>RL: Ooh! Tell me about it.
>DB: Yeah.
>RL: It ain't the turkey, it's the dressing, brother!
>DB: That's right! That's right! Get the stuffing! Damn the turkey!

The stuffing duly arrived. Beavers received his $4,000 share in the mail. He phoned Lee – from an FBI office – to say the money had arrived. The call was placed to Lee's office in East Orange, New Jersey.

>RL: Hey Beavers.
>DB: My man!
>RL: How you?
>DB: Better since Federal Express got here.
>RL: Oh, you're on the ball, huh?
>DB: Yes ... Hey, was that from Fuzzy Wuzzy?
>RL: Yup.
>DB: Was that the turkey? Hey, the turkey's good.

Beavers used what he called his 'magic pencil' to change the ratings list. He spent about 30 hours rating boxers each month before he and Lee fixed the final list. He said he often gave his boss cash at hotels in Virginia, where he also arranged for hookers to visit Lee. But Beavers told the FBI that the IBF conventions, where promoters and managers lobbied for better rankings, were the real bazaars of bribery. Beavers and Lee also used a coded list in which the names of certain boxers represented dollar amounts, so they wouldn't have to mention figures over the phone. Each had a copy of a list with boxers' names and numbers next to them, signifying the amount each one stood for: for example, 'Alexander Zolkin, Larry Barnes, Tony Martin, Darryl Tyson, and Ross Hale' meant $10,000.

Lee was very cagey. Though the hours of secret recordings mounted up, he rarely dropped his guard in conversation. He even had some advice for Beavers: 'I remember Ramone Jordan from down in Puerto Rico told me years ago, you never bring the enemy into your house. And that's the truth. You don't bring the enemy into your house.' But it was already too late.

For the investigators, one of most dramatic moments of their hours of video and audiotape came when Beavers met Lee in a room at a Holiday Inn on 18 December 1997 to hand over a portion of a Pancho Fernandez pay-off – with FBI consent. A hidden camera caught Beavers taking the wad of cash from inside his sock. He unstrapped it from cellophane on his leg while Lee talked on the phone to his daughter, Cheryl, who was ill in hospital.

'Christmas cheer,' Beavers said, handing the cash to Lee. It would become one of the most powerful images of the entire IBF case.

'How much is this?' Lee asked.

'This is five thousand,' Beavers said. 'We got twenty-five hundred apiece. We got ten thousand total.'

'Five grand for me and Rob, for Robby [his son]?'

'Twenty-five for you and twenty-five for Robby,' confirmed Beavers.

The Feds continued to amass evidence and by 21 October

1998 prosecutors decided to shut down the operation. Beavers, who had agreed to meet Bill Brennan and Lee in the Portsmouth Holiday Inn, brought a $1,000 pay-off for the Lees to split. As the secret camera rolled, he again pulled the cash from his sock. Moments later, Lee handed envelopes to Beavers and Brennan. Inside Beavers's envelope was $4,000 in cash.

'What's this? Turkey?' Beavers said.

'Big daddy, a little turkey,' said Lee.

'This from Fuzz?' asked Beavers.

'From who?' interjected Brennan.

'Fuzzy?'

Lee nodded.

'How was big daddy's big day?' asked Brennan.

'It was very good,' Lee said. 'That's for you.' After some chitchat, Brennan and Beavers left. Then Lee heard a knock at the door. It was the FBI.

If the FBI probe needed any extra impetus to make a case, it came in March 1999 when Lennox Lewis was robbed in a title unification fight against Evander Holyfield. The bout was declared a draw despite Lewis's clear superiority. Five separate investigations were launched into the affair and the mood was summed up in a letter written to the US Senate committee by no less a figure than Muhammad Ali. 'The Greatest' pulled no punches: 'What occurred will surely go down as the biggest fix in fight history. Professional boxers have for too long been the target of unscrupulous managers and promoters. The sanctioning organizations that award the title belts have joined the list of abusers. I pray justice will be done and somehow along the way honour can be restored to this sport.'

At the same time prosecutors began presenting witnesses to a grand jury in Newark in the IBF case. George Foreman testified in April 1999 for an hour. He later told reporters he had never paid a bribe. Eugenia Williams, the IBF judge who had ruled Holyfield the winner in his controversial clash with Lennox Lewis – and whose expenses were paid by Don King, Holyfield's promoter – also gave testimony. Her lawyer denied she did anything improper or was offered anything for her decision.

In June FBI agents executed search warrants at Don King's office in Florida. Agents carted away hundreds of boxes of documents. Speculation grew that King, who had already beaten two federal trials, would be indicted again. Yet he wasn't.

Against this backdrop of impending indictment, Bob Lee gave a rare interview to *On The Line*. He firmly denied ever accepting kickbacks and saw the reasons for his troubles as part of a racist conspiracy: 'Well, I think one of the major reasons is I'm an African-American. They give the white guys immunity, they indict the African-Americans.' By 'the white guys' he was referring to people like Beavers, who he now knew to have betrayed him, and also promoters like Bob Arum and Cedric Kushner, who had made statements in return for immunity from prosecution.

Lee saw himself as victim, not villain, and railed against the very boxers whose interest he was supposed to uphold: 'Everybody thinks that the fighter is mistreated. Maybe they ought to take an honest-to-goodness look at some of the manner in which these fighters function when they sign a contract and then fail to live up to it, where they're supposed to be present at a weigh-in and they haven't trained to fight for a title. Or when these fighters decide that they want to take off on a hiatus and never show up again. They don't realize the money that they cost the manager and the promoter by doing some of the things that they do. And everybody thinks that they're being mistreated. Well, some of them are. But a lot of them are not.'

Despite his problems, Bob Lee remained upbeat. When asked if he expected to be indicted, he laughed: 'Listen, I hope not. That's a tough question but I tell you I hope not. I don't think that I've done anything to be indicted for. But there's one thing for sure, indictment is only the charge and then they have to prove what they're talking about.' On one point he was adamant. The former police officer said he would never testify against other people: 'No. I'm not a snitch, I'm not a rat.'

At the time of that interview Lee had still not been charged. But it did not take much longer. A few weeks later he was arrested at his home in Fanwood, New Jersey. His son, Robert Junior, who had a crack cocaine habit, was also picked up. Outside the court-house at his arrangement, Lee Snr told reporters he was 'inno-cent of these outrageous charges'. He took a leave of absence from the IBF to fight his case, and the court appointed an impar-tial monitor to oversee the organization.

A main plank of the defence became apparent even before the trial began – race. 'One can legitimately ask why the IBF, the only professional sports body dominated by African-Americans, was selected for this prosecution,' Lee's attorney, Gerald Krovatin, told reporters. Two of the twelve jurors finally chosen were black.

On 11 April 2000 federal prosecutor José Sierra opened the trial. He said boxers were the real victims of IBF corruption and said that Lee 'placed himself in a position to corrupt the IBF, to demand and accept bribes'. Sierra outlined many bribes, includ-ing a $100,000 payment by promoter Bob Arum in 1995 to get George Foreman a special exception to defend his heavyweight championship against unranked Axel Schulz. Sierra said Arum had agreed to pay another $100,000 but demurred when he learned that Foreman gave promoter Butch Lewis $250,000 to lobby the IBF. He also said the tapes showed Don King's domi-nant role.

Krovatin, one of New Jersey's top defence attorneys, attacked the charges in relaxed, conversational tones. He wanted the jurors to question the motives of witnesses, knowing that few of those testifying would be squeaky-clean themselves. 'Just because somebody calls it a bribe doesn't make it a bribe,' he said. He made out that this was just the way things were done in the big bad business of boxing and said cable television networks held the real power and didn't want the IBF to force champions into title fights against mandatory challengers. The networks wanted to pick marquee names like Mike Tyson and Oscar de la Hoya, who were not mandatory challengers in the IBF rankings but who would pull in big audiences.

In particular, Krovatin attacked Doug Beavers. Lee had given Beavers a job and lent him money. 'What did Lee get in return from Beavers?' asked Krovatin. 'He hated him. Resented the man. Not to his face.'

Beavers's chance to respond came when he took the witness stand. He testified that he took his first bribe, of $500, from Lee in 1985. Why? 'Greed, I guess,' he said. He added that if he had refused the bribes, Lee wouldn't have trusted him as ratings chairman. He took dozens of payments over the next 13 years. Beavers said he routinely collected bribes from promoter Cedric Kushner, beginning in the late 1980s when Kushner contested an IBF ratings ban imposed on South African boxers as a protest against apartheid. Kushner paid $10,000 to end the ban, Beavers said. After that, Beavers visited Kushner three or four times a year to pick up bribes so that Kushner 'was allowed to do IBF title fights without being harassed'.

Beavers said his biggest shakedown came after George Foreman beat Axel Schulz in April 1995 to retain the IBF heavyweight title. Kushner and Swiss businessman Wilfried Sauerland backed Schulz, and they wanted a rematch. Beavers said Lee told him to demand $100,000. 'Kushner thought I was joking at first, but I told him no, this was serious, serious business,' Beavers said. Kushner agreed to pay and Beavers arranged to collect after the IBF convention. He said Kushner gave him four packs of $25,000 because he knew he would split it with Bill Brennan, Lee and Robert Jnr. This bribe made Beavers uneasy. 'I thought it was a real travesty,' he said. 'I didn't think he should have to pay either but I also was a realist. I knew that was the only way he was going to get the rematch.' Yet despite the payment, the rematch never took place.

Gerald Krovatin went straight on the offensive.

'Mr Beavers, do you tell lies?'

'If there's a reason,' said Beavers. It was a poor start for the key prosecution witness.

Another important man for the prosecution was Colombian boxing manager Ivan Feris. He recounted paying 19 bribes. But under pressure from Krovatin, he came across as petulant, erratic and slightly odd. He likened the IBF to the mafia and referred to Lee as 'Don Vito Corleone'.

Bob Arum was far more impressive. As the only serious rival to Don King as boxing's most powerful promoter of the 1980s,

Arum spoke with authority and biting wit. He described the millions of dollars he had made promoting the likes of Muhammad Ali and Sugar Ray Leonard. He also told how George Foreman, then 45, was looking for a soft touch to defend his IBF title. A meeting was arranged with Lee at a Manhattan hotel. Lee said he would give Foreman dispensation to fight a lowly contender in return for $500,000 more than the usual three per cent sanctioning fee. The request was 'totally crazy and out of the question', Arum said. But he agreed to pay $100,000 before the fight and $100,000 after it. Arum also said Lee wanted $800,000 to arrange a Foreman bout with Mike Tyson when the latter got out of prison.

Then there was Cedric Kushner, the 300lb promoter with a drooping moustache who was known on the tapes as the 'Fat Man'. Kushner, who once promoted rock acts such as Queen and Fleetwood Mac, gave a convincing account of routinely paying bribes to the IBF, with $10,000 the going price to have a fighter rated. Beavers was always the bag man. Kushner admitted that he never spoke to Lee directly about bribes but insisted that the IBF was fully aware of the situation.

After three months of testimony, the prosecution case against Bob Lee Snr seemed very strong, though the evidence against his son was weaker. But in the US justice system, nothing is that simple. Race, so important an issue in other trials such as the O.J. Simpson case, was an unpredictable factor here. Prominent black leaders the Reverend Al Sharpton and Martin Luther King III held a news conference to attack prosecutors for failing to charge Arum, Kushner and Dino Duva, all white promoters who admitted crimes.

Lee's defence hinged on the theatricals of Krovatin, who played the race card without shame, smoothly discredited the government's star witnesses and managed to create sympathy for Lee, an ageing African-American with diabetes and a bad heart. 'I submit to you that this case breaks down along racial lines,' he declared. 'Did the government intend it that way? Did they set out to go after African-Americans? Well, I certainly think Don King has a role to play here in our thinking.'

Krovatin also punched holes in the various bribe accounts, while outlining a governmental conspiracy. He said prosecutors aligned themselves with the 'powerful commercial interests' backing HBO – like Arum, the Duva family and Kushner – in a battle against black promoters Don King and Butch Lewis and the rival pay-per-view broadcaster Showtime. 'Whether unwittingly or not, they and this prosecution have become another weapon and another tool in this battle of these giant promoters,' he said. Forced to explain the cash that jurors saw on videotape, Krovatin likened it to waiters' tips. 'Mr Lee is entitled to receive gifts and gratuities from people with whom he does business and that is not a crime,' he said. 'Even if King or Lee gave gifts at Christmas, they were not lawbreakers.' Finally tears streamed down Krovatin's cheeks – as they had in his summations at other trials – as he asked the jury to acquit his client. As he sat down, six jurors had tears in their eyes.

The emotive plea worked. The jury found that the prosecutors proved only a $5,000 payment from Fernandez for welterweight Hugo Pineda, and a $2,000 payment from Colombian manager Manuel Povea for junior featherweight Edison Valencia. In both cases, jurors could listen to Lee discussing the pay-offs on audio tapes, and watch him take cash on videotape. Yet the jurors did not believe the $5,000 payment from Fernandez for junior featherweight Victor Llerena. Fernandez delivered that money with the Pineda cheque and discussed it on the same tape as the Llerena payment. 'For a lot of counts, the majority of us believed that it occurred, but without any type of reference on any of those tapes, we couldn't find him guilty,' one of the jurors later said.

They found that the prosecutors proved a money-laundering conspiracy but found no pattern of racketeering activity by Lee. They bought Krovatin's view that the prosecutors misapplied the Racketeer Influenced and Corrupt Organizations Act, the so-called RICO law, which was meant for mobsters and drug dealers. The jury also found Lee guilty of three counts of interstate travel in aid of racketeering, a money-laundering conspiracy and filing false tax returns for 1997 and 1998. They rejected the other charges, including all of those against Lee Jnr.

Despite what many considered a very sympathetic series of acquittals, Lee immediately moaned that his convictions were based on race. Some of the jurors were livid. 'I thought, we cut you a major break, buddy, and this is the way you express your gratitude,' said one. Despite the racketeering acquittal, several jurors believed that bribery was routine at the IBF. Another said, 'There is no integrity in the IBF or its ratings. I don't think there's any integrity in the sport of boxing. I looked at this as a case of commercial prostitution and Bob Lee as a pimp. He had a stable of something he could prostitute, which was his ratings. You had people who had more money than they knew what to do with, and they wanted something they couldn't have. The clients, like in a brothel, were all too happy to spend their money to get whatever they wanted.'

New Jersey regulators moved to revoke the licences of Arum and Kushner to promote shows in casinos. Both men agreed not to do business in New Jersey while they fought a permanent ban. The Nevada Athletic Commission accepted a settlement with Arum in which he agreed to pay a $125,000 fine and abide by a six-month ban on staging fights in the state. Kushner was fined $175,000. The IBF now has a new president and continues operating under the scrutiny of a court-appointed monitor.

Beavers says he bears no ill will towards Lee: 'I like Bobby Lee. I don't like what Bobby Lee has done to boxing, and I feel sorry for him. I feel sorry for all of us, actually. I hate what I did in taking the bribes because it wasn't good for the fighters, and the fighters have always been the most important thing to me. The majority of boxing people don't want to be corrupt because the majority are good people. If you get one or two powerful people who are corrupt, then the other people have no choice. You have to pay to survive.'

In his final year in office, US president Bill Clinton signed into law the Muhammad Ali Boxing Reform Act. This aims to sweep away the kind of corruption revealed so dramatically in the IBF case. Lawyer Paul Feeney, who helped to draft the Act, says it will be a big step forwards for the sport. 'We would prohibit these ratings organizations from receiving any payments from promoters, managers or other entities in the industry except for their publicly reported sanctioning fee; we would require them to release the names of all of their officials who vote on the rankings of boxers. We would also force them to explain publicly when they change their rating of a boxer in the top ten.

It will require promoters to open up their books at least in their treatment of specific boxers; it will require financial disclosure so that state commissions can know more about some of the financial arrangements that are going on in their jurisdiction; it will stop a promoter from being able to grab unending long-term contractual rights from every boxer who tries to fight for a title. We need everyone to take a look at this industry and recognize that things can be done much better, for the fans, the athletes and the industry members themselves.'

CHAPTER TWO

They Drug Horses, Don't They?

How America's Acceptance of Drug Culture is Splitting Horse Racing

Like many other people with a guilty conscience, the men and women who run horse racing hate to admit they have a drug problem. But every year their embarrassing secret presents Britain's top trainers with a moral dilemma: what matters most, animal welfare or winning?

The clip-clop, tick-tock of the horses' hooves pacing patiently about the yard underscores the general sensation that time walks slowly at Jack Berry's racing stables. The facilities here are some of the most modern available and are busy for 16 hours a day, but there remains a wonderfully peaceful atmosphere of duties carried out unhurriedly. Moss Side Stables are on the flat plain of the Fylde Coast, halfway between Lancaster and Blackpool. Bright white horseboxes skirt a square concrete yard from which narrow paths lead onto all-weather gallops and then mile after mile of lush farmland. The rectangular fields are paragraphs of green script, punctuated by the pencil lines of drainage ditches leading to the nearby coast. Freshly mown grass, manure and sea air blend to create a unique smell. This is not the heartland of horse racing; it's miles from the nearest rival trainer or the well-worn paths of Newmarket or Lambourn – and that's just the way Jack likes it.

Following his career as a national hunt jockey, Jack started training deliberately away from the masses. It was not a decision based on having secrets to keep – he has nothing to hide – he sought to avoid the equine viruses that circulate the closely packed yards of racing communities as easily as tummy-bugs circulate around children in a playground.

Isolation brought rewards. Jack Berry soon became one of

the most successful trainers in the UK with a specialism in young sprinters, two-year-olds that dart like jets for seven furlongs or less. His cheery smile, along with that of his wife, Jo, was well known on the courses of Britain, as were the red shirts he always wore. He joked that red shirts were lucky, but he is not unusally lucky.

He is a stickler for animal welfare, especially when it concerns chemicals. 'I'm opposed to any kind of drug whatsoever,' he said shortly before handing the management of his yard over to his son, Alan, in 1999. 'I wouldn't even give one of our horses a small pill from the vet unless I absolutely had to. I'm dead against it.'

Such a stand is easy to keep when competing in the UK, where racing is widely held to be the cleanest in the world. But with a calender of racing events that demands ever more globe-trotting, the temptation to employ the expertise of the chemist is rising all the time. This is particularly true if you send your horses to run in the USA, where the drug culture is completely out of step with the rest of the racing world. 'In the States the horses are allowed to run on lasix and bute,' continues Mr Berry. 'Over here we're not.'

Of all the substances in the pharmacy, lasix and bute are the drugs which cause top trainers the biggest heartache. There is no doubt that they enhance performance. There is also no doubt, in this country at least, that it is harmful for a horse to run while using either of these readily available drugs. But every time British-trained thoroughbreds travel to America they are competing against horses who are boosted by chemical assistance. The dilemma is simple: do you run clean or compete on equal terms? Should you use drugs which you believe might be harmful, just because you can?

It is a choice Jack Berry faced himself: 'We ran Bolshoi in a sprint at the Breeders' Cup and I wouldn't let us use anything. We ran a big race but were beaten by about four lengths and finished out of the money, but we ran well. If we'd have run him on lasix or bute I would have worried all my life.' Asked by *On The Line* if Bolshoi would have run faster with the drugs he replied:

'I'm sure he would, but I don't believe in it personally and we wouldn't put our horses on anything. I'd fall out with an owner if they wanted to use a drug, I'd just oppose it.'

Clive Brittain went one better than Jack Berry. He trained Pebbles to a famous victory in the Breeders' Cup in 1985. Pebbles was without doubt one of the best fillies ever trained in Europe, and all her wins were achieved without drugs, even those in America. 'I wouldn't use drugs unless they were necessary – if it's not broke don't mend it,' says Brittain. 'But if I trained in California and had problems there, I've no doubt we'd have to use drugs to compete. But in the short term I think it's a bit short-sighted for us to say, they're there, we can use them, when really you don't have any need to.' He continues, 'I know for a fact that horses have gone from England on lasix and suddenly their form has turned round. There's no magic in the training that can do it so it has to be something else and the medication is the obvious factor.'

Many of the 19 European-based horses that went to America for the Breeders' Cup in November 2000 are known to have used at least one of the controversial substances. Christian Wall, a respected Newmarket trainer and near neighbour of Clive Brittain, has some sympathy for his colleagues: 'The thing is that it's such a pressure competition that if the American horses are racing on it and are thereby conferred an advantage, it's slightly unfair to our horses not to be running on a level playing field. If you don't do it and you get beaten by a short head then you might think, "Well, if I'd done it then I might have won." So I think that you're under pressure to do the same as the Americans.'

Up until the late 1980s lasix and bute were not really an issue. Then the Breeders' Cup meeting, which had been founded as a domestic event in 1984, promoted itself to become an unofficial world championship of racing. The top horses from Europe are now routinely flown to the USA every November to try and boost their prize winnings and stud value. Lasix and bute are commonly used treatments in Europe, widely recognized for their medicinal value. It is perfectly legal for horses to be treated with either product provided there is none of the substance remaining in the animal on race day. If a trace remains it will be detected by racing's dope testers.

Dr David Marlin works in the Centre for Equine Studies in Newmarket, analysing the health of horses. He's very familiar with both lasix and bute. 'Lasix is a diuretic,' says Dr Marlin. 'It acts on the kidneys to produce much more urine. It tricks the body into thinking it's had a large intake of water. The kidneys will then get rid of a lot of water and salts from the body and will effectively make you dehydrated.'

The short-term benefit to the horse's backers is that their mount is carrying less weight in a race. The long-term cost to the animal is that it undergoes maximum physical exertion with minimum fluids in the body. As Dr Marlin explains: 'In racing everybody is very concerned about the amount of weight the horse is carrying and trainers and jockeys know the implication of a few pounds here or there in the handicap. If a horse had been given lasix it could shed up to ten kilos, around twenty-two pounds. If you said to a trainer, "I'll allow you to run your horse carrying twenty-two pounds less," most people would be quite excited about that prospect.' *Quite* excited? They would be delirious!

The therapeutic reasons for using lasix are that it reduces internal bleeding when a blood vessel bursts in the lungs. But Dr Marlin even disputes this: 'It's interesting that when you examine the scientific evidence for this, there is actually very little hard evidence to suggest that it really is effective. So there's not really good evidence to suggest that lasix either reduces the severity or the frequency of bleeding in the lungs of horses after racing. In fact there's a lot of evidence to suggest that that theory is wrong.'

The medical merits of bute (more properly phenylbutazone) are less contentious. It is a non-steroidal, anti-inflammatory drug, in short, a painkiller. It was used for humans until fears emerged about possible links to stomach ulcers and its application was restricted. Trainer-turned-writer Charlie Brooks is aware of bute's palliative powers: 'It is extremely effective in relieving the aches and pains that racehorses are susceptible to,' he wrote in his newspaper column. 'If a horse has been jarred up on fast ground or is generally suffering from the wear and tear of racing, its freedom of movement and subsequent willingness to give everything in a race will be transformed by bute.'

It is precisely because bute is such an effective treatment that horses are banned from running with it in their system. Quantifying the effects of allowing a horse to run on painkillers is tricky, but some figures from the USA might give an indication of the long-term consequences. In Kentucky the average number of horses destroyed each year after racing incidents is 1.64 per thousand. In New York, one of the few states where bute is banned, the figure drops to 1.2 horses per thousand. Could this be because horses in Kentucky run when they are not fit to do so? It is impossible to say for certain, but it is unreasonable to ignore the circumstantial evidence.

Dr Marlin says this: 'The concern over using drugs like bute while racing is the same as it would be for a human using a painkiller while performing sport. Pain is there to tell you to stop doing something. If a knee is painful it is because it is injured and needs treating. If the pain is hidden and a horse runs on an injured knee then the damage could be long term. In this country drugs like bute could be used in the short term on a horse being trained to get through a minor problem. But a trainer must have that information recorded so that if he then receives a visit from Jockey Club security services who might want to test horses in a yard, it must be clear which horses are on which medication.'

The American dope temptation to which so many of our trainers succumb is at least eased by the timing of the States' main event. The Breeders' Cup takes place early in November, right at the end of the European flat-racing season. Christian Wall says there is, therefore, no risk of a horse testing positive for lasix or bute administered in the USA at a race meeting in Europe. 'If they were to race within ten to fourteen days of the Breeders' Cup back in England then there is every chance that they would fail a dope test because that's how long it would stay in the system,' reveals the trainer. 'The fact of the matter is that this is an end-of-season event for us and unless you're going to send a horse to Hong Kong or out to Japan in the coming months then as there is nothing taking place in Britain now, it is the end of our season. These horses will be going into winter quarters and quite a few of the older ones will be going off the stud to be bred, so they're not going to hit the track again. Certainly if you were looking to run a horse again quickly then there would be concern.'

There is concern because the racing industry has recently launched a glamorous intercontinental series of meetings where the same horses compete in Europe, the USA and all over the world. In the majority of the venues the horses have to run clean, but in North America lasix and bute are allowed. Imagine a Grand Prix of athletics meetings where steroids were banned in some races and not in others. That is what is happening to the most prestigious horse-racing development in decades. There are two sides in a global struggle for a united stance on drugs, only one can win. Either the Americans will ban drugs, or the other countries will allow them to be used.

Top-class flat racing takes place all over the world, with America, Japan, Australia, the Middle East and Europe all boast-ing prestigious events. These are the meetings which gave rise to the glamorous lifestyle of the jockey jet set, hopping around the globe to ride in races which are the highpoint of the season in their respective countries. In the mid 1990s the International Racing Bureau (IRB), a company set up in 1968 to develop links between racing nations, started to talk about connecting all the top events together into a formal series – similar in style to motor racing's Grand Prix circuit. The company's chief executive, Nick Clarke, says, 'International racing has developed very rapidly over the last 15 years. If you go back to 20 years ago the number of horses travelling between continents each year could be counted on the fingers of one hand, two hands at the most. Now we're talking about around 100 top-quality horses moving between continents each year for the major races in Europe, North America, Asia (including West Asia) and Dubai. So clearly, this was one of the most dynamic areas of thoroughbred racing on a world-wide basis and there was clear merit in making a world series in the same way soccer and cricket and golf and rugby and everything else has gone for a global championship.'

The IRB now has offices all over the world, including Africa and South America. Nick Clarke first presented his dream of a world series of racing in 1996. 'It was a question of getting the authorities together and seeing whether the idea appealed to them,' he continues. 'We had our first meeting in Toronto at the time of the Breeders' Cup and simply introduced the notion to the people attending that meeting, and people were fascinated and very enthusiastic and gave me the authority to take it to a development plan and just look at the numbers and implications and we've really marched forward pretty rapidly since then.'

It is not hard to see the appeal of the scheme. A global circuit of thoroughbred encounters joining together a series of already world-famous races like the Dubai World Cup, the King George VI and Queen Elizabeth Diamond Stakes at Royal Ascot, the Prix de L'Arc de Triomphe, the Cox Plate in Melbourne, the Japan Cup and the Breeders' Cup. Television companies and bookmakers love it, as Nick Clarke enthuses: 'We're looking at which horse is going to accumulate the highest number of points and become champion of that series. Of course he will then automatically make his owner the champion owner and possibly the trainer and jockey as well, plus the breeder. What will be really interesting is at the end of the year just which breeder and which trainer and ultimately which horse is going to prove an undoubted world champion.'

Nick Clarke's proposals had the backing of the International Federation of Horseracing Authorities, whose chairman, Louis Romanet, is passionate about a world-wide link-up. 'Racing needs new events and new ideas,' said Mr Romanet from his Paris office. 'But it's very difficult at the top level to create new races, so the concept is to use existing races and mould them into something we can market around the world.'

For years this grand idea was held back by the drug-friendly rules of Kentucky, where the Breeders' Cup is held. Despite intense pressure from all around the world, officials in the States refused to fall into line by banning lasix and bute. Every nation outside Northern America thinks it is unsafe to run horses on these drugs but the USA disagrees. Most race organizers recognize that the integrity of a world series is compromised if the rules are different in each country, especially rules regarding performance-enhancing drugs. The USA held firm. As a result the nation which stubbornly refuses to acknowledge the dangers of running a horse through the pain barrier was able to enact a veto over the world series of racing.

Louis Romanet tried on many occasions to persuade the racing authorities in the USA to see sense: 'There was a debate and we came to the conclusion that it was nearly impossible to oblige racing authorities to change and it's even more complicated in the USA because each state racing commission would decide which rule should be applied in their state. So we adopted a situation where each country would apply its own rules, which I think is regrettable. I am absolutely convinced that any world series should totally exclude medication and that it will partially harm the project if some of the countries allow medication.' Mr Romanet was asked why a series could not go ahead without the USA, he said: 'I think that is one possible approach but we are facing a situation where if you exclude the Breeders' Cup you take out the richest day of the year and harm the project. I think it's now a matter of opinion for each country whether they think it's acceptable or not. Some countries could eventually decide not to participate because they don't want to take part in a series where horses can run under medication.'

In the autumn of 1998, at a conference near to Mr Romanet's base in Paris, more than 30 nations signed up to a new set of drug rules. They approved random out-of-competition testing and automatic disqualification for any horse which tests positive after a race. Once again, with the equine world moving towards a united front to keep the sport drug free, the USA and Canada refused to join in.

So the Emirates World Series was launched in 1999 with different rules in each country. The website for the event fails to mention in its fulsome praise of the idea that every year some trainers from across Europe risk their top horses by racing them on drugs which most of the world knows are harmful. Daylami was the first horse to be crowned world champion, a fact known to few sports fans other than the racing fanatics. As the series gathered momentum in 2000, the victory of Fantastic Light gained a little more recognition.

Faced with the accusation that they jeopardize the health of horses, the Americans shrug their shoulders. Nick Nicholson is the executive director of the US National Thoroughbred Racing Association, a coalition of interested parties including racetracks, owners and breeders. On The Line suggested to him that the current state of affairs was a shambles. 'I would not agree with the word "shambles" because shambles implies that some-how or other it's not working,' he bullishly replied. 'Racing in the United States is growing and we're able to work around these complexities reasonably. The allowance for lasix and bute has been something that has evolved in this country and it's just the way that it is over here. It's part of the everyday life over here and I'm not sure there's more to it than that.'

In fact both drugs were banned throughout the United States until the mid 1970s. Then some trainers who had used lasix away from the racetrack claimed that they had noticed remarkable improvements in a horse's performance in training, sometimes by as much as ten lengths over a race distance. The temptation was huge and before long there was a clamour among trainers to have access to this apparently miracle-working injection. In a short space of time scientists had been recruited who were willing to claim that racing a horse treated with a diuretic didn't risk any harm – a claim still rejected in every other country. Staggeringly, they also argued that numbing an animal to pain in order to make it run faster was also acceptable. Both lasix and bute became as common as carrots.

North America's stance on lasix and bute doesn't just cause problems for trainers taking horses to the USA and Canada. American trainers face a far greater dilemma when considering taking their animals overseas to compete. Will their horses still perform without the drugs they have come to depend upon?

Will all traces of the drug be out of their system when they race abroad? Two American-trained horses were banned before the start of a race in Hong Kong when they tested positive for lasix on arrival. It is clear that until there is a uniform approach stating which drugs are allowed and which are banned, there can never be a credible world series of racing. And while indecision holds up progress, those trainers who are willing to use drugs are getting more and more inventive.

Michael Gill is one of the hottest trainers in America, with a number of top horses. His career is enjoying a second lease of life following a juddering setback when, in 1995, one of his horses tested positive for clenbuterol. Racing investigators found syringes and bottles of drugs in Gill's barn. The young horseman pleaded that he had been framed by one of his rivals, but the New Hampshire racing commission took a hard line and Gill was banned for three years. Clenbuterol abuse has also led to the punishment of trainers in Los Angeles, New York and Maryland. In 1998 17 positive samples were discovered in California. Dr David Marlin says clenbuterol is a well-known performance enhancer: 'It has two main effects. Firstly, it is a bronchodilator: think of people who have asthma, their airways can constrict, leading to difficulty breathing. Clenbuterol can help to open up these airways. We have horses with a similar problem, therefore clenbuterol would be a way to treat that. The other effect is on muscle. Many studies show how long-term use of clenbuterol can increase the muscle bulk and can change the fibre type within the muscle. So potentially there are two different effects.'

In terms of stimulating muscle growth, clenbuterol has the same effect as a steroid. Faced with the kind of drug use which has besmirched many human sports, the equine authorities might have been expected to take a tough stance. Instead they caved in. Racing commissions in the USA have responded to the increasing use of clenbuterol in the same way that they did in the 1970s with lasix and bute – by going soft on it. In September 1999 the state of Kentucky – the home of American racing – liberalized its approach to clenbuterol, allowing horses to escape punishment so long as the amount of the drug in their blood was below a given threshold level. Trainers were told that they were safe to administer Ventipulmin syrup, the oral form of clen-buterol, up to 72 hours before a race. As the campaign grows for other states to follow Kentucky in weakening their approach to clenbuterol, there is anger among some American writers who claim that what is happening with this drug now is exactly what happened with lasix and bute in the 1970s. It seems the gap in attitude between the USA and the rest of the world towards chemically assisted horses is widening.

European racing has a reputation for being clean, and with a small number of notable exceptions, that is true. While some cases come to light concerning performance-enhancing drugs, the Jockey Club's main concern is with a substance called ACP, which has been used to stop horses running to the best of their form. This was the drug which prompted a wave of arrests by Scotland Yard in 1998 and 1999. Two horses were tested positive for ACP, Avanti Express at Exeter and Lively Knight at Plumpton. In a 12-month period from January 1998 14 men were arrested in connection with the doping of the two horses, which was thought to have been done to fix races. Both of the nobbled horses were short-priced favourites which would have lost the bookmakers significant sums. Twenty months later the biggest inquiry into racing fixing ever held in Britain ended with no con-victions whatsoever, other than a man being jailed for 18 months for trying to blackmail an innocent jockey. Who did nobble Avanti Express and Lively Knight will probably never be known.

Since then it has been business as usual with just the occa-sional transgression for bute and lasix. In January 2001 the Jockey Club investigated a positive test on a horse called One Won One, who had won one race at Haydock Park. The gelding, bred in the USA and trained in Ireland by Joanna Morgan, had won the John of Gaunt Stakes the previous June and tests showed traces of bute in its urine sample. The disciplinary hearing at Jockey Club headquarters in London was unable to establish the source of the bute, and a statement said that the committee could not be satisfied that the administration of the substance was accidental and that the trainer had taken all reasonable care.

One Won One was disqualified and Joanna Morgan was fined £600. Even at the time of this case the Jockey Club was keen to emphasize the overall probity of racing and point out that as long as bute is allowed for treatment away from the racetrack its presence should be seen more as evidence of neglect by the trainer than as a sign that cheating is taking place.

But cheating does happen, and it can be practised far away from the racecourse, years before a horse is ever entered for an event. Louis Romanet, the senior racing administrator in Europe, says some unscrupulous breeders build up their yearlings with illegal supplements to make them look stronger at auction: 'I would say the main present concern for all sports organizers, human or horses, is growth hormones,' he warns. 'Clearly they have been manufactured by laboratories to treat humans and have then been produced for other purposes, certainly for both humans and horses. We are funding several projects, working very closely with all those doing the same work for human athletes, to have the possibility to detect them in the near future. But it is certainly the greatest challenge.'

Clive Brittain says he has seen the results of equine growth hormone at auction: 'Well, that's been going on for years. They overdid it at one time. You went to the sales and you were buying bullocks. Nature has a way of turning round and blowing back in your face. You see more lean, well-prepared yearlings now than 10 to 15 years ago when the hormones first started to get widely used. I remember going to certain sales, it is not fair to mention which ones, and there was a batch of horses which looked like they'd won three races, they were big burly horses you'd think were three-year-olds. When you got them home and they were weaned off hormones they fell to pieces.'

Exactly how many horses have been pumped up with hormones, no one can know – until the summer of 2000 there was no reliable test for the practice. When a trustworthy procedure was developed, it came from an unlikely place.

Three hundred miles south-west of Sydney, Wagga Wagga (it means the City of Crows) hasn't contributed a great deal to racing's development. In fact, other than being the birthplace of

Australia's most famous jockey, Scobie Breasley, the New South Wales settlement didn't even merit a mention in the sport's credits. Until, that is, a couple of scientists in the agricultural department of the Charles Sturt University came up with an almost foolproof way of detecting growth hormone abuse.

Martin Sillence, a son of Cheshire now working as a professor of animal science in Wagga Wagga, says he and a colleague, Glenys Noble, started their pioneering research as a result of a phone call from the Australian Racing Board. 'In 1998 a company in Adelaide announced it wanted to market equine growth hormone,' he explains. 'The Racing Board was concerned about misuse and asked us to try and find a way of testing for it in the blood.' The professor's task was made harder because growth hormone occurs naturally and is produced by the body in spurts – mimicking the spurts caused by injections. Furthermore, it only remains detectable in the bloodstream for about 20 minutes.

As with all the drugs causing problems for racing, growth hormone has legitimate uses in medicine. Administered in the right quantities it can speed up the healing of wounds. But, as Professor Sillence warns, the fear is that some trainers will deliberately overdose their horses because of the side effects of growth hormone injections. 'The effects it can have on muscle production are similar to those of a steroid,' he continues, 'but the consequences of overdoing it are far more serious. At a clinical trial in Newmarket they had to put a horse down which was given too much growth hormone by accident. It's very detrimental to bone strength and young horses are particularly vulnerable.'

Sillence and Noble discovered that when growth hormone is administered, another hormone, IGF-1, is produced by the liver. They found that IGF-1 levels increased abnormally when a horse had been injected, and the level remained high for up to 36 hours after growth hormone had been given. Tests on more than 2,500 animals around the world showed that normal levels of IGF-1 were easy to establish. The Wagga Wagga scientists then created a test which they say has a one in thirty thousand chance of giving the wrong result, and so a reliable test for hormone abuse was made available for the first time. Dr Sillence is thrilled.

'High doses of growth hormone can damage growing bones and could eventually cripple young horses,' he said. 'Hopefully we can prevent that happening by helping the authorities detect hormone abuse.'

In addition to the worries regarding growth hormone, horse racing's major drugs problems come from an attitude in America that seems to put winning above welfare, and the interests of a few US trainers above expanding the sport around the world. The matter is not helped by European trainers who so readily reach for the syringe when competing across the Atlantic.

It is worth noting that it was the drug cheating of a few American trainers at the start of the twentieth century which prompted England to ban doping for the first time in 1903. Now, at the start of the twenty-first century, racing is once again being betrayed by America's continued liberal attitude to chemistry. Until the rest of the world is brave enough to tell the United States to either get clean or get lost, the Americans can do as they please.

Louis Romanet's wish is that the clean countries should extend their influence into America, with perhaps a trickle of individual states turning against drug use. But he says the opposite is already happening. As the super powers of racing, Europe and America, are split over their stance on drugs, the less-developed racing nations have so far climbed onto the moral high ground inhabited by the Europeans, the Australians and the Far East. But Mr Romanet says that faced with dollar-backed pressure from the USA some of these nations, such as those in South America, are siding with the liberals: 'Unfortunately, this trend [the USA's lax approach to drugs] is progressively going to South America because South America is doing a lot of business with North America, and countries like Argentina and Brazil, who used to allow no medication, are progressively allowing some medication, which is a pity and means you have the American continent on one side and the rest of the world on the other.'

When it comes to choosing between welfare and winning, it appears the financiers speak louder than the vets.

CHAPTER THREE

Academy – Schmacademy!
The Sorry Tale of Britain's Attempt to Build a Sports Academy

The British Academy of Sport was to be the envy of the world – the finest facilities turning out the best athletes on the planet. Here is the story of how this bricks-and-mortar approach to sporting excellence ended up as a suite of offices in London instead.

It was 23 July 1996 and hopes of a glorious summer of sporting success for Britain seemed to have been dashed. Our footballers had failed at Euro '96, our cricketers were being flayed by Pakistan, and at the Atlanta Olympics the TV presenters' expectant smiles were beginning to crack along with the nation's patience.

It was relief rather than joy that was the dominant emotion when Paul Palmer, after nearly four days of barren competition, broke Great Britain's duck by winning its first medal of the games, a silver in the 400-metres freestyle. In the Georgia twilight the swimmer spoke of his delight at the medal but also his resentment at the level of needless slog and self-sacrifice he'd endured because of the poor support athletes received in Britain.

Hours later, in the sunshine of his Downing Street garden, John Major, the then Prime Minister, announced a new direction for British sport. He pledged £100 million of lottery support for Britain's first Academy of Sport. An edifice, he said, that would open its doors in time for the millennium. The likes of Paul Palmer would never have to worry about hardship again. 'The purpose of the Academy,' declared the Prime Minister, 'will be to provide the best training, the best coaching, the best sports medicine, the best sports science for elite sportsmen and women.' He added that on top there would be 200 scholarships offered to over-18s who demonstrate 'exceptional talent'.

The Academy project came wrapped up in a policy announcement called 'Raising the Game'. In simple terms the plan was to revive sport in schools and harvest the resulting elite for what amounted to a sports university, whose graduates would then go out onto the world stage better equipped to win cups, gongs and titles for the greater glory of the nation. It was well received in the press. And why not? Usually the lot of the British sports fan was to suffer national defeat and the resulting pain and humiliation with only morose conversations among the similarly blighted for comfort. For the government to throw its weight unambiguously behind the quest for success was novel indeed. Traditionally, administrations of either hue had not bothered themselves very much with sport.

Back in the 1970s Denis Howell (famously minister for droughts as well as sport!) presided over something called 'Sport For All'. But this proved to be less of a policy and more of a logo. It can still be seen, a quintessential piece of 1970s graphic art retained by Sport England to this day.

Under Margaret Thatcher the policy changed, unofficially at least, to 'Don't Give a Stuff About Sport'. Admittedly the sickening images of Heysel and Hillsborough stadiums during that period cast their unwelcome shadow over all sport; but that was no excuse for the accelerated sell-off of playing fields, or the privatization of council recreational services which led to a devastating decline in facilities and pitches.

But at least John Major was genuinely keen on sport and there can be little doubt that the cricket-loving premier meant it when, on that sunny morning in Downing Street, he said he wanted to see Britain where she belonged: at the top of world sport. Having invented or codified many of the world's popular sports, however, does not bestow any right to be the best. That must be earned; and the sad truth is that typically we have performed well below our punching weight, set against those nations with whom we could reasonably expect to compete.

The farcical tale of the British Academy of Sport is as good an example as any of our ability to screw up at sport off the park as well as on it. Be it our comical performances at Euro 2000 or the hash we have made of simply trying to build a national stadium, it is a sorry tale of cock-ups, broken promises and the unerring ability of people who do not understand sport to prevail over those who do.

On the face of it 1996 was an excellent time to announce a sea change in sporting policy. After the awful 1980s Britain was in love with sport once more. Just as the poetic drama of Italia '90 and images of Paul Gascoigne's tears had faded from the national consciousness, along came Euro '96. England may have been cruelly deprived in the semi-finals by Germany (again!) but the whole experience of hosting the championships gave a new fillip to sport in general.

But below this fresh outburst of enthusiasm flowed an undercurrent. Having suffered outright failure, and then heroic failure, there was a hunger for success. Why was it that our cricketers crumbled, footballers flunked it and athletes became anonymous in the face of merely credible opposition? There was a feeling that the rest of world had moved on and left us in its wake. England may have won rugby's Five Nations with back-to-back grand slams in 1991–92 but that meant nothing when faced with southern hemisphere opposition. Our cricketing bigwigs had stalwartly opposed test match status for the likes of Zimbabwe and Sri Lanka, but it was Sri Lanka who won the ICC World Cup in January 1996, while our boys beat their most ignominious retreat from the competition yet. Our athletes travelled to the Olympics or World Championships brandishing any number of global superlatives but were invariably disappointed.

Now that the National Lottery was supporting sport there could be no whinging about a lack of resources. Prior to the lottery launch in 1994 the most the Sports Council could disperse in support of British sport was £50 or £60 million. Now sport was a lottery 'good cause', and that figure had swelled to more than £300 million a year. Most of this was earmarked for capital projects aimed at improving recreational sports facilities – swimming pools, new pitches or clubhouses. Still, the idea of channelling some of that cash towards satisfying the yearning for success seemed a good one, not only from a sporting perspective but from a political one too. Granted, the dividends would be limited – people do not elect governments on the basis of their sports manifesto – but a little of the feelgood factor never did a government of the day any harm.

The man charged with turning John Major's dream into the kind of reality that would leave our rivals slack-jawed in admiration was Iain Sproat, Minister for Sport. Iain Sproat is a cultured man with a love of cricket and a fondness for the poetry of Pushkin, on whom he is something of an expert. But, like most sports ministers, he was yet another in a long line of politically anonymous figures appointed to the post. As irrelevant as sport was in the greater political scheme of things, the Academy project, because it carried the Prime Minister's personal stamp, gave Sproat the rare opportunity for a minister of sport to leave a mark.

The prospect of a decent ribbon-cutting ceremony at the end of it all surely had its attractions, but what probably sealed Iain Sproat's enthusiasm for John Major's vision of a temple to athletic excellence was a trip to the Australian Institute of Sport (AIS) in Canberra.

The AIS was dreamed up in the aftermath of the Montreal Olympics in 1976 when calamitously, from an Australian point of view, their Olympic squad failed to clinch a single gold and won very little else. The government determined that such a thing would never happen again, and it is hardly an exaggeration to say that becoming world beaters in sport became an arm of Australian foreign policy. The AIS opened its doors in 1981.

There's no doubt that the AIS makes a pretty spectacle, festooned as it is with impressive pools, pitches, tracks and other facilities stuffed full of machinery going 'bip'. But it was not buildings that were behind the rise and rise of Australian sport. It was people and money. As Jim Ferguson of the AIS explains, 'I think it is imperative to establish a set of principles. If you have a set of principles right, the actual mechanism should flow from that and I think it would be wrong to put it the other way around because then you are trying to force your principles onto something which exists in a material sense.'

Think of it in political terms. State-of-the-art parliamentary buildings do not make a democracy. People do. The AIS only works as a finishing school for excellence because there is a strong network below, promoting sport at the grassroots. In Australia playing sport is a fundamental part of the culture to a much greater extent than in Britain. The excellence programmes feed off this fertile ground and are fully funded by tax dollars.

Sproat and his advisers were dazzled by what they saw – and paid less attention to what they could not see. They could not, or would not, grasp the importance of the 'people' part of the mix. Thus it was that the bricks-and-mortar aspect of the Australian Institute of Sport loomed large in the published specification for the British Academy that John Major brandished in July 1996.

Sproat claimed to have a clear vision of what he wanted. This is odd because if he really did, why not simply pay someone to build it and cherry-pick the best sports brains in the world to run it? Instead, a competition was launched. One hundred million pounds from the lottery was pledged to the project. One impact of this approach was to dilute the existing expertise in the business of elite sport across nearly three dozen consortiums that answered the call to build and run the British Academy of Sport. What was even stranger was that the very people whom this project was supposed to benefit had already told the minister in no uncertain terms that they did not want his Academy.

In late 1995 the Sports Council had commissioned a polling firm to find out what athletes wanted to make their lives easier. There was a high degree of unanimity. They wanted cash. Cash, so top athletes did not have to hold down jobs as well as train to be world beaters; cash to pay coaches; and cash to be invested in a credible network of sports science and sports medicine support. And they wanted these facilities to be no more than an hour's drive away. There was absolutely no room for misunderstanding. In addition to the questionnaire, three consultation exercises were held in London, Birmingham and Edinburgh in January 1996, and the same message came through loud and clear. Only ten people out of the five hundred who attended the three events expressed any enthusiasm for the idea of a central academy of sport.

Sue Campbell, founder of the National Coaching Foundation, renowned world expert in coach education and, incidentally, a frequent visitor to the AIS, summed up what sport was looking for: 'All you have to do is put within one very simple office building someone who can coordinate coaching education, someone who can coordinate sport science support, ditto sports medicine, and someone who can provide athletes with career and counselling advice. That is an academy.'

But not according to the prospectus. And it was the overblown and flawed vision contained therein from which the competing consortiums were taking their cue in the late summer to early autumn of 1996. It really was a bizarre document. On the one hand, true to Sproat's vision, it was almost prosaic in its detail, laying out precisely the numbers and dimensions: 'indoor, 8-lane, 50-metre swimming pool; outdoor, floodlit, 8-lane, 400-metre land running track; 2 indoor halls big enough to contain 8 badminton courts; 250 medium-stay study bedrooms, 3-star hotel standard ...' And so on.

On the other hand, the appendix to the document included the thoughts of the various governing bodies of sport in the UK. Almost all expressed outright opposition to the idea. In a sentence, their sentiment could be summed up thus: 'You can build it if you like but we won't use it.' For example:

ATHLETICS: The British Athletic Federation does not believe that all the specialist facility needs of athletics can be met at an Academy.
CANOEING: There is a general willingness to develop a national training centre but the sport has a general preference to develop this independently of the Academy.
GYMNASTICS: There is a strong view for gymnastics to be developed around existing facilities.
ROWING: There is a preference in rowing to develop its centre of excellence around its current base at Henley

In the Hollywood movie *Field of Dreams* the lead character, played by Kevin Costner, is told in a dream to build a baseball field in the middle of a cornfield on his remote farm. The voices he hears in a dream reassure him: 'If you build it, they will come.' It seemed to be pretty much the same principle with the British Academy of Sport. Despite a clear warning from the very people it was being built for that they did not want it, the hope was that, once built, it would be so impressive it would quickly win over the sceptics, and athletes would soon be queuing up to spend their money. This tendency to ignore awkward issues or gloss over obvious problems characterized much of the sorry history of the Academy.

For example: although John Major had said there would be up to £100 million of lottery money made available for the project, the prospectus made no mention at all of the figure – and actually the Prime Minister had no power to direct lottery spending. Sports spending had been delegated by Parliament to the Sports Council, where there was even more fun and games going on.

The Sports Council was going through one of its customary reorganizations. The body had not long since been broken up from a single quango into four separate ones – one for each of the home nations; now it was decided there was a need for an umbrella organization. UK Sport, as it was to be called, would 'Identify sporting policies that should have a UK-wide application and apply them.' Lord McLaurin, formerly of Tesco's and at the time chairman of the England and Wales Cricket Board, was drafted in to head up the organization.

Clearly the scope and aim of the Academy fell within the UK Sport remit, but as the home sports councils controlled the lottery cash, UK Sport had to go cap in hand for any funding it might require. Given that any academy would almost certainly be built in England, there was no guarantee that the Welsh, Scots and Irish would willingly open their coffers. Even the English did not see the Academy as a priority in the greater scheme of things. Chairman of the English Sports Council at the time, Sir Rodney Walker (omnipresent in the world of sport, holding posts on dozens of bodies and boards ranging from Leicester City to the Rugby League to Wembley National Stadium Ltd), warned the government, 'No one should be in any doubt that if we do not like what we see in the final analysis we have the right to say no.'

And just to make the bid assessment committee's job even more complex, Iain Sproat announced that the government reserved the right to cherry-pick between bids: 'These are going to be open envelope bids. We look at them and say this is a great bid except for that two per cent that we don't like very much and we will change it or we might say this bid is 95 per cent rubbish but five per cent is terrific, so why don't you two get together.' Welding together disparate elements from multiple bids would have been a nightmare, and is one more reason why the government should have hired the expertise, put up the money and let them get on with it, instead of fishing for ideas with no idea of what it would net.

Thus it was in the late summer of 1996 that politicians attempted to breathe life into a project nobody wanted by publishing a prospectus that stood no chance of achieving its aim. But such was the prestige vested into the Academy by the government there was hardly a city, university or management consultancy firm that did not hook up with one bid or another. Even as 28 bid teams charged off trying to tie into their teams' governing bodies and anybody with perceived sporting clout, wiser heads from sport continued to repeat that this was all madness. What was required was relatively simple and inexpensive in terms of infrastructure. For instance, Geoff Cooke, former England rugby union coach: 'I think the thing we are not addressing is that in any performance the thing that makes it happen is people. No one is talking about the people aspect of the whole situation and how the services are delivered and sadly what we are doing is bypassing that and concentrating on facilities.'

At Sheffield University, Professor Peter Taylor from the Leisure Industries Research Unit had studied what athletes wanted. He found that no matter how fantastic or glittering an academy was to be built, and no matter how central the location in the UK, it would never attract through its doors the very people it had been built to serve: 'It is ridiculous to expect elite sports people throughout the UK or even throughout England to travel to one central site on a regular basis. A lot of these people have jobs, are in education and need the strength of family, friends, coaches and their own personal infrastructure nearby.' (Interestingly, the Australian Institute for Sport soon discovered the same and started to develop a regional network within a couple of years of opening its doors at the Canberra HQ, thus bringing the expertise to the athletes rather than doing things the other way around.) These were not marginal views whispered from the sidelines, they were shouted loud and clear every time government came within earshot of any serious sports expertise in the UK.

The consortiums that had set out on this wild goose chase to run the British Academy of Sport submitted their bids, which were to be whittled down to a shortlist of 13 for first-round interviews in December 1996, from which three were to be selected for second interviews in January 1997. It was envisaged that work would start on-site in 1998, with the doors opening for business on the eve of the Sydney Olympics in 2000. If this timescale seems wildly optimistic, it moved into the realms of fantasy when the assessment committee caught sight of the bids. A selection of civil servants, management consultants, sports administrators and representatives from the AIS, the committee members were appalled by what they saw and heard when they sat down to the first set of interviews at the beginning of January 1997.

The Academy had been sold as one of the greatest, most prestigious state-of-the-art sports projects ever in this country, but it soon became clear that the bids which plopped through the postbox at the UK Sport HQ in December 1996 were well short of the right stuff. One consortium, fronted by a well-known British athlete of the time, when quizzed about the apparent lack of catering facilities in its plan, replied, 'I thought the athletes might bring their own packed lunches.' Another, when it was pointed out that, despite proposals for indoor and outdoor facilities of every technical ilk proudly detailed in their weighty document, there did not seem to be a budget or facilities for maintenance, said, 'A handyman with a well-equipped shed could cope with that.'

More seriously, a member of the panel later wrote to the minister: 'The panel was not impressed by the vision put forward by most of the consortia. It was difficult not to hear behind what was said and written, the ambitions and goals of the academic, health, local government and commercial organizations that made up these groups. None had anything to say in detail about how the Academy could produce change. The services that they planned to offer appeared to a great extent to be extensions of what they provide at present.'

It was all so perfectly in keeping with how the project had stumbled out of the blocks, spreading thin the nation's sporting expertise with the demand for competition and turning to builders and academics for the final word on sport. But a decision had to be made and in the last week of January a list of three finalists was on the way to Iain Sproat at the Department of Heritage and Lord McLaurin at UK Sport. These were the Upper Heyford Consortium, a bid supported by the British Olympic Association and the Football Association and based at a redundant air base in the Oxfordshire countryside; the Central Consortium based around Loughborough University; and finally a bid to be wholly based on a greenfield site just outside Kettering in Northamptonshire.

As the panel made clear, none was ideal, but these were the only three that did not contain any 'show-stoppers'. In contrast to the generally accepted meaning of the word as a *good* thing, the panel defined a 'show-stopper' as an aspect of a bid that could not be moderated or improved or planned around. A 'show-stopper' killed the bid dead in their eyes. Only three consortiums survived this test. Whatever sheen the Sproat/Major vision for an academy of sport had was now tarnished by a shortlist made up not so much of the best but rather the least bad.

UK Sport was due to announce the shortlist on 19 February but the decision was delayed a week. When it finally came the Kettering bid was nowhere to be seen. Until a couple of years later, when *On The Line* revealed to the people of Kettering that they had in fact made the original shortlist they had no idea they had been successful. They assumed they had been eliminated at the interview stage.

Kettering was bumped in favour of Sheffield, a bid that the evaluation panel had identified as having at least two show-stoppers and the longest list of other concerns surrounding any of the 13 bids that went to interview. First, a portion of the proposed site in the Don Valley was poisonous; more seriously, the core facilities around which the Academy was to be constructed, namely the Don Valley Stadium and the Pond's Forge swimming pool, belonged to the people of Sheffield in trust. In fact, the people of Sheffield were still paying for them through their council tax bills, thanks to the massive losses incurred when the World Student Games were held in the city in 1991. Yet here was a proposal to take these communally owned facilities and turn them over for the principal use of a small minority of people from all over the UK.

Neither Lord McLaurin nor Iain Sproat has spoken about this behind-the-scenes tampering with the shortlist, despite being asked by *On The Line*. Sir Rodney Walker, who was close enough to events, explained it thus: 'The reason Sheffield was brought back into the equation was simply because of the massive investment it had made in sports facilities.' Faced with the reality of just how much a state-of-the-art academy would cost, the politicians were already looking for cuts – and what better potential to make money go further than to press-gang existing facilities into the process, never mind their suitability? Another reason Sheffield sat well on the shortlist was politics. Iain Sproat feared that if the Conservatives lost the next election and there was no candidate for the Academy in the North, the whole project might be killed off. Certainly, Tom Pendry, New Labour's shadow sports spokesperson, was unimpressed and had rubbished the concept on a number of occasions.

By the early spring of 1997 the civil servants at the Heritage Department had seen which way the political wind was blowing and were becoming increasingly unwilling to proceed with a project that an incoming Labour administration might change significantly or simply scrap. In March Sproat put pressure on UK

Sport's chief executive, Howard Wells to hurry the process along. He refused. Then, in a rather desperate attempt to pick a winner while he was still in office, Iain Sproat telephoned the three competing teams and invited them to second interview at the beginning of April. As the teams gathered their paperwork to head south they received another call, this time from civil servants at the Heritage department telling them to stay put. There would be no interviews.

Iain Sproat ran out of time. New Labour swept to power and those in the know confidently expected that the new minister of sport would kill off the whole sorry project. Quite unexpectedly Tony Banks, the maverick, football-mad, left-wing vegetarian was appointed to the post ahead of the favourite for the job, Tom Pendry. Equally unexpectedly, Banks picked up Sproat's academy baton and ran with it.

Three weeks into his job, in June 1997, Banks toured the three shortlisted sites, helicoptering between Oxford, Loughborough and Sheffield in a single day, looking at a variety of green fields, campuses and second-hand sports facilities and trying to imagine the world's finest sports institute rising up before his eyes. Wedged in by civil servants from his department (now called Culture, Media and Sport instead of Heritage), Banks looked bewildered. At a ghostly and windy Upper Heyford he said, 'No one is talking about scaling the bids down.'

They were. Sir Rodney Walker noted that lottery sales had been falling and the decision to introduce a fifth good cause would inevitably mean less money for sport and the Academy. He said, 'We can't ignore the likely development of having less money to fund the headquarters ... if, as may be the case, we lose anywhere between 30 and 40 per cent of our budget then all existing commitments will need to be reviewed. Above all else we must keep up our commitments to community sports and indeed the athletes themselves.'

Asked about the Tory-inspired university of sport concept, which Labour had vehemently opposed before coming to power, compared to the scaled down multi-centred regional model which they had championed, Banks replied, 'We are clearly looking for a centre. The British Academy of Sport is not going to be built on wheels and pushed around the country. The all singing and dancing model looks good to me, that seems the way to go. We want to try and get as much together because we can see all the ways the different sports can provide facilities for each other.'

One of the political problems that dogged the Academy project was that the politicians who championed it consistently made promises they could not keep. Meanwhile the Sports Council, the right and proper body to have provided leadership in this issue, seemed incapable of getting through to them that they were embarked on a course that was not just wrong but doomed to embarrassing failure. So, the politicians said they could have the lottery money but it was not theirs to give away. The politicians said the athletes could have the finest sports facilities known to man but the athletes made it quite clear they did not want them on those terms. To help with the running costs and to make it attractive to the bid teams, the politicians said the academy of sport would be a charitable trust. The Charity Commission took a different view.

Janice Munday, director of policy at the Charity Commission, at the time told *On The Line*, 'Sport is a very difficult area for us. The courts have ruled that the promotion of mere sport is not a charitable purpose in its own right. But there is quite a lot of sporting activity that is charitable: the creation of recreation facilities open to the whole public, that's charitable and there is no problem with that. Sport for the disabled, sport for the unemployed – these things are charitable. The key thing is that it has to be of benefit to the community as a whole not to the benefit of individuals – that's the test.'

The whole point about an academy of sport dedicated to excellence is that it *is* all about 'benefiting the individual'. Elite programmes, by definition, are precisely the opposite of open access. There was little chance that any successful candidate in the bidding process could have claimed charitable status without making massive alterations to the plans for the use of facilities. Yet charitable status was vital to the future revenue plans of all three consortiums.

Back in London, Lord McLaurin, who had predicted something close to economic Armageddon should New Labour be elected, cleared his desk at UK Sport and soon a familiar face would take his place: yes, Sir Rodney Myerscough Walker, who with his close relationship with Derek Casey, the chief executive of the now rebranded Sport England, at least had a fair chance of finding the money to support UK Sport's projects. Sport England, which would be asked to stump up most of the money for the project, reacted to the lull in activity by doing what it liked to do best. It commissioned a survey to discover what exactly sport wanted from an academy – as if it did not know. Predictably, it told Sport England the same things the first survey on such matters had told them back in 1995 – more cash, more support, stuff the Academy.

As if for the want of something to do in this increasingly embarrassing vacuum of activity, the project was rebranded. From now on it would be called the United Kingdom Sports Institute (UKSI). But it would take more than a spot of rebranding to introduce impetus into the project, especially as in October 1997 all attention shifted to something else. The home sports councils unveiled their latest lottery-funded programme for excellence. The World Class Performance Fund (WCPF) made available up to £50 million a year in cash grants to athletes and coaches. It was what our world-class performers had been clamouring for: the opportunity to go full time and concentrate on excellence free of the worry of how they were going to pay their mortgages.

There were and are problems with the WCPF and its operation, but it was this element of lottery support that athlete after athlete gave praise and thanks for at the Sydney Olympics. The idea had been around for as long as the Academy. The mystery was why the relatively simple task of putting money in athletes' pockets had not happened a lot sooner. But more than anything, the WCPF meant the end for the UKSI project as originally conceived in the prospectus. What is remarkable is that nobody noticed, or at best they were in denial. Not even the professional sports administrators at the Sports Council. They blundered on for another two years as if the UKSI, as outlined in the prospectus, would one day be a reality.

The athletes, however, now flush with WCPF money, were able to go full time and train on their doorsteps, stay with their family and their friends, or even go to universities offering scholarships at home or abroad. There was not a snowball's chance in hell that they would flock to the UKSI, no matter how flash it looked.

Two years later Derek Casey, still chief executive at Sport England, professed surprise at the impact of WCPF on the UKSI: 'While the development of the UKSI was going on, the development of revenue support for athletes [WCPF] arrived and once given that flexibility demand changed.' There are two things to say about this. Firstly, demand did not change. It was the same as two exhaustive Sports Council surveys and any number of academic studies had told them from way back when the athletes had asked for time and money not bricks and mortar. Secondly, how much of a surprise can it have been that when athletes finally got their hands on direct funding they then lost all interest, if they ever had any, in the UKSI?

Although the government had promised a decision on the UKSI headquarters by August it was not until December 1997 that Sheffield, the bid originally counted out of the running as having too many 'show-stoppers', was declared winner. It was a poisoned chalice. Apathy had clearly set in regarding the project at the Sports Councils and there was no obvious driving force championing the project in the government or at the Culture, Media and Sport Department either.

Crucially, Sheffield was allowed to go at it full pelt, believing that the Major/Sproat dream would actually happen. The project team on the ground was either unaware of or unwilling to pick up on the obvious disinterest elsewhere. There was no chance of Sheffield pulling it off. Almost immediately it began to suffer death by a thousand cuts. Budgets were subject to frequent downwards revision and key actions to progress the project were consistently postponed.

Abroad, where academies *have* worked, the state has funded them fully from concept to execution and underwritten the risk.

Here, entirely in keeping with a project to be funded principally by the proceeds of gambling, our government wagered that a big lottery cheque would trigger the delivery of an academy of sport to be the envy of the world.

One of the UKSI's most outspoken critics every step of the way was David Sparkes, chief executive of the Amateur Swimming Association: 'Someone had plucked a figure out of thin air and said we will spend £100 or £150 million on the UKSI without defining what it was. And to make matters worse no one had defined how revenue funding was going to be delivered. Would the athletes have to pay? Would there be a government or Sports Council grant? If so, how much? Could the lottery contribute to revenue costs? Nobody seemed to fully get to grips with these questions.' It is true that the 'income question' was unwelcome. All the consortiums *On The Line* spoke with tended either to be excessively woolly on the subject or instead became irritated and answered along the lines of, 'We'll cross that bridge when we come to it.'

Despite the general air of apathy, there were some people on the inside who viewed the whole process with a mounting sense of real alarm. Howard Wells had helped to set up and become chief executive of the Sports Academy in Hong Kong, which runs along similar principles to the AIS. That is, the government built the facilities and put up the scholarships, and the coaches picked the talent to work with.

Wells had arrived at UK Sport just as the chickens were coming home to roost in December 1996. Six months later he admitted to *On The Line* that there were big problems with moving the British Academy forward: 'I think that the major concern is that we are not working in a situation in other parts of the world where the government has paid for everything, and we are relying on many different agencies coming into the piece ... but that is the way it has been structured and we have to move forward.'

But he found that he could not move forward and so he resigned soon after. Meanwhile, in Sheffield, a company optimistically named Phoenix Sport had been created to manage the transition of the UKSI from a concept in the pages of the consortium's bid document to a reality on the site surrounding the Don Valley Stadium. It had its work cut out as the team grappled with local planning problems, tried to tie down the cash promised from the Sheffield bid which had failed to materialize, and worked with the government land-use and environment quango English Partnerships to get to grips with the supposed show-stopper of poisoned ground. It also employed law firms to discover how it could reconcile the seemingly opposed interests of the people of Sheffield, who had right of access to the site that was to benefit elite performers. Never mind selling the concept to the people for whom the UKSI had supposedly been designed.

For the future epicentre of British sport there was an alarming lack of commitment from governing bodies. Only netball and table tennis had agreed to move lock, stock and barrel to Sheffield and even then table tennis later stalled and decided to stay at the Holme Pierpoint national sport centre near Nottingham. Squash was supposed to come too but opted for Manchester instead. Both swimming and athletics were playing wait and see.

Two years down the line in October 1999 the two projects which it had been envisaged would complement one another – the WCPF and the UKSI – had diverged so hopelessly that it was obvious the Major/Sproat-inspired UKSI had to be killed off once and for all. In Sheffield, Phoenix Sport and other interested parties must have been aware of the inevitable but the *coup de grace* when it came was still a bitter pill to swallow. As a sweetener the city would get around £30 million to improve its sports facilities. Lovely as this may be, even the UKSI's most ardent Sheffield supporters had recognized that tempting the world's best sports coaches, scientists and doctors would be a great deal easier with London as bait rather than the seven hills of Steel City. (Actually it proved to be something a grim time for lottery projects in Sheffield – weeks later the much vaunted museum of pop music closed its doors too.)

Not surprisingly, there remains a great deal of anger in the aftermath of the demise of the Academy/UKSI project. Iain

Sproat still believes that Britain is poorer for not having an impressive, identifiable 'capital of sport' in this country. The members of the team who hammered out the detail in the winning Sheffield bid are mostly back in further education or local government, chastened and shocked, like the many individuals who touched the project, at our inability to organize for sporting excellence.

On the positive side, what has happened is that some universities have recognized there is money to be made in sport and have increased their commitment to elite athletes accordingly. They have courted top athletes and coaches, given them budgets and built facilities at places like Bath, Birmingham and Loughborough, which in turn has led some sports to base themselves near these centres of excellence. In effect they are getting on with the job instead of talking about it.

The Sports councils have belatedly attempted to corral these centres together and present them as some kind of cogent network of their own rather than the loose organic federation that they are. Of course, the World Class Performance grants dispensed by the US Sport and monies from their facilities budget are key to the universities' ability to get on with their sporting agendas but there is still tension and resentment towards the 'suits' from London. Rightly or wrongly, they are seen as bureaucratic and interfering – a hindrance rather than a help. Many governing bodies feel the same way. Most sports in this country have no choice but to live by Sport Council rules because they need the money but given half a chance most would have nothing to do with them. One of the more successful sports at the Olympics last time round told *On The Line* that they plan on giving up on some applications to the World Class Performance Fund because it was more trouble than it is worth.

But not everything can be laid at the doors of the sports councils. People do not join the sports administration with the idea of making a mess of things. They themselves are subject to control and must operate within parameters laid down from above. And above them there is a real vacuum of leadership and no obvious evidence of any national sporting philosophy.

Sport in this country suffers from a diffident attitude from the government and wider establishment. The Sport portfolio remains outside the cabinet and runs across three departments, Culture, Education and Health. Government has never seemed to have quite worked out what sport is for or what international success is worth to the nation. Funding is typically as woolly and capricious as policy. It is generally a hotch-potch of the lottery, local authority funding and private sponsorship. And in most instances this works fine if you are building local facilities for local people. But elite sport is a different matter. It is expensive and requires a long-term commitment. It requires the government to get its cheque-book out, like they do everywhere else in the world.

While there is a consensus that success in sport on an inter-national stage is good thing, it is still treated as too trivial an aim to warrant serious planning at the highest levels. Projects like the England World Cup 2006 bid, the National Stadium, and the UKSI, only seem to concern Cabinet ministers when they go wrong. There is confusion abroad sports administrators as to who they should turn to in any given situation. What exactly is the role of Sport England, as opposed to UK Sport? Add to this mix what has become of the UKSI and the problem is clear. Each nation now has its own sports institute, in effect, an office full of consultants. It may be no surprise, given our thrall to anything antipodean that, should you phone, the chances are it will be an Autralian accent that you will hear on the end of the line.

So a sport that operates UK-wide but also under home nation colours, that runs both recreational and elite pro-grammes, must now choose between which one of five sports councils or sports institutes it speaks to depending on which hat, elite or recreational, it is wearing at the time. Confused? Well, to be fair, it is not rocket science but add to this a culture of high staff turnover and the endemic reorganization and rebranding , and you'll see that running sport in this country is clearly a des-perately complex business.

The clamour of agencies and federations pulling in all directions that so alarmed Howard Wells still resounds down the corridors of Britain's sporting powers. Agencies, experts and management consultants continue to chuck in their opinions and while the rest of the world seems to find it relatively easy to build a stadium, or decide on a budget for elite sport, or where to build facilities or understand the importance of coaching, in Great Britain everything is an agony and there is no better illustration of that than the Academy/UKSI saga.

On the eve of Howard Wells' departure from the Hong Kong Sports Institute to take up his post as chief executive of UK Sport he chatted to an Australian colleague who was a veteran of the AIS in Canberra and had worked in Britain: 'He warned me, "You will write a paper, do a consultancy, write another paper, talk to 300 people and four years down the line you won't have delivered anything." I think it is sad but that is pretty much what happened.'

CHAPTER FOUR

No Pain, No Game
Ninety Per Cent of Fast Bowlers Rely on Drugs to Keep Going

Ninety per cent of fast bowlers in county cricket rely on a daily diet of drugs to take to the field. These aren't the drugs that make the head-lines and draw the usual condemnation, but the very same drugs we all take, peddled to them by their employers desperate to keep them out of the treatment room

Angus Fraser composes himself at the end of his 25-pace run-up; the red, half-shined ball is clasped in his large hand. It's a warm summer's evening, late in the last session of a county champi-onship match, the professional cricketer's bread and butter. A modest smattering of spectators is dotted around the vast white stands of Lords as Fraser prepares himself for the next ball. He lumbers rather than glides to the crease, but it's rhythmic, grooved out over 15 years at the top of the game. He passes the umpire and contorts his body into its now familiar but highly unnatural position, before pounding his foot into the ground with full body weight and hurling the ball at 70 miles an hour towards the opposition batsman.

In the 2000 county cricket season Fraser repeated this 2842 times. Add to this the rest of his long, distinguished career of 46 test matches, plus overseas tours, the burdens of one-day cricket, bowling in the nets, batting and long days in the field. No wonder the years he has spent in the game have taken some toll.

'I think the first injury I had,' he explained 'was a strained side or something like that when I was younger, and then I had a stress fracture in my back after a couple years of being a pro-fessional cricketer. After that I have been OK until my hip ail-ment came along in 1990–91, that was a major problem and it took me a couple of years to get it right. Since then I just had a groin operation.' He stops himself as he realizes that his definition of luck may differ from the rest of ours and laughs: 'It sounds like a casualty ward, you obviously get niggles, but they're the main injuries I have sustained throughout my career, so there is not many really.'

Fast bowlers are the cart-horses of this country's peculiarly structured domestic game; they willingly punish their bodies for no more reward than a hot bath and the chance to do it again the next day. When the next day comes, though, it isn't all will-power and professional pride that gets them out of the dressing room and onto the field. The vast majority are reliant on chemical assistance, the type that only comes in a bottle or box. Not, however, the performance-enhancing drugs that make the headlines, but the performance enablers found in every bathroom cabinet.

Yorkshire's Darren Gough has probably benefited more than any other from the recent introduction of central contracts for England's top players. He relies on short bursts of hostile fast bowling for his effectiveness, difficult to maintain when a test match may follow a four-day county match, which in turn follows a one-day cup game. It was Gough who highlighted the legal drug problem of his fellow fast bowlers by declaring that he was free from injury and 'not taking painkillers, which 90 per cent of fast bowlers do'.

His fellow cricketers, just to get out onto the field day after day, are popping potentially addictive pills, giving them a short-term remedy but long-term problems. Angus Fraser recalls the first time he turned to the bottle as a youngster at Middlesex: 'I just remember pulling a muscle in my back just before I got in the Middlesex team,' he says, 'and basically the physiotherapist saw me and gave me a couple of anti-inflammatory tablets. I took them, and lo and behold the injury disappeared overnight so all of a sudden you'd found this almost cure to your problems and I was out and playing in two or three days' time.'

Like Fraser, Graham Dilley can reel off a stomach-churning list of injuries to most parts of his body. His action was unique, hurling the ball javelin-style while dragging his back foot through. He explained how taking anti-inflammatories and painkillers became a routine: 'That's just the nature of playing English county cricket, you never go out onto the field, or very rarely anyway, 100 per cent fit. There is always something wrong and it's just a question of what degree of injury you have got as to whether you can go out there and do what you are supposed to do.' He went on to explain a familiar scenario: 'The doctor would say, "Right, you have got to have an operation in six weeks' time or at the end of the season," and you would muddle through the best you could until you could do no more, and then you would go and have the operation.'

Dilley is now a coach, most recently with the England women's team and the 1999 Scotland World Cup squad. Naturally, the standard of medical care has improved since he won the last of his 41 caps: 'The injuries I have had are the usual sort of things that are part and parcel of the job. I suppose the most serious was having a disc removed, taken out of my spine, then the disc below that gave way, plus two others in my lower back that have gone as well and then four knee ops.'

One incident, though, highlights how much attention was paid to the players' physical wellbeing. 'During my last year with Worcestershire,' he says, 'I had an Achilles problem. They sent me off to have an x-ray on it. I had been strapping my ankle up for eight years and it got to the stage where I thought it was just psychological, there is nothing wrong with it, so they did some x-rays.' To his astonishment the radiologist looked at them and asked him when he broke his ankle. 'I said I never have broken my ankle and she said, "You can see the fracture on the chart!" So I had been playing for eight years with a broken ankle.'

After leaving Kent, Dilley played in the star-studded team assembled at Worcestershire, which included Ian Botham and Graham Hick. Dave Roberts was then the physio at New Road, before going on to work with the England team. He says that reaching for the medicine bag was the easy way to get players back onto the field: 'A lot of these players by the time you get to mid-July or August you are giving them anti-inflammatory tablets. Some are having injections, which isn't really the best way to prepare players for playing at the top level. It's something you don't want to do. If somebody needs an injection or somebody needs a painkiller you tend to stop. If you were going to work during the day and you needed a painkiller to type you'd think twice about actually going to work, wouldn't you? Well, not these lads, they just put up with it.'

The walls of the waiting room in Manchester where Dave Roberts now practises privately are liberally covered with pictures of his time touring with the England team around the world. He agrees, he says, with Darren Gough's chilling statistic: 'I would probably say that by August 80-90 per cent of fast bowlers are probably taking some kind of anti-inflammatory or painkilling tablets from time to time. They don't have to be taking it every day, but they will be taking it from time to time.'

Graham Dilley admits he is familiar with this 'patch 'em up and get 'em out' philosophy: 'It was "Right, physio, what's the problem?" "This is what's wrong with you." "What have I got to do?" "Well, start off with here's a glass of water and a tablet. Take that and we will just assess it." The painkillers start taking effect and whether you can get out there or not, it was a "Patch you up, get you out there, do a job, see what happens the next day." All the time we are asking people to play the amount of cricket they are now playing, people are going to have to take painkillers and anti-inflammatories to get them out there and get them through the game; that is just a fact of life.'

The worry confronting a player is that just taking a tablet is not going to solve the injury but make it worse. The pain may have disappeared but the problem that is causing it hasn't – the painkillers have simply numbed the body's message that there is a problem and all the time the injury keeps deteriorating.

According to Roger Odd of the Royal Pharmaceutical Society there are other serious side effects: 'Stronger medicines and painkillers can be addictive, and the actual quantity and the length of time people have to take it before they become dependent or addicted to it varies from person to person. A lot depends on how often it is used, for example how often it is taken and the strength taken, of course. The higher the dosage and the longer the period of time, it is much more difficult to wean off.'

Neither Fraser, Gough nor Dilley has suffered an addiction to painkillers, but in sport generally it is not uncommon. In the United States one of the highest paid players in American football, Brett Favre of the Green Bay Packers, was admitted to a clinic to deal with his addiction. And the *New York Times* reported in 1998 that match tickets are a valuable currency for players to 'buy' pills from employees of drug companies. Estimates in the US are that ten per cent of players in the NFL are addicts, understandable in a game that is not so much a contact sport as a collision sport, but not in the sedate world of county cricket.

Repeated use can also lead, according to Roger Odd, to long-term internal problems, 'if a large quantity is taken over the dosage that is usually given because people feel that they need a stronger painkiller. The worry is that they can be extremely harmful and they certainly do cause irreparable damage and particularly if they are taken over a great length of time. Similarly, anything that is an aspirin-based product, for example, or an ibuprofen-based medicine can cause stomach or gastric-based irritation, if taken in large quantities.'

The added side effects of painkillers which contain drugs called narcotic analgesics can be: drowsiness, nausea, constipation, sweating, a loss of balance and coordination, fainting, palpitations, restlessness, mood changes and a decreased breathing rate. Not ideal for a professional sports player – but there is not much of a choice, according to Angus Fraser. 'Yes, you are aware of certain side effects,' he explains. 'I mean the way that they can cause damage to your stomach, for instance. Mike Atherton takes them and they upset his stomach from time to time so he has to take something to correct that. You have got a short enough cricket career as it is and you want to play as much cricket as you can while you're young.'

Dependency on drugs sold in every high street or handed out by a physiotherapist is made all the easier, according to Roger Odd, because of their very availability: 'The problem with taking painkillers which are much stronger is that not only are you on a much higher dosage but there is sometimes a dependence on taking large dosage of those medicines. For example, much more medicine is needed to try and deaden the pain, and of course some of them, especially if they are morphine or codeine based and taken over any length of time, can also become rather dependent or addictive.'

Addiction to over-the-counter (OTC) medicines was a huge part of life for Scotsman David Grieve. For years he went to enormous lengths to satisfy his own need for cough mixture. Cured of a dependency which cost him around £18,000, he set up the help group Over-Count, where he has encountered addicts like himself. Disturbingly, he says, some of them are cricketers. 'One in particular, I remember, had an injury to his knee and he actually didn't want to go to his own doctor or the Sports Council doctor to be treated because he felt it may be detrimental to his career.' Not surprisingly, the player didn't want to be named and risk being identified by his club.

'He went to a local chemist's shop to buy a very popular product which contains a drug called ibuprofen and codeine combined,' Grieve says, 'It stopped the pain and reduced the swelling in his injury but he liked the effects so much he carried on taking it when the swelling went down. He contacted us because he couldn't stop taking it. He was very worried that he would have a random drugs test and because the product contains codeine he was worried that with the presence of opiates he could end up getting a ban.'

Reflecting on the cricketers who have come to him for help, Grieve says: 'Of the nine or ten that I can think of, approximately four are nationally known professional cricketers. You would be very surprised and you would recognize their names like I did. They're doing it on the daily basis – that's the worrying point. They are not just taking it on a five-day period; some have been doing it for the past three or four months, constantly, day after day.'

Should we really be so shocked? The pressures on a cricketer are no less than in any other sport. The way the game has been structured for decades, with the players' welfare well down the list of priorities, is a huge factor in this. Having been involved in the game both domestically and internationally, Dave Roberts has witnessed its ills from both sides. 'Worcestershire is a fantastic place to watch cricket,' he recalls. 'It's their biggest crowd-puller. When I was there we had Hick, Botham, Dilley, Phil Neale, Damian D'Olivera, Phil Newport, Richard Illingworth, Steve Rhodes, we had a lot of good players – England "A" or England players – and playing on a Sunday was Worcestershire's biggest day.'

Like all counties, Worcestershire had one eye on the gate receipts, and they needed the big names on the field, injuries or not, and it was Dave Roberts's job to get them out there. 'Often the trouble was the test side was announced at eleven o'clock on a Sunday morning,' he explained. 'And if you had two or three players involved in the test on the following Thursday, you would watch them go out at two o'clock on the same Sunday afternoon to throw themselves about New Road in an effort to stop a four or whatever, putting themselves at risk a more important match on Thursday.' Come Thursday, Roberts had his international hat on; in his opinion the sensible and preferred option was rest and a few days on the treatment table. Unfortunately, that was an option seldom available to him or his fellow physios.

'You know it masks the injury,' he continued ruefully. 'There's not a lot of choice ... players cannot stand up and say, "I am not playing," they are either going to lose face or lose their income, they are under contract to play cricket and they have just got to get on with it. There's pressure on you from the club, the captain initially depending on the player, depending on who he is and what his motivation is. There is pressure particularly with an overseas player where you are paying him a lot of money, and if they are sat in the physiotherapy room they are not out on the pitch earning their money and bringing the crowds in.'

Even off six languid paces Graham Dilley is still able to trouble England Women's cricketers in the nets. He says it was pressure from his peers which had the most effect: 'When I was playing you were looked at almost as if you were weak if you missed a game. People said, "There's something wrong with that fellow, he's missed a game, he's got another injury." There is certainly not the understanding of what it actually takes to get somebody out on the field and what sometimes they actually *take* to get out onto the field. There is definitely more of an understanding of fast bowling in this country now, but all the time we ask them to go out and do it every single day we are not going to make strides forward.' He can certainly recall decisions on match fitness that have been made by men in blazers and not the men in whites.

'There were occasions when there was a little bit of pressure put on in terms of "What's wrong with him again, is it the same injury or is it another one?" I don't know whether there was ever any occasion where a committee man said, "You will get out on that field and play", it was left to the physio and the individual as to whether he thought he could get through the game. If he thought you could, you went on the field; if he thought you couldn't, you didn't. It's not the direct pressure, more like the indirect pressure of knowing for a fact that people sitting in that committee room are moaning at the fact that you are not on that field again, because you are waiting to go and have a major operation or something like that, but they don't realize or certainly didn't realize what it took to get you out onto the field.'

A study revealed that two thousand people die in the UK every year from dependency on OTC painkillers. And one in ten of those who take them continuously for over two months will die. The study also highlighted the serious internal side effects of the pills. In order for the body to deal with a regular intake of drugs it needs to have even more drugs. Ian Botham, for example, went into great detail about his pill-popping routine in one of his books, explaining that he drank huge amounts of Gaviscon, a thick, syrupy liquid, to counter the effects on his stomach of his constant diet of painkillers.

Luckily, however, the next generation of fast bowlers this country is producing is entering a more enlightened and understanding game. Research into injuries and prevention is becoming more and more common, rendering the injury-masking drugs redundant. At the forefront of this is Professor Roger

Bartlett, head of the £5-million Centre for Sport and Exercise at Sheffield Hallam University. He says that the sworn enemy of the fast bowler is the mixed technique. His theory is that bowling actions fall into three categories: the front on, the classic side on and the mixed action where the bowler is caught between the two – where the inevitable result is injury.

Bartlett uses high-resolution video images and computer-generated figures to illustrate the stress placed on the body. Judging by the wince-inducing, high-resolution pictures, it is no wonder that injuries are such a huge part of a cricketer's life. Professor Bartlett continued frame by frame: 'He then lands on his left foot, which will impose a force of somewhere between six and eight times his body weight. All of these taking place at the same time cause high stresses in the lower back, which can lead to a whole myriad of injury problems.'

Unfortunately, a fast bowler's action is ingrained by the time he or she reaches professional standard. They could no more change it than the rest of us could our signature. It may be too late for Angus Fraser, one of our most durable bowlers, to take his action apart and start again. 'No, nobody tried to change my action,' he says. 'Really, you know, they have tried to point you in the right direction and little things you might be doing wrong from time to time. No one's got hold of me and said, "You should do this, you should do that". I think essentially I have got a fairly classical action in a lot of ways – there isn't arms and legs going everywhere, so I have been left to work things out for myself.'

One bowler who tried to reconstruct his action was Essex and England left-armer Mark Illot. He took a year off from the game after injury problems but did tell *On The Line* that he still needed regular doses of anti-inflammatories. Graham Dilley also says he was advised to change his action when he was a young player: 'When I first started playing I bowled very much chest on, then I got told by some of the senior players at Kent and one of the coaching staff there that if I wanted to be a success at test cricket, then I had to change what I did and get the ball to move away from the bat. In those days in order to do that you had to change your bowling action totally. I went from being chest on to being side on. I sometimes wonder whether if I had been left to my own devices, as it were, I would have had so many injuries.'

Professor Bartlett certainly possesses some real video nasties in his collection. He talks through another film, this time of another international bowler with over 300 test wickets, whose front leg actually bends backwards at the knee as he delivers the ball at nearly 90 miles an hour. He reveals that the bowler, who wanted to remain anonymous, suffers a lot of pain while bowling. 'But,' he added, 'he suffers more while watching himself bowling on tape.'

Lancashire's indoor cricket school sits behind the plush executive boxes at Old Trafford. It's an excellent facility where the county's players from youngsters to first-teamers train. Professor Bartlett is a regular visitor here, called in by Lancashire's development manager, John Stanworth. 'We are just starting to use experts in the bio-mechanical field,' Stanworth explains, while casting a paternal eye over the young hopefuls. 'And what they have told us is that there is a conflict between the axis of the shoulders and the axis of the hips, in effect a mixed action. There is potential, therefore, for problems in the back area. By identifying those as soon as possible from under-13s and then upwards we can address potential problems they may have in the future, so that they are solved by the age of 14 or 15.'

This is the key: spotting the problem while players are young and before they cause irreparable damage. Research carried out by Professor Bartlett and fellow 'bowling boffins' at the University of Western Australia in Perth estimates that nearly 25 per cent of fast bowlers at 14 years old suffer from career-ending damage to the back. It is the sad experience of one young player that provides the incentive for John Stanworth.

'The lesson we have learned came with one very gifted bowler,' he recalls. 'He played representatively for us and at national level, but he'd got a technically poor action which wasn't diagnosed. He'd had back problems and when he joined the staff there was nothing our physiotherapy unit could do, the damage had already been done. He had an operation two weeks into his professional career and after six weeks his career was over, and I think the lessons there were learned by us so we could prevent this sort of thing happening in the future.'

As the youngsters John Stanworth hopes will go on to play for the county's first team go through their paces in the nets, next door Professor Bartlett assesses them using a video link. They are then called in one by one to review the tapes. It's encouraging that clubs like Lancashire are being so proactive with their young players, but Professor Bartlett says he knows that asking a fast bowler in his twenties to tinker with his action is unrealistic. 'I can very much understand bowlers at that stage of their careers who do not want to change, because somebody happens to come up with some evidence that suggests they could be injured at some stage. But certainly younger bowlers who have learned that the mixed technique could lead to injury for them ... ' he stares at the screen as the young bowlers try and put his advice into practice. 'These younger bowlers are very receptive and they want an action that will enable them to bowl fast and to bowl well until they are into their thirties, not until they are into their late teens.'

As an ex-pro himself on the county circuit, John Stanworth agrees with physio Dave Roberts where the problem lies: 'One of the big problems with our game in producing quality quick bowlers is that there aren't enough rest periods, the demands on players' time is too great and the quality that is produced is affected by the quantity that is played – and until we address that amongst other things as well I don't think we will have genuine quick bowlers in abundance.' Would the highly paid stars of professional football put up with that? Probably not. Central contracts and a reduction in one-day matches are moves in the right direction, but the treadmill of the county circuit is a difficult one to get off.

Back in the macho, big-hitting, bone-crunching world of American football's NFL the sport has been forced, in some part, to face up to its drug problem. Walt Sweeney, a former player with the San Diego Chargers, successfully sued the League for $1.8 million after he was repeatedly given painkillers during his career: he claimed they were guilty of helping him become an addict. In this country, anecdotally at least, painkillers are widely used in rugby and football – addicts thankfully are not so common, or at least not so willing to come forward

There is little chance of us aping litigation-mad America, but for years cricket and gridiron have shared a culture of clubs dispensing tablets to players only too willing to take them with scant regard for the future. When asked, neither Graham Dilley nor Angus Fraser can say that as a young player he considered the side effects; but neither does a boxer dreaming of becoming World Champion reflect that the price he might pay could be the loss of his faculties, when the time comes to reap the rewards of being pummelled in the ring.

It may be, however, that the painkillers and anti-inflammatories taken so regularly could become a thing of the past. In Sydney the German Olympic team were the latest to use 'systemic enzymes', a natural treatment for pain and swelling. Research in Austria has confirmed their effectiveness in treating injuries in sport, without the side effects, and they should soon be widely available over the counter in Britain.

And yet there is still a startlingly 'matter-of-fact' attitude in the game towards this high level of dangerous drug-taking. In any situation there has to be a villain: in this case it's the game itself – county cricket. It is the way that the game is structured, the way that our top athletes are asked to perform at their best day after day, the way they are patched up and sent out onto the field, aware that if they admit injury they will be seen as weak and unreliable, in a game of short-term contracts and limited opportunities. Addiction is much easier when your dealer isn't the seedy-looking bloke who hangs surreptitiously in a back street, but is behind the door marked physio, and behind the counter in the local chemist's.

CHAPTER FIVE

Board and Confused

Murder and Mystery as Chess Tries to Join the Olympics

As the kings of the Olympic Games consider making chess an Olympic event, the pawns in the House of Commons prepare to deem the game a sport in order for it to qualify for generous public handouts. On the one hand these developments are the laudable and overdue recognition of an activity loved by millions; on the other they are the outworkings of a global plot by the cunning and corrupt president of world chess. He is also the flamboyant head of state of a murky little tax haven on the shores of the Caspian Sea.

Charismatic, debonair and ostentatious, Kirsan Ilyumzhinov leads the campaign for chess to be recognized by the Olympic Games and receive cash from the British government. He has had meetings in the House of Commons and played chess with the president of the International Olympic Committee (IOC) for the benefit of press photographers (although neither seemed to notice that the pieces were on the wrong squares at the start of their game). Ilyumzhinov bankrolls chess to the tune of US $25 million that, he insists, comes from his own personal fortune. But he fixes elections, rips off the poorest people in Europe and is linked to the murder of a journalist. Where the money really comes from, nobody knows. Where he comes from is public knowledge: he's from the southern Russian state of Kalmykia, where the people are called either Kalmyks or Kalmykians.

Dina Newman, a Russian-born journalist who has travelled the area extensively for the BBC's World Service, explains: 'Kalmyks themselves are Mongolian tribespeople who came to Russia from China in the seventeenth century. At that time the Kalmyks were a fierce tribe and the Chinese did not really want them, so they went to the Tsar of Russia, Vasily Shuysky, and offered their allegiance to him. He was impressed by the ferocity of their soldiers and gave them a part of Russia near to the Caucasus so they could protect the Russians from the Caucasians and the Chechens. So the Kalmykians formed Europe's only Buddhist state on the lower Volga, with a small part of the Steppe along the Caspian Sea.'

The present-day state of Kalmykia skulks unobtrusively between Chechnya and Azerbaijan, a largely anonymous consequence of the break-up of the Soviet Union. It is 80 per cent desert with nearly half of its 300,000 people inhabiting the drab capital, Elista. 'Nothing grows there, it is very, very dry and all that you have there is a kind of grass that is very bitter and very tough. Only sheep will eat it, so this is what the Kalmyks do traditionally, they raise sheep, which is the only thing they can do in this climate,' says Dina Newman. Visitors speak of the Kalmyks as being a friendly people, proud of their distinctive heritage and welcoming of outsiders.

Kirsan Ilyumzhinov spurned the dust-coated life of a Steppe shepherd to seek his fortune Dick Whittington style. In 1989, aged 27, he graduated from the Moscow State Institute of International Relations. Within a year he was a member of the Russian Parliament. In 1991, when the voracious and unregulated free market of post-communist Eastern Europe emerged, he was ideally placed to take advantage. Exactly how he made his millions is not clear. His own account is that he was part of a joint Japanese and Russian venture importing cars and computers to Moscow.

One of Ilyumzhinov's business associates then and now is Artem Tarasov, founder of Russia's first lottery, sometime Muscovite restaurant owner and now a London-based businessman. 'I've known him for ten years, we are friends,' he says. 'The sources of his money are his participation in, and personal investment in, different companies like television. He has a substantial holding of stocks in Russian television and he has stocks in trading companies and in a bank. He's a big businessman. He's a politician.'

Certainly, when Dina Newman asked Ilymuzhinov about

the source of his wealth he gave a very political answer: 'When I asked Kirsan this question he said "Why are you looking in someone else's pocket?"' His autobiography, *The President's Crown of Thorns*, is a little more forthcoming. It tells of how difficult it was for an outsider from an ethnic minority to prosper in the Russian capital. Against the odds he gained a place in the prestigious Foreign Relations Institute where he learned Japanese. He then set up the Sun Corporation, of which he wrote, 'Together with French partners we started producing animated films, arranged exhibition sales of paintings, started new newspapers and organized a Russian commodity exchange. However, the sheer size of the operation generated new problems. We could no longer keep track of the money.' So he started a bank – the Steppe Bank of Kalmykia.

Dina Newman says the Kalmyks regard Ilyumzhinov, the local boy who went to Moscow and successfully sought his fortune, as a hero: 'They are incredibly proud of him. I cannot think of anybody else of Kalmyk origin who has ever been famous outside Kalmykia, not a single person comes to mind.' Fame and fortune secured, the rich young star needed a power base. In 1993 he stood for election as president of Kalmykia. Boasting by now more than 50 companies to his name with a combined turnover of more than $500 million a year, Kirsan (as both friends and foes know him) showed a fantastically populist touch in campaigning. He promised to turn impoverished Kalmykia into the new Kuwait, equip every shepherd with a mobile phone, give all voters a hundred dollars and recruit Diego Maradona to play for Elista FC. None of these outlandish promises has been kept, but, according to Dina Newman, his people still adore him: 'All of a sudden to have a leader like this, young, dynamic, good-looking, charming, literate, able to speak Russian and Kalmyk, proudly announcing he is a Buddhist, but he is also a capitalist, you know, all these things make the Kalmyks incredibly happy.'

The presidency of Kalmykia earned Kirsan complimentary elevation to the Upper House of the Russian Parliament as a senator. He was made president of the Russian Chamber of Enterprises and acquired all the diplomatic trappings of high office, the most notable being a complete immunity from criminal prosecution. This Soviet get-out-of-jail-free card was to prove most useful. Sarah Hurst is a former chess reporter who for some time watched Kirsan's gameplan from the vantage point of neighbouring Azerbaijan. She says he moved swiftly to make maximum benefit from his new status: 'He established a kind of one-party state. He banned political parties from Kalmykia, saying they could only return when the standard of living there was twice as high as that of Russia. He has also established a personality cult with posters of himself on all public buildings.'

Just two years into his presidency he sought re-election and allowed no opposition to stand, a practice illegal under Russian federal law although Kirsan's connections in the Kremlin ensured no action was taken against him. The so-called election was permitted to go ahead and he secured 85 per cent of the turn-out. Quite who the other 15 per cent voted for has never been made clear. President Kirsan took the opportunity to pass a new law lengthening his term of office from four years to seven. His next move was an economic masterstroke of typically imaginative opportunism: he declared the barren, mid-continent state of Kalmykia to be an offshore zone, a tax-free haven for international business.

Any company that relocates to Kirsan's discount economy is exempt from local taxation. In return it pays a flat fee of $1,200 a year into the President's Fund, administered by Kirsan. He is lord of his own manor, and has created a feudal tax system in keeping with his pseudo-mediaeval status. 'We now have investors from South Korea, Germany, England and the USA,' he bragged in an interview for the BBC. More than six thousand businesses raced to take up this generous offer of tax-free trade, contributing nothing at all to the Kalmyk exchequer – and seven million dollars a year to the President's Fund.

Kirsan is an absentee landlord, choosing to live not in the rural backwater he claims to be so proud of but in a palatial residence in the heart of Moscow. When Dina Newman arranged an interview with him she was told to arrive after 11 o'clock at night. 'He likes to work overnight and disappears during the day,' she remembers. 'I found the address he suggested and it turned out to be a huge, luxurious residence right in the middle of Moscow, situated privately in one of the courtyards so you wouldn't be able to see it from the street. It is an incredibly beautiful and elegant building. He met me himself, just wearing a normal suit, nothing flashy, and he was very charming. He gave the impression of being someone you have known for a very long time and that he's your best friend.'

Slim and dark-haired, with Asiatic features hinting at his Mongolian ancestry, Kirsan Ilyumzhinov has the soft hands and gentle voice of a smooth-talking charmer. He seemed at ease with his power and wealth, eagerly exhibiting photograph albums to his late-night house guest. 'He was showing me photos of fleets of flashy cars, holiday villas in far-flung places which he said belonged to him, pictures of him with Saddam Hussein, telling me they are the best of friends and somehow this all seemed perfectly normal coming from him,' Dina Newman recalls.

Sarah Hurst was also granted an audience with the president, during which he explained his philosophy of leadership. 'I try to live as if I'm in a five-minute blitz chess game,' he told Hurst. 'I have to constantly raise my professional level, first to Master, then to Grandmaster, then a Champion. So every day I study important subjects like economics, business and wool. Previously I knew nothing about wool, but I read books about sheep farming in Australia and New Zealand so that I would become an expert.'

Boasting that each year he visits around 80 countries and is always entertained by heads of state he confesses that running an autonomous ex-Soviet state as it nurtures a free market is not as tricky as it might appear. 'It's not difficult because there is the telephone and the computer,' he modestly explains. 'I could be in Africa or Indonesia; I turn on my computer and modem and straight away I see on the display how much money there is in the national bank. I know how much wool is in the warehouses, how many people have been paid and how many haven't.'

Like Dina Newman, Sarah Hurst was shown the photographs of Kirsan and his pal Saddam. 'From the media it seemed he [Saddam] was a dictator, that he was crazy,' said the Kalmyk ruler, digging himself a little hole with his words. 'In person he turned out to be very cultured and educated. He knows history and politics very well,' he continued to tunnel away. 'I had the same sort of impression of the Pope,' he concluded, getting about as deep as is possible. Quite how much Saddam Hussein and Pope John Paul II have in common is unknown, but they share at least one admirer. On his official website of Kalmykia there is a subsection for his 'friends'. The President reflects on his Catholic leanings, 'When people ask me why I have built a catholic cathedral in Kalmykia I say it is for the children. Also the Pope paid for a library in Elista,' he reveals.

Along with His Holiness and Saddam Hussein, Buddhist Kirsan claims more than a passing acquaintance with the Dalai Lama. While describing himself as a capitalist he openly toyed with standing for the presidency of Russia as a communist and, in the right company, tells of his respect for both Marx and Lenin. He confided in Hurst that he models his leadership on both Napoleon and Jesus Christ. Yet Kirsan's hobnobbing does not come from being king of the Kalmyks but from becoming the big cheese of chess, gaining him the profile he craves outside of the former Soviet block.

FIDE (the *Fédération Internationale D'Échecs*) was founded in Paris in 1924 – *'Échecs'* being French for chess. The game's popularity saw FIDE establish national bodies all over the world. But splits and bad business meant that by the mid 1990s FIDE was broke. A game with complete global appeal encompassing all ages and abilities, which could be staged anywhere and which is perfectly suited to the internet, was in need of a saviour. It was plump and ripe for the taking by a charming and brilliant young politician with international ambition and access to enormous wads of cash. Kirsan Ilyumzhinov was elected president of FIDE in 1994. Chess got its injection of funds, Kirsan got an international platform.

The change at the top of chess was marked; elite players were earning big money and few of them seemed bothered where it was coming from. 'Chess has always been somewhat like the wild west: it's rather splendid in many ways,' says Jon Speelman, Grandmaster and newspaper chess correspondent. 'Players have always been individual; if you are playing for a sponsor you don't enquire where the sponsor made his money. All we require is an organization that works, that arranges tournaments and makes sure that they are funded,' he admits.

Speelman's ambivalence to who runs chess is shared by Nigel Short. One of the best British players of recent years, Short broke away from FIDE with the then World Champion, Gary Kasparov. He says most players have a straightforward ask-no-questions approach to Kirsan. 'We all know Ilyumzhinov is corrupt,' he told Sarah Hurst. 'But at least he's corrupt and *giving* money to FIDE. The previous FIDE president was corrupt and *taking* money from FIDE. If people are starving in Kalmykia it is sad, but it is not my problem. Chess is my livelihood,' he said.

Sarah Hurst is disgusted: 'Supposedly intelligent chess players who you would think would support human rights and be against corruption have pledged their allegiance to him simply because he gives them huge prize funds, and chess players aren't used to winning huge prizes.'

With next to no funds of its own and little commercial flair FIDE could find nowhere to host its grandly titled Thirty-third Chess Olympiad of 1998. Kirsan not only offered to put up all the prize money but also promised to build a sparkling new venue especially designed to be the home of chess. The outrageously lavish Chess City on the outskirts of Elista is an oasis of opulence in a desert of deprivation, a glistening gold tooth in the mouth of a tramp. The *Los Angeles Times* described it as part Disneyland, part Oz. Dina Newman went there soon after it was built and describes what she saw: 'It is incredibly luxurious by Kalmyk standards, because in the city itself there is still a lot of poverty, and in the rural areas poverty is acute. But if you look at Chess City alone it seems that this project was very generously financed. It was built to European standards with fountains and plenty of water splashing around. In Kalmykia there is a shortage of water and supply is rationed in the summer months, so the locals aren't happy seeing all these fountains in Chess City.'

Not that the locals ever do see the opulent townhouses interspersed with lush green rectangles of lawn and elegant statues of Kalmyk shepherds and warriors. Armed guards keep the people out. Impoverished tax payers who live within a stone's throw of Chess City's walls have been denied the pleasures experienced by foreign chess players, journalists and dignitaries. And where did the money come from to build this? A local journalist found out what you get for asking questions like that on the streets of Elista.

Larissa Youdina wrote and distributed *Sovietskaya Kalmykia Segodnya (Soviet Kalmiya Today)*, the only opposition newspaper in Kirsan's Kalmyk kingdom. She wrote a number of articles asking why Chess City was built at huge expense when election promises to bring prosperity to the people had been broken. Why, demanded Youdina, was the income from the tax haven being spent on furthering the political ambition of the president when state farmers had not been paid for five years? She was also keen to find out what had become of a $70 million grant for wool production paid by Moscow to a company owned by Ilyumzhinov, by this time a well-read wool expert of course. The company was disbanded shortly before he became president and the money has never been accounted for. Kirsan responded to these perfectly reasonable questions by outlawing Youdina's publication. Undaunted, she relocated to Volgograd, two hundred miles away in Russia, and smuggled the papers across the border in the boot of her Lada each week. In June 1998 Larissa received an anonymous phone call promising documentary evidence of corruption within Kirsan's regime. She excitedly arranged a meeting.

The dark alleyways of Elista held no fear for the 53-year-old reporter, an experienced and streetwise operator. On the night of 7 June Larissa drove alone to the Kalmykian capital for a secret rendezvous with the person she hoped would be her most revealing source. The precise detail of the evening is unknown, but the outcome is certain. The following morning, at the bottom of the hill which elevates Chess City to the sky, Larissa's body was face down in a pond. Her skull was smashed and she had been stabbed repeatedly.

Within a week three men were charged with the murder of Larissa Youdina. Two of them were members of Ilyumzhinov's staff. According to the reports of local newspapers, all three admitted to the murder. No trial has been held. There have been no convictions and no investigation into who, if anyone, ordered the killing. Kirsan, wallowing in his diplomatic immunity from prosecution of any kind, dismissively distances himself from any connection to the crime.

As Sarah Hurst explains, these events leave a sour taste: 'He is very unpopular in Russia. He is believed to have embezzled hundreds of thousands of dollars [the wool grant] and he is also known to have spent millions of dollars on Chess City, but no one knows where that money came from. He also drives around in a white Rolls-Royce and jets all over the world.'

The murder of Larissa Youdina did achieve something. It finally made a small minority of chess players question the man at the top. Australian Grandmaster Ian Rogers was one such conscientious objector. 'I missed the Elista Olympiad in 1998 after the murder of Larissa Youdina. A few other Australian players had the same point of view. We just didn't feel it was right playing an event organized and sponsored by someone who we thought should be at least investigated to see if he had any connection to her death. So we just stayed away. It's only something small, but it makes me feel better,' he said. Grandmaster Rogers is contemptuous of those who say chess is too poor to start asking questions of its benefactors: 'You could also argue that if the Carli Cartel [Colombian drug dealers] decided to put $20 million of heroin funds into chess, that would also be good for the sport. Should chess accept money like that? It's very easy for Ilyumzhinov to spend money that perhaps should have gone to the people of Kalmykia. It's easy to be generous with other people's money.'

Other players who seemed capable of tolerating the stabbing of a reporter and the ripping off of a national electorate found it harder to accept their own money drying up. It happened a year after Rogers's mini-boycott of Elista, at a tournament arranged by Kirsan in Las Vegas. Much to the embarrassment of all concerned, the prize cheques bounced. Even a man of his colossal resources had failed to avert a cash-flow problem at FIDE. After much growling from the unpaid participants, new cheques were issued and honoured by the bank. The paid-off players returned to their lairs, sated.

By this time Kirsan's position at the top of FIDE was almost as untouchable as his sovereignty in Kalmykia. OK, so he hadn't managed to change the constitution like he had at home, but he had managed comprehensively to squash the only person ever to stand against him. 'When Kirsan Ilyumzhinov was elected president of FIDE one of his tasks was to set up a match between Anatoly Karpov and Gata Kamsky,' explains Hamman Harmas, head of the Dutch Chess Federation. 'He announced that this would be in Baghdad, the capital of Iraq. This was in 1995 when the whole of the western world was boycotting Iraq.'

The Dutch were angered by the suggestion that Kirsan's new chums in chess could come and meet his dear friend Saddam. They were also unhappy with what they perceived to be an undemocratic style of leadership. They called a congress in Utrecht. As Mr Harmas recalls, the gathering had two purposes: 'The aim of the congress was to first of all prevent the match in Baghdad from happening. The second was to form a presidential ticket to stand against Kirsan in elections the following year.' The first aim was successful, the Baghdad trip was scrapped; but the second objective – to mount a viable challenge to Kirsan's presidency – floundered. 'We asked Mr Sunyanato, the president of the Brazilian Chess Federation, to be a candidate for the presidency of FIDE,' continued Harmas. 'We also had support from the Russian Federation and the USA.'

Everything looked fine until the very last minute. With all the delegates gathered in Armenia to choose between Kirsan's leadership and the alternative organized by the Dutch, Mr Harmas's ticket crumbled away. Three of the most prominent people in his campaign, candidates for top posts within FIDE, stepped down and refused to be part of the process. The depleted Dutch had an incomplete set of nominations and under FIDE election rules were forced to withdraw. Kirsan was returned unopposed and he immediately gave top jobs in his new administration to the people who had left Harmas in the lurch.

'Yes, it was rather surprising,' says the Netherlander with irony. 'I can imagine people have reasons to step down from a ticket, but when they later joined Ilyumzhinov it was rather surprising.' What was it that tempted the trio to leave at the last minute? What enlightenment visited them during their short Armenian trip causing such a dramatic change of heart? No one knows, but whatever it was, they were at least lucky enough to secure a place in the jet-setting elite of world chess. So their trip wasn't unrewarded.

Having humiliated the opposition in 1996, Kirsan's position is impregnable, according to Ian Rogers: 'I think most potential candidates for FIDE president would not dare to stand against him now. It would take a crazy person to stand against Kirsan.'

Throughout all this turmoil the British Chess Federation (BCF) has taken every opportunity at the ballot box to vote for Kirsan Ilyumzhinov. There has been no protest from the UK about the lack of democracy that so upset the Dutch, the Australians, the Americans and the Russians. There have been no questions about where the money comes from or why associates of Kirsan have admitted to the murder of a reporter who was investigating his financial dealings. The British Chess Federation did not support the Dutch-led opposition to Kirsan or the boycott of the Elista Olympiad.

On The Line asked to speak to someone from the BCF about its seemingly blind loyalty. Their international director, David Anderton, stepped forward. This is a section of the interview:

OTL: What do you make of Kirsan Ilyumzhinov?
DA: I've never met him.
OTL: Are you aware that there are serious allegations about where the money he is putting into chess has come from?
DA: I've seen rumours, I've heard innuendo but I have seen no hard evidence.
OTL: Don't the rumours make you uncomfortable?

DA: I don't think you can act of the basis of insub-
stantial allegations. I think in practice you have to
presume someone is innocent until there is firm
evidence that they are guilty.

OTL: As a member of the Russian Parliament he is
immune from investigation, so hard evidence will be
difficult to come by. We do know that a reporter in
Kalmykia who stood up to him was stabbed and
beaten to death. Three of his associates have been
charged with murder. Does that concern you?

DA: I have no hard evidence that he is personally
involved in that matter and it is extremely difficult
for someone sitting in England to do more than
follow the national press and international press on
such issues.

OTL: Shouldn't the British Chess Federation be
trying to find out more?

DA: I can't see how the BCF could possibly be
involved in seeking evidence of what might have
happened in Elista.

OTL: Does the BCF pay money to FIDE?

DA: Yes, the BCF has to pay membership fees to FIDE.

Somehow the people entrusted with caring for chess in Britain
have contrived to bury their heads in the sand while holding out
their hands for a grant and running a campaign for government
and Olympic recognition. The BCF's attitude is the same as many
of the players: never look a gift-horse in the mouth. Not only did
the BCF choose not to look into the background of the man who
runs their sport, but such was their allegiance to him, they
actively banned anyone who did.

Before Sarah Hurst took up her post in Azerbaijan she was
editor of the BCF's in-house publication, *Chessmoves*. She recalls
her time there as being ruined by interference from above: 'I
wrote two articles for *Chessmoves* and they were vetoed by the
[then] BCF chairman, Stewart Rueben, who said that we didn't
want any kind of politics, we didn't want to upset FIDE. He told

me to take the articles out.' She says it was old-school political censorship. 'Even though I was editor of their newsletter, there were certain things that I was not allowed to write about.'

While chess players are individuals with complete freedom to follow their conscience, the BCF is a publicly-funded body. Under the current system, chess gets around £50,000 from the government every year direct from the Chancellor of the Exchequer. But, thanks to a Kirsan-backed campaign by the BCF, the government is bending over backwards to find ways of giving more money. It is even willing to change primary legislation, with far-reaching consequences, just so that lottery money can be given to the BCF. Could this be why the BCF is so reluctant to upset the man who not only channels funds into chess himself but is also helping them in their campaign for lottery money?

In the early hours of a Wednesday morning in March 1999 Sports Minister Tony Banks is stoically addressing the hardy few members of parliament who have remained in their seats: 'I congratulate the honourable member for Oxford West and Abingdon on securing this debate,' he enthuses. 'Chess is a great sport where there are no barriers and I have publicly expressed my support for chess to become a sport.' The member receiving the congratulations of Mr Banks is Dr Evan Harris. His motion for discussion calls for the government to change the Physical Training and Recreation Act of 1937 so that chess can be classed as a sport, and so qualify for lottery money through the Sports Council. Chess, indisputably a noble and worthy pastime, is not physically strenuous enough to claim sporting status as the 1937 Act defines it. It also fails to qualify as an art or a good cause. Since lottery funds are paid to arts, sports and good causes, chess is ineligible for cash. 'It seems unfair,' says Dr Harris, 'that young people who play chess, disabled people who need access to chess, simply are not allowed even to apply for these funds.' Hence the motion calling for sport to be redefined.

The redrafting of the 1937 Act would have to be worded with great skill or all manner of games from Scrabble to snakes and ladders could be after a handout. Dr Harris has this covered, though. 'We're not calling for all mind games to be recognized as sports,' he explains. 'But certainly chess and duplicate bridge would qualify because there's no element of chance and secondly because hundreds of thousands of people play these games every week.' Duplicate bridge is a version of the game which minimizes the luck-of-the-draw element until it is negligible.

'Physical fitness is required to play chess and duplicate bridge at tournament level,' continues the MP with missionary zeal. 'We don't have to argue that. The brain is an organ. What we find is that young people who play chess and duplicate bridge develop themselves in terms of the ability to play in teams, they develop mathematical skills and it does allow boys and girls to play at an equal level and the able-bodied and the physically disabled to play at an equal level in the same tournaments. That's very rare in sport, and if we're trying to be inclusive as the government talks about, then it's logical that we shouldn't exclude or discriminate against sports of the mind.'

Double-heading the parliamentary assault is Charlotte Atkins, the MP for Staffordshire Moorlands. Together with Dr Harris, Ms Atkins accompanied Kirsan Ilyumzhinov on a visit to the House of Commons. 'Well, he came with us to a meeting with the Sports Minister and indeed seemed very concentrated on the issue of having chess recognized as a sport and I was delighted that his support was coming through strong and clear to our campaign,' she said.

The president of chess has been fulsome in his support of a plan to get the British lottery players' money channelled into chess. Do the MPs who joyfully welcome his help know of the accusations that he himself is already diverting the Kalmyk people's money into FIDE ? What does Atkins know about Kirsan Ilyumzhinov? 'No, I, I can't really answer that question. No!' declared the flustered politician.

Dr Harris knows a little more, but not much: 'As I say, I'm not an expert on his background, I've only met him once when I took him to see the Sports Minister, and I only see what the International Chess Federation (FIDE) has done for chess. I would rather have an even more democratically elected chess federation that didn't revolve around wealthy people putting in funds, but chess has always lived off philanthropy because it doesn't have access to the funding and professional chess players need to earn a living. It's impossible for me to comment on the rumours and allegations against the World Chess Federation president because I haven't looked into them. I'm the MP for Oxford West and Abingdon, not for southern Russian republics.'

There are many who will agree that chess is as valid a destination for lottery funds as many of the activities which already receive support. But shouldn't MPs be instructing their researchers to make sure they don't get too close to unsavoury characters, whatever the cause? Dr Harris says this: 'If he's infringed human rights, I don't know that, or if he's earned his money wrongly. I think the issue is what should his future be as president of Kalmykia, not whether he chooses to be a benefactor of and a leader for world chess; I don't think that's the main issue. As I say, I campaign on various human rights issues, and I've not had any correspondence from Kalmykians about whether they're downtrodden or not.'

Provided parliamentary time can be found, the 1937 Physical Training and Recreation Act will be amended so that chess and duplicate bridge can be funded as sports. In the meantime, Kirsan has plans to generate a fortune on the web. 'Chess is the only sport in the world that can be shown on the internet,' claims Artem Tarasov, the long-time confidant of Kirsan Ilyumzhinov who is now the head of a new company called FIDE Commerce PLC. Confusingly, the official records show that Mr Tarasov is not Russian but a citizen of the Dominican Republic. This, he explains, is merely a personal flag of convenience. He bought the passport from the Dominican government by investing $25,000 in their economy. It allowed him freedom of international movement not afforded to Russian passport holders. Tarasov is currently based in a suite of offices in London's Piccadilly, where he plans FIDE's internet fortune.

'Chess on the internet is developing and that is the key for future development,' he coolly asserts. 'I'll give you one idea. We showed the World Championship from Las Vegas on the web.

We showed it *virtually* on our internet site, and during the one month of the championship we received 35 million hits on our website, which was incredible because it was a new address. We did not receive any money for this, but if we'd put some sponsors or banners on such a grandiose website we could have received a lot of money. In America, for example, for each thousand hits they are paying up to $32, so if we can make this £20 per thousand we will already have a lot of money in sterling.'

The charm offensive with the Olympic movement has been similarly successful. Fervent lobbying and glad-handing of the Olympic decision-makers seems to have paid off. FIDE has been recognized by the Games as a bona fide sporting body and it seems likely that chess will appear as an Olympic sport before long, probably at the less-crowded winter games in Turin in 2006. That will mean that Kirsan Ilyumzhinov, as head of FIDE, will automatically become a member of that most powerful and globetrotting of sporting coteries, the International Olympic Committee. His rise from membership of an impoverished ethnic minority on the dusty steppe of the lower Volga to the top table of world politics and sport will be complete. Few people have questioned his motives or methods. The person who questioned most vigorously was found face down in an Elista puddle.

CHAPTER SIX

Taking the Piss
Bad Law and the Misappliance of Science Are Undermining Drug Testing

The courts are filling up with athletes taking to the law to overturn positive drugs tests. Are they taking the piss or is there something rotten at the heart of drugs testing and sport's governing bodies' procedures?

Michele Verroken loves to catch drugs cheats. It's nothing personal, it's just her job. She runs the United Kingdom Sports Council's drug-testing programme, and she runs it with enthusiasm and conviction. What drives her crusade is not, as she is quick to point out, a personal distaste or moral outrage at cheats but a firm belief that clean competitors need to be protected. In this aim there is no doubt that she enjoys a strong consensus of support, not only among athletes but also among all those who have an interest in sport.

'We must protect athletes' rights to participate in a drugs-free sport,' she explains. 'That is not the same as being tough on drugs. That sounds as if we are trying to police and coerce. The only issue here is protecting athletes' rights.'

Verroken is the director of ethics and anti-doping at UK Sport and under her watchful eye the UK is acknowledged as having one of the most comprehensive and rigorous testing environments in the world. She is a frequent speaker at the increasingly fashionable 'Whither Sport?' type conferences that have erupted into the working diaries of lawyers, sports administrators, academics and anyone anywhere who makes sport their business these days. Her line is always the same: drugs are not good for you, cheating is bad for you, but most of all, both are bad for the clean athlete. If you are an athlete of any ilk in the

United Kingdom, you are quite likely to have come across one of her people.

The drugs testers, as portrayed in the UK Sport training video, are not exactly the sort you imagine would make for a wild night out, despite the character in the video looking like a member of the hirsute rock band ZZ Top. Still, it takes a straight-faced sort of character to approach a total stranger and ask him or her to wee in a bottle.

The training video, produced by UK Sport for the instruction of testers, presents an idealized version of the process. It goes something like this: up pops a tester in a gym or at the athlete's home or workplace, politely introduces himself and asks for a sample. The tester whips out all the appropriate gear from a customized briefcase and off goes the athlete, closely monitored by the tester, to provide the sample. The urine is then split into two bottles, marked A and B, in the presence of the athlete, then they are sealed, given a number and signed for. They are then tracked and signed for every step of the way until received by an International Olympic Committee (IOC) accredited laboratory. Here the sample, identified only by a number, is kept in a controlled environment before the content of bottle A is analysed. If it is found to contain any substance on the IOC banned list, the testing agency should be informed. They in turn tell the athlete's governing body, which finally breaks the bad news to the athlete. The second sample is then analysed to provide confirmation, or otherwise, and the information turned over to the governing body, which decides what course of action to take against the athlete. Up until that point the information must be treated in strictest confidence.

On the face of it a rigorous but simple process. However, it does not always work that way. Diane Modhal, the Sale Harrier whose international career was killed off at its peak by what was subsequently found to be a flawed procedure, is the most famous victim of a glitch or two in the testing system. But then her sample was taken and tested in Portugal. It could never happen in Britain, could it? Well, yes it could and it has. But as *On The Line* discovered, this has done little to shake the anti-dopers' faith in their system. The result is that over the last few years some athletes have had their careers ruined, their reputations tarnished and their bank accounts wiped out by legal bills, all because the anti-doping system is not as perfect as it makes out.

In August 1998 one of Michele Verroken's testers turned up in Wythenshawe, a vast, sprawling council estate in south Manchester. It is, in character, not unlike dozens of other disastrous postwar housing projects, it is just a lot larger than most. It once held the dubious distinction of being Europe's biggest council estate. But it does have at least one thing going for it: a decent leisure and entertainment complex at its geographical heart.

Not many local people patronize the theatre company, despite its national reputation, but the swimming pool and sports halls are popular. And in the bowels of the complex, if you have a memory for directions, you will come to a pit-like room with mirrors down three sides, harsh uncompromising lighting and a stench of sweat and Deep Heat in the air.

This far from glamorous facility is home to the Forum Weightlifting Club and its star member is Paul Supple. Paul Supple is a local lad made good in the world of weightlifting, so much so that in August 1998 he was the UK amateur champion in his class.

British weightlifters rarely get the chance to shine in the international arena. The Olympics, World and even European Championships are dominated by Turkey and a selection of nations that were either former Soviet republics or eastern bloc countries. The Commonwealth Games was to be Paul's big opportunity, the event he had been training and aiming towards for four years.

Paul had been tested many times before so a tester announcing himself in early August 1998 was nothing out of the ordinary. 'He comes in the gym,' recalls Paul, 'he asks for a test. I say, "OK, no problem. I will be with you in an hour." I finish my training, have a shower and fill in the usual paperwork. Because I had been training, I was dehydrated. I went up to the sports bar. Had some orange juice and also a couple of pints of lager to help me wee quicker, so that the chap would not be hanging around for hours.'

It was all so routine that he soon forgot about it. Towards the end of August he was down training at Bisham Abbey, the national sports centre where squad members for the Games, from a variety of sports, were going through their final paces before flying off to Kuala Lumpur in September. He was pulled out of the gym by a member of the British Amateur Weight Lifting Association (BAWLA), who told him that he had failed a dope test. He says he went numb: 'I just could not believe it. I thought, "There must be some kind of mix-up"; I was just in complete shock. I thought, "I have had samples taken before and even since and there were no problems at all, so why should this one be any different?"'

But it was. According to the IOC accredited laboratory at King's College in London, excessive levels of testosterone had been detected in his urine sample. He was told that a B test would take place to confirm the findings but, perhaps because BAWLA was anxious to avoid any potential scandal out in Malaysia during the Games themselves, he was suspended from competition there and then. Paul Supple would be not be spending September as planned in Kuala Lumpur but in Wythenshawe. His dream of a Commonwealth Games medal was in tatters. He vigorously denied the doping charge and he got support from his local club. They helped get him a lawyer.

'Paul came to me in September,' recalls Fraser Reed, a lawyer who specializes in sports tribunals. 'I looked into the background of the case. Paul said he was innocent and I believed him. We asked the governing body to set a date for the analysis of the B sample, which they did.' When Fraser turned up with Paul to witness the second sample analysis they encountered a problem. 'We had asked to see the documentation from the governing body and UK Sport so we could see the evidence that the sample to be tested was the same sample taken at Wythenshawe, nearly a month before. I was surprised then when we turned up at the laboratory to find no such documents.'

The UK Sport dope tester's training video stresses the

importance of keeping a written and contemporaneous account of what happens to a sample from when it is given to when it arrives at the laboratory. This is known as a chain of custody. 'The chain of custody,' explains Fraser, 'is the key document to prove that the sample is in fact your sample and has not been mixed up with anyone else's.'

Now if this sounds an unlikely scenario, in 1992, the 400-metre runner and world record holder, Butch Reynolds, proved to a US court that his sample was mixed up with a positive test at the IOC laboratory in Monaco. The International Amateur Athletics Federation (IAAF), refused to quash the ban it had imposed and the resulting legal wrangle remained unresolved when the suspension expired after four years.

The point is that the chain of custody is no mere detail among the battery of paperwork that accompanies every test. It is a key part of the process and should be uppermost in every tester's mind, but when Fraser Reed and Paul Supple turned up at the King's College laboratory on 13 September neither BAWLA nor UK Sport could provide a chain of custody. Despite this major breakdown in procedure, Paul Supple and Fraser Reed agreed that the B sample test could go ahead, on the proviso that they might challenge its findings in court at a later date. As with the A sample, the B sample contained a high level of testosterone – twice the IOC limit. Paul Supple and his lawyer demanded a hearing with the governing body to explain and a medical investigation to discover how this might have happened.

The Paul Supple case went on to be troublesome to UK Sport on a number of counts. It offered a real challenge to the claim that the integrity of the testing system in Britain was watertight.

When *On The Line* challenged Michele Verroken over the chain of custody irregularities that were apparent in the Paul Supple case, she played a particularly straight bat.

> *OTL*: The first thing that was strange about the Paul Supple case was that the chain of custody was not produced. Can you explain why not?
> MV: I really cannot comment on individual cases.

OTL: But you know there was no chain of custody produced.

MV: I can't comment on individual cases.

OTL: But this is one of the issues you spoke of at a conference I attended the other day and it is in your training video; it is vital that there is a contemporaneous chain of custody. Now, in this case you know there was not.

MV: I will not comment on individual cases.

As our investigations progressed it became clear that the process of catching and convicting a drugs cheat can be far from the straightforward and simple affair projected in the UK Sport training video.

The Supple case also threw light onto another irregularity at the heart of the dope-testing system in this country: that testing should be random. In other words, the chance of being tested in one sport must be pretty much the same as in any other. But it would seem some sports are treated more randomly than others, especially weightlifting.

UK Sport gets a grant from the government to pay for around four thousand tests a year. They do not come cheap at £200 a pop. Around one thousand of the grant-aided tests are aimed at competition testing, targeted on the basis that if people use drugs, it is to gain an edge in competition, so dope is more likely to be detected in the run-up to or at major championships.

Additionally, some sports governing bodies – the Football Association, the England and Wales Cricket Board and the Rugby Union – pay UK Sport to test their members. All in all, they are testing on behalf of a hundred governing bodies, some British, some international, some home nation.

Given that weightlifting is a minority sport, with no more than 750 people competing in all age groups, there are some who are outraged at the level of testing to which weightlifting is subjected. In 1998 this amounted to 492 tests. Over 10 per cent of the total tests on athletes in the UK were carried out in one of its smallest sports.

Anthony Banks is a member of Paul Supple's Forum Weightlifting Club in Wythenshawe. He is also an orthopaedic surgeon and specializes in treating sportsmen and women. 'When you have 490 tests,' he complains, 'in the space of a year and some of those tested have been done twice in a single day, how can you call it random? How can it be random when everyone has been tested?'

In some cases more than everyone. At the British Weightlifting Championships in Manchester in 1998 there were 39 tests carried out on 37 competitors. In all it cost the taxpayer £150,000 to carry out the 492 tests in 1998, which was more than BAWLA received in grants from the Sports Council. And the result of all this appliance of science? Paul Supple's false positive.

Banks added, 'Weightlifting is not perfectly clean, just as rugby, athletics and most other sports are not perfectly clean. But I think if we are to get to grips with drug abuse then we have to be fair and random must mean random.'

Michele Verroken would not take this one on either when we asked her, except to say, 'We do not measure our success in positives, we measure our success in protecting the reputation of athletes who are negative.' Far from feeling protected, some within weightlifting believe that they are being hounded. In March 1999 Anthony Banks wrote to Sir Rodney Walker, chairman of UK Sport, accusing the doping unit of carrying out an 'almost vindictive level of testing in the sport'. Something Michele Verroken vehemently denies.

The failure of chain of custody, and the argument about what exactly constitutes random in the context of dope testing and sport are just two examples of the need to tighten the procedural framework around dope testing.

Tony Morton Hooper, who defended Diane Modhal, says there is massive room for improvement: 'I think for the last 15 years there has been a real need to play catch-up. There is a kind of sloppiness in the way drug testing is carried out. I would say that in Britain standards are much higher than elsewhere but problems still arise. Sport is a major international business now. Careers, livelihoods, reputations are at risk. The temptations are huge and you have to have a more sophisticated system and the rule book needs to be more sophisticated.'

But it does not require a sophisticated rule book to correct two of the most pernicious aspects of the dope-testing process in this country, because they are both enshrined in common law: that like should be treated as like, and that an accused person should understand the due process to which he or she is subject in the determination of guilt, innocence or a sentence. There is great inconsistency in the manner in which different governing bodies react to people who return a positive dope test. Take the way Paul Supple was treated by BAWLA and compare it to the manner in which UK Athletics handled the case of Dougie Walker, who failed a dope test around the same time.

'Athletics UK took three months to make a preliminary investigation before they suspended Dougie,' explains Supple's lawyer, Fraser Reed. 'In our case Paul was suspended immediately; we had no hearing for three months, after which we were told that the suspension would be upheld. Dougie Walker was granted a hearing and medical examination by his governing body. No such medical examination or hearing was granted to Paul Supple.'

It might also be added that while Dougie Walker's identity was protected until he appeared before UK Athletics, Paul Supple's case was leaked and fully aired in the press, even before he had received written confirmation of the positive test. As a result Fraser had no difficulty in outlining a fairly powerful case to be heard on appeal. He claimed that BAWLA had failed to follow its own rules by not seeking further medical evidence that might have explained the high testosterone reading. Some members of BAWLA were beginning to have severe worries about how the whole case had been handled and it was pretty clear that there was a sentiment that a line ought to be drawn under the matter and that Supple should be cleared.

When the appeal committee gathered at Bisham Abbey on 13 March 1999 they were surprised that Michele Verroken suddenly turned up and, according to one committee member, began grilling the members.

'She said she wanted access to the meeting,' recalls Geoff

Platt, an appeal panel member. 'She wanted to know who was on the committee; she wanted to prevent a shotgun defence, whereby the accused would try and wear down the committee by denying everything and raise objections at every turn. She insisted that his attitude to the charges be clear from the start and his answers pursued.'

Platt claims that Verroken made it clear that if the procedure followed was not acceptable to the Sports Council, then BAWLA would be in danger of losing its grant. We put this version of events to Michele Verroken.

> MV: I will not comment on a specific allegation that has not been put to me personally.
>
> OTL: Well, we are putting it to you now.
>
> MV: The issue is, whether a governing body is following its own procedures. Where there is a suggestion that a governing body is failing to act, well then that is a matter for the Sports Council to consider if the continued investment of public funds is desirable.
>
> OTL: So you were just advising them of the danger?
>
> MV: Where there was a suggestion from a governing body that they did not want to follow a line that was part of an agreement for both lottery and exchequer funding, it would be a principle that the funding could not continue to a body that did not want to implement the funding policy of the UK.
>
> OTL: So you do not deny that you brought this up with the weightlifting people at Bisham Abbey on 13 March 1999.
>
> MV: I won't comment on a specific allegation about the meeting that certainly, as I understand it, is a private governing body meeting.

As it happened, BAWLA's grant did cease. But not because it refused to implement UK Sport's dope-testing policy, rather because an audit of its affairs revealed 120 counts of administrative ineptitude.

Paul Supple's suspension was dropped because at appeal it was decided that the rules of the testing procedure, previously agreed by all parties, had not been followed: the chain of custody documentation was inadequate, and Supple had been denied a further medical examination and denied the opportunity to explain himself.

For Anthony Banks the very point of dope testing is under threat if the procedure continues to leave itself open to legal challenge: 'Tests have to be carried out impeccably and I think if someone is positive then the punishment should be great, but let's get it right! For example, if you get done on a drunk-drive charge, the police have no difficulty about getting the procedure and the science right. They bring the charge and make it stick. I cannot see what the difference is.'

But it is not just the procedure that is frayed around the edges. There are big questions to be asked of the science at work too. UK Sport has a short, and reasonable, answer to that: 'We are in the hands of the IOC scientists.'

But just because an IOC laboratory is accredited does not mean its work is always beyond reproach, as Diane Modhal found out. Modhal, one of Britain's best 800-metre runners of the time and a favourite for a medal at the 1994 Commonwealth Games, was pulled from the track after failing a dope test. She was sent home in a blaze of publicity and the general belief was that if the sample was positive she must be guilty. Only, as we now know, she was not guilty.

According to the Lisbon laboratory that analysed Diane Modhal's sample, she had what is known as a T/E ratio of 200:1. A normal T/E ratio would be 3:1; the maximum permitted by the IOC is 6:1; Paul Supple's was 13:1; Diane Modhal's was the highest T/E ratio ever recorded. If she really had such a ratio, then either she would have been suffering in the final stages of a massive cancer, when quite often the body produces vast quantities of testosterone in a last bid to attack the disease, or she would have had a beard, been knotted with muscles, and spoken like a man. None of which applied to the svelte and smooth-skinned Diane Modhal.

What happened to Modhal's sample, as a programme in the first series of *On The Line* exclusively revealed, was that it was left unrefrigerated on a shelf in a laboratory, in the middle of the Portuguese summer for two weeks. Subsequent tests in Britain on a clean control sample of urine put through the same conditions proved that Modhal's positive reading had happened because those conditions caused her sample to degrade and mutate to give such incredible readings.

Despite this evidence, her first appeal failed and the press branded her a drugs cheat for a second time. Because it was an IOC accredited lab that tested the sample, there was a refusal to believe that such a place could get it so wrong. When it all came out in the wash in 1995 it not only bankrupted the British Athletics Federation but also showed that the science could be wrong .

The Modhal case highlighted one reason why a positive drugs test could lead to a charge against the athlete concerned failing; Paul Supple's case highlights another and it goes back to the first step in the process.

Simon Davis is a research scientist who specializes in drug sample analysis in the pharmaceutical industry. He was drafted in to Paul Supple's defence team. 'One of the big problems with Paul Supple was the consumption of alcohol immediately before he gave his sample,' Davis explains. 'Alcohol increases your T/E ratio and Paul was encouraged to drink alcohol by the tester, or at least, not discouraged from doing so, because he had been training, was dehydrated and could not provide a sample – so alcohol stimulates urine. It seemed to make sense but unfortunately it meant the reading would be wrong.'

Just as the Lisbon laboratory could be wrong about Modhal, it might be argued Davis is not necessarily right about Supple – except that he is no lone voice in asserting that alcohol can produce a distorted T/E ratio. The man who invented the T/E test, Manfred Donike, believed it too and the German IOC accredited laboratory operates what is known as the Cologne Protocol. 'What this protocol does,' explains Davis, 'is that if, after analysis, alcohol is present, then that sample is discarded because it can produce a false positive.'

Professor David Cowan, head of the English IOC accredited laboratory at King's College, London, says a protocol is not the same thing as a published fact, accepted by peer review in scientific journals, so he does not observe it. *On The Line* asked him whether, given the debate over the protocol, testers at least should not allow athletes to drink alcohol before producing a sample. He told us, 'Well, that is just common sense.'

We put the same point to Michele Verroken, who again played her increasingly tiresome straight bat: 'I would not comment on a particular case because the evidence you are giving me, I have no evidence myself to support that that was the case. It would certainly be worthy of my investigating if that happened.'

The American sprinter Dennis Mitchell gave a similar defence to the US Athletics Commission when his T/E ratio proved above the limit, as did Mary Decker Slaney. Both were exonerated by their own association, although Decker remained banned by the IAAF. The point is, despite alcohol consumption having played a prominent part in the defence of well-known athletes, British testers were knowingly allowing samples to be given by athletes who had drunk alcohol.

The problem for British sport is that it is not the UK testing agency that gets sued should they slip up. It is the governing body which, in law, is the party that imposes the penalty and is thus the target of any resulting legal action. The whole Paul Supple saga has cost upwards of £50,000 in combined legal fees, money that neither Paul Supple nor the impoverished BAWLA could afford.

We have already seen one governing body go to the wall as the result of legal action following a false positive. Modhal's pursuit of damages bankrupted the British Athletic Federation, as her lawyer, Tony Morton Hooper, well knows. 'The ultimate problem for a governing body,' he warns, 'is that if it has a bad set of rules and if it is challenged successfully, they could face extinction. It could wipe out a small sport. They have to be prepared to spend a bit of money in the short term, get a proper set of rules rather than pay out a colossal sum if someone makes a mistake.'

Perhaps some money should be spent assessing the chosen borderline between guilt and innocence in the first place. Professor Rod Bilton was employed by Diane Modhal's defence team. He is a specialist in the chemical properties of steroids, a body of knowledge he usually applies to the treatment of cancer. 'It struck me as rather strange the way arbitrary limits of the amount of a particular substance an athlete can or cannot have in his body are arrived at,' says Professor Bilton. 'I would not think it was possible to set such a thing without first doing a lot of testing on people with different body shapes and metabolic rates, to see what levels of circulating hormones, particularly steroids, there are. It seems to me to set an arbitrary level for everybody is not really scientific. '

In other words scientists outside sport would question benchmarks, like the 6:1 T/E ratio that the IOC committee has declared to be evidence of guilt. 'Until the various authorities devote more time to the actual science behind these problems in sport, I do not think you are going to get anywhere,' says Professor Bilton.

The problem for the national dope testers and the sports governing bodies is that, having come out all guns blazing to show the world how serious they are about drugs, they now find themselves with a set of protocols and procedures that are being challenged and knocked down in courts all over the world. The era of the no win, no fee lawyer, the introduction of the Human Rights Act, the perverse attitude that puts the onus on the athlete to prove he or she is innocent that is the rule in many sports tribunals, legally suspect internal procedures and disciplinary codes, increasing financial losses surrounding a ban – all these are ammunition to the athlete toughing it out through the courts, whether guilty or innocent.

Far from giving athletes the comfort that they are competing on clean fields, the impact of imperfect science and procedure is to have sown both fear and confusion: fear among the innocent that they may unwittingly be snared by some aberration of analysis; and confusion among the public who, because testing procedures and science have been shown wanting recently, now do not know whether the civil courts are filling up with chancers exploiting science for all they're worth to cover the fact that they are cheats, or whether dedicated honest athletes are having their careers and reputations destroyed by over eager and incompetent 'drugs police'.

It is clear that there must be a workable system to determine guilt or innocence otherwise there is not only no point in testing but also the integrity of sport will be dealt a terrible blow. A stab at consistency would be nice, as would international scientific consensus as to what constitutes a performance-enhancing drug and what does not.

There is no doubt that until these issues are addressed many governing bodies in the UK feel they are in a lose–lose situation. They must accept the UK Sport drugs-testing protocols if they are to claim lottery and taxpayers' support, as most sports in this country must, but they are aware they could be sued out of existence if the law or science subsequently lets them down.

To be fair to Michelle Verroken and her team, doping is an international problem and ultimately a fair system of dope testing that enjoys the confidence of both athletes and the public will probably require an international solution. The UK Sport anti-doping unit can only ever be as good as the science it is given to work with.

Governing bodies have had a tendency to make up their procedures as they go along. The overriding concern has not been for the rights of the athlete but damage limitation for the sport. The result is knee-jerk reactions and a subsequent lack of consistency in the manner in which positive tests are dealt with.

It is a principle of sound law the world over that it is better that the guilty go free than the innocent be caged. Economically there is a law of diminishing returns – there comes a point when the cost of chasing the dopers may outstrip the value of the peace of mind dope testers claim to deliver. Bad law and bad science will lead to an ever-increasing caseload of expensive legal spats. These are all lessons that any international drugs body that might be constituted in the future would do well to learn when it comes to framing its protocols.

104

CHAPTER SEVEN

National Enquirer
A Catalogue of Cock-Ups in the World of Work Permits

The Overseas Labour Service decides which EU non-nationals can or cannot play in this country. It stands accused of inconsistency, a lack of transparency and startling ignorance of how sport operates.

As the clock counted down the last few seconds of the game, veteran Marty McSorley of the visiting Boston Bruins skated up behind the unsuspecting Donald Brashear of the Vancouver Canucks and in one scything swipe of his stick knocked him to the floor. Players from both sides traded punches around the unconscious Brashear as he lay, the blood from his horrific gaping wound quickly spreading on the ice. Brashear was taken to hospital and recovered. After the game McSorley declared his embarrassment and regret, and was immediately suspended by the National Hockey League (NHL) for 23 games, in effect the rest of the season. The career of a man who made his living as an 'on-ice minder' for players with skill (most famously Wayne Gretsky) was, it appeared, over.

Indignation across a sport never entirely shy of embracing violence was as swift as the blow from McSorley's stick. No sporting hyperbole was left unuttered. The *Los Angeles Times* thundered: 'It is not exaggerating to suggest that Brashear could have been killed. The NHL should definitely suspend McSorley for life, it was the act of a damn nut. If his McSorry self is never on the ice again it would be too soon.'

Yet thanks to the government department charged with policing who can or cannot play sport in the United Kingdom, McSorley's sickening act of violence actually helped him in his quest to take to the ice over here.

The Overseas Labour Service (OLS) is based at the Department for Education and Employment (DfEE) building on the outskirts of Sheffield city centre. It is difficult to miss: just off one of those roundabouts where there is usually at least one car going round for the second time. It's a clean, new, modern building, competing for the skyline with drab high-rise council flats and the imposing gothic spire of St Mary's Church.

Anyone who has been within shouting distance of a pub philosopher will be familiar with the arguments about the number of foreigners plying their trade in this country, whether in football, cricket or rugby. The Overseas Labour Service is at the very heart of this controversy, satisfying no one with the way its decisions are made.

In the spare bedroom of an attractive, secluded house in the heart of Surrey's commuter belt opposition to the OLS is at its strongest. The bedroom has been converted into an impressively kitted-out office and it is here that solicitor Jo Collins runs the British Ice Hockey Players Association. British ice hockey is actually something of a misnomer: examine the team sheets before any game and you will see that home-grown talent in the country's premier competition, the Super League, is alarmingly scarce. Most of the clubs, rather than develop talent here, import players from North America, some of them too old, most of them just not good enough to cut it back home.

'We have seen the number of domestic players trained here drop to ten within the UK,' Collins explained, sitting in front of her computer, ice hockey caps and other memorabilia scattered around. 'Of the rest we are looking at about 90 to 100 players and they are mainly Canadians with European Union qualifications, although we do have a smattering of Scandinavians, Ukrainians and Latvians, plus other bits and bobs. At the moment we can bring in players on work permits who are the equivalent of, say, third division football in this country.'

The OLS drives the normally mild-mannered Jo Collins to desperation. Each year she travels to Sheffield to negotiate the criteria for foreign players who want to play in the UK, and every year she returns down the M1 disappointed.

Currently a player wanting to step on to British ice must have been available for 75 per cent of competitive matches played by his last team in the previous season. 'We are quite happy with that,' she concedes. 'Our members who we consult with on this are perfectly happy with it also, so there is not a problem with that. The problem that we are experiencing is where players who have received substantial bans and suspensions in the previous season are being counted towards the 75 per cent and this is wrong.'

Before McSorley hit Brashear and then the headlines, this rule was highlighted by the London Knights, who hired ex-National Hockey League player Darren Banks. The previous season back in America, Banks had been given a 12-match suspension for violent conduct. This meant he had not played the required 75 per cent of games in that season. Jo Collins, fearing an alarming precedent, contested Banks's being awarded a work permit.

'The Knights argued with the support of the League,' she explained, 'that a suspension is to be treated the same way as an injury, and should be counted towards a player who has played 75 per cent of games. We asked the OLS to discuss this as we felt it was an important issue. However, they chose not to consult with anybody, they moved the lines and they told us that a disciplinary problem and suspension in ice hockey is the equivalent of a bad tackle in football, which we totally disagree with, and represents in our view the fact that the OLS does not understand sport.'

The London Knights were overjoyed: a new player in ice hockey with a violent reputation inevitably means more bums on seats. 'Overseas Labour Service rules actually improve the chances of a violent player being deemed suitable to play over here,' Collins continued. 'The club admitted to me privately that it was great for them and it was great for other teams because they looked at the precedent that had been set and we saw a flurry of work permits being brought in by different clubs for players with the same reputation as Darren Banks. It was a kind of evening-up process that went on, we warned the DfEE what would happen but they failed to heed our warning.'

Government responsibility for the OLS lies with the department of Education and Employment, the minister at the time was Margaret Hodge. She is adamant, she says, that the current system is the best one: 'The purpose of work permits is to ensure that we do give opportunities to UK residents, so it is to ensure that there are opportunities to play in games for home-grown talent. I think we have a very difficult task and balance, which I think we strike appropriately.'

Shortly after the McSorley incident in Vancouver the London Knights sensed another marketing coup. Marty's brother Chris is the Knights' head coach, and if anything was to get the sports fans of the capital off their couches and down to the London Arena this was. The rumours spread quickly – the latest most hated man in US sport was on his way.

Jo Collins knew immediately that under the OLS rules there was nothing to stop the third most penalized player in NHL history from taking the ice over here. A year after his vicious swipe at Brashear, frantic negotiations to allow Marty to join his big brother in London continued as the 2001 Super League transfer deadline drew to a close. But just as it seemed as if the Knights would get their man, the move was stopped. Had the civil servants of South Yorkshire seen sense? Actually no, the Ice Hockey Super League vetoed his move, not because the player was deemed unacceptable, but because they couldn't be seen to be allowing clubs to sign players after their transfer deadline. He stayed in Canada, where he picked up his career with minor-league team Grand Rapids Griffins, making the headlines again when he was sent off for fighting in his first game.

'I am not sure how many games McSorley played in the regular season,' Jo Collins explains, 'but the 23-game suspension he was handed would be taken off the total number of games the Bruins played, so you are looking at 75 per cent of what was left and I am sure he would have qualified.'

McSorley appeared in court in Vancouver in November 2000 and was convicted of assault with a weapon and put on probation for 18 months. Around that time Jo Collins again travelled to the OLS offices in Sheffield to discuss the criteria for ice hockey work permits – also there were two civil servants from London. They were not, however, from Margaret Hodge's Employment Department, but representatives of the then Sport Minister Kate Hoey. They told the meeting that Hoey would prefer it if suspension were not treated like injuries, and that if a player like McSorley missed games due to foul play then that was his fault. Opinions in government were split. The OLS ignored Hoey's pleas and sided with Margaret Hodge.

Jo Collins left the meeting angry but again not entirely surprised. 'The OLS have no practical working knowledge of sport from the inside,' she says. 'They are on the outside looking in, they are interested in having nice, neat, tick-box criteria, moving files from in-tray to out-tray as quick as possible with the minimum amount of fuss and bother, and I don't think they understand any sport at all. They take responsibility for issuing work permits without consultation and then hold up their hands and deny responsibility for any problems that occur because of that. They want to turn the work permit scheme literally into a rubber stamping exercise, they have made it clear, and Margaret Hodge has made it clear that all they want is a fast, efficient service for employers.'

This view is not restricted to ice hockey. The OLS has jurisdiction over who can come here to play all sports. In football, too, there is concern about how it reaches its decisions. In the spring of 2000, MPs of the Education and Employment Select Committee heard evidence about how the work permit system affects the game. What they heard made uncomfortable listening.

Gordon Taylor, chief executive of the Professional Footballers' Association, told the committee: 'We have lawyers who are established, and part of their advertising now is that they work in the field of work permits for professional sport. They will advertise and they have bullet points and one of those bullet points is: "Don't worry if you have been refused. We can find ways round it." We'll start by pressurizing the local MP and making sure the club knocks on his door and says, "You get tickets for our game, we now want you to get us a work permit." This

player will be the saviour of our club and he will win us the
League and we'll get promotion and you'll be voted in forever
more.'

How widespread 'seats for permits' is isn't clear, but there is
one case where political pressure from the very top of government was used, leaving one second division club high and dry.
Blackpool's Bloomfield Road ground has witnessed much better
times, and much better teams than it sees now. The proud orange
grandstands once packed with fans of Matthews, Mortenson and
Armfield are now tatty and decrepit. The club will soon move to
a new home, which hopefully will do justice to it's rich history.

In a vain effort to stave off relegation to the third division
in 1999–2000 season, Blackpool felt they needed some foreign
influence. They turned to Indrek Zelinski from the ex-Soviet
republic of Estonia after receiving good reviews about him from
Scotland manager Craig Brown. In order for him to qualify,
Zelinski, like all non-EU players, had to satisfy two OLS criteria:

*1) A player must have played for his country in at least 75 per cent of
its competitive matches that he was available for selection during the
two years preceding that date of the application.*
*2) The FIFA ranking of the player's country must be at or above 70th
place in the official rankings list when averaged over the two years preceding the date of the application.*

In Zelinski's case Estonia was placed around seventeth in the
FIFA rankings and he was a regular in their side. The Blackpool
chairman, Karl Oyston, was confident that there would not be
any hitches and his new player would soon be available.

'If we had brought Indrek over a month or two months earlier, we would have been able to sign him,' he says, standing on
the terraces behind one of the goals. 'We were aware of the criteria, but the pace at which Estonia were rising through the
world rankings we thought would have gone in our favour, even
though they were two or three places below a very arbitrary cut-
off point. He had certainly made the necessary number of
appearances for the team and had made a significant effect on

the results of the team when he played.'

Blackpool's initial application was turned down, so they launched an appeal, which was heard at the OLS offices in Sheffield. On the same day two other appeals were heard: one for Bury, who wanted to make an Indian player, Baichang Bhutia, the first from that country to play in the League, and one for Middlesborough, who wanted to re-sign the mercurial Brazilian, Junihno. Of the three players, two were handed work permits, the third was forced to return to Estonia.

Karl Oyston left the meeting feeling angry and confused. 'In both instances there were other factors that went against us and in their favour, they are the hidden aspects we do not know much about,' he mused. 'But there are definitely reasons that those two applications were approved and I would say by the same token why ours was turned down. Without it seeming like sour grapes we want to abide by the rules, but the rules have got to apply to everyone and it doesn't seem that that's the case.'

Despite seemingly having the stronger case, Zelinski missed out on his move. At that point, though, India were lying in one-hundred-and-seventh place in the FIFA rankings and Junihno, who was playing for Atletico Madrid in Spain, hadn't played for Brazil for two years. Although there is no evidence that Bury or Middlesborough did not abide by the rules, the hidden aspects Karl Oyston refers to are possibly not so hidden after all. Newspapers at the time reported that two local MPs, the member for Redcar, Mo Mowlam, and the member for Sedgefield, Tony Blair, were both pushing for the initial decision to be overturned, despite Junihno not qualifying under the government's own rules. Middlesborough did admit to *On The Line* that it received political assistance, but from another local and unnamed MP and not, as speculated, from Blair or Mowlam.

At the Education and Employment Select Committee the Football League in a written statement admitted that the Bhutia case did concern them: 'There is suspicion amongst Football League clubs that the Bhutia application was looked upon more favourably because there is a marked absence of Asian role models within professional football. Whilst the special circumstances surrounding this sensitive issue were understood, the credibility of the work permit arrangements have been seriously undermined, and as these decisions were taken in private, a marked lack of transparency now prevailed. This despite the objectives ministers set out to achieve.'

Back in her Whitehall office Margaret Hodge disagrees that the system is anything but transparent. 'I think the criteria around football are absolutely clear,' she maintains. 'I can't think of somebody who's been refused a work permit because they meet the criteria. What we do have is an appeal mechanism so that the people that don't meet the two criteria of quality thresholds that we lay down for football have the chance to appeal, and then we have an appeal panel, which has three people who are experienced in football. They sit together and I see the minutes of these panels and I think they take their work very seriously. They then make a judgment on the quality; those people in football who meet the criteria get a work permit.'

The concern in this case, however, is not about the people who meet the criteria getting work permits, but those who despite blatantly not deserving one get one anyway – with a little help from their friends, of course.

Around the same time Sunderland frantically chased the signature of the Honduran international Milton Nunez. So desperate were they to get their man, the deal was rushed through just hours before the March transfer deadline. Honduras were, at that point seventy-fourth in the FIFA rankings, outside the OLS's own seventieth place cut-off point. Unlike Indrek Zelinski, Nunez got a permit. Just over a year later the player that the Black Cats were so desperate to pounce on that they paid £1.6 million, had played a grand total of one hour in first team colours. By the end of the 2000-2001 season, 'Tyson', as he was called, was on his way out of the Stadium of Light – a failure.

The confidence Margaret Hodge has in the two 'quality thresholds' is not shared by the FA Premier League. Mike Foster gave evidence on their behalf: 'On the face of it,' he told the assembled MPs, 'it seems that it is a League table so the countries below a certain level must be worse than the rest, and I suppose to a certain extent that is right. But those countries are likely to have the odd star playing in the team. We had a situation recently, without naming any names, where a player's application had been turned down because the country was ranked seventy-first, at the moment the cut-off is 70, and the club brought forward evidence showing that if you calculated the average standing in a different way they were actually sixty-fifth, and if you waited another two months they would actually come below 70. So it strikes me as being an arbitrary decision that is difficult to justify.'

Clint Marcelle knows all about arbitrary decisions. He sits and listens to his son explain what he has done at school: it seems mostly to consist of lots of drawing and some playing outside. For a long period Marcelle wasn't sure whether he would have to uproot his family from their home on a modern housing estate, and the school where Clint Jnr, too young to understand, draws his elephants and tigers.

Marcelle is a Trinidad and Tobago international, but in early 2000 he was forced out of the Barnsley team after helping them to promotion to the Premiership. When *On The Line* visited him he was in limbo, unable to play for anybody. It all started when his former boss, John Hendrie, made it clear that Clint's face didn't fit, despite him being a hero of their historic promotion to the Premiership.

'I had to leave Barnsley because I wasn't getting a fair run,' he says. 'My career in this country was basically being stifled. I went to Scunthorpe for a month and it was really good to get back playing, a lot of people were happy to see me playing again, and I was really happy to be playing again.'

Having left Oakwell, he was allowed by the OLS to go on loan to Scunthorpe United, but this was breaking its own rules, which state that work permits cannot be issued to clubs 'for the purpose of having players on loan or giving them trials'. Despite this, Marcelle says that he had no problem transferring his work permit from Barnsley to Scunthorpe: 'No I didn't, I thought I would have done. Brian Laws, the Scunthorpe manager, called me and I said, "You know I am on a work permit and my work is for Scunthorpe," and he said, "Don't worry" – I should leave that with him. He spoke to me on Friday and he said he would call me on the Monday and the next thing you know it is all sorted. I couldn't believe it, I told my wife it is real, I am going to play! And lo and behold the work permit was transferred over from Scunthorpe. For a month we had a great spell, I will always be thankful to Scunthorpe for that. We had a five-game winning streak and the club moved from the bottom of the table to the middle. I would have liked to have gone there permanently; unfortunately, it didn't work out between us. I wish it had; if it did I wouldn't have been in this problem like I am now.'

A short walk away from the OLS headquarters is Gary Dickinson's office. Dickinson is Clint Marcelle's solicitor, and it was his job to try and work out what his neighbours were going to do next. At that time Trinidad and Tobago were involved in the Gold Cup international tournament, which coincided with a surprise at Oakwell.

'He was called into the first team squad at Barnsley,' Dickinson recalls, 'and he thought he would now get his chance and he would be able to prove himself to Dave Bassett. So he decided not to take up the international call and of course Barnsley then decided to release him. Trinidad and Tobago then got to the semi-finals of the competition and they played five or six games, which meant he would have played enough to get him an extension to his work permit.'

Clint then got a call from West Bromwich Albion offering him a chance to kick-start his career. He went to the Hawthorns to train and impressed the manager, Gary Megson, enough to be offered a two-year contract. Clint was excited and relieved at the prospect of the move: 'I went there expecting to play in the next match, because when I went down to sort things out at Albion on the Wednesday they said they could not see any problems to get the work permit.'

Gary Dickinson was also confident that things were moving on. 'We went down to West Brom,' he said, 'and we all believed that we had been given the green light; indeed Dr John Evans, the West Brom secretary, was very helpful and I believe he had looked into this with the Barnsley secretary, so as we understood it we had got the green light.' The light, though, was still on red and it didn't seem likely to change.

All Clint wanted to do, he says, was to play football: 'I was all geared up to go that weekend, but it didn't happen so I set my sights for the next week and the next thing you know they phoned and said the work permit is being denied and we would have to appeal – and that was another long waiting process.'

So despite breaking its own rules by allowing Clint to go on loan to Scunthorpe United, the OLS denied him the chance to sign a contract for two years at West Brom. In its letter to the Midlands club explaining its decision, the OLS stated its reason was that 'they were not convinced he would make a significant contribution to the game in the UK'. Despite the fact that Gary Megson was willing to offer Clint a two-year contract, and the OLS had allowed him to go on loan to Scunthorpe where he helped them to a good run, they didn't feel he could make a 'significant contribution'. No wonder he was confused.

'When you look at a movie and you see a guy in jail,' he says, reflecting on his fate, 'and he is on death row – that is how it feels, you don't know whether you are coming or going. That was rejected as well and that was the biggest disappointment in my entire life.' He continued looking at his young son playing on his living-room floor. 'My kids are getting older and they want to settle down. They have been moved around from place to place and want a place to call home.'

Employment Minister Margaret Hodge rejects the claims that the OLS is making ambiguous decisions: 'We sit down every year and we negotiate with the football bodies,' she maintains. 'We have established what I think are clear, transparent and consistent criteria and I think they're not working badly. They are giving us the right balance between bringing in talented players but allowing home-grown talent to grow, and we will continue to talk to the sporting bodies to ensure that we get that balance right.'

The Football League disagrees, and did so to the Education and Employment Select Committee. It accused the OLS of 'arbitrarily determining issues', of an 'unacceptable level of interference from OLS officials' and of 'ignoring Football League protestations over the crucial aspect of the FIFA rankings', which they felt the civil servants were 'imposing unilaterally'. Not, it seems, the words of a body that has been negotiated with, and feels that 'the balance is right'.

As football enjoys its rapidly contracting summer break, cricket takes up the reins as the national sport. For years ex-Lancashire spinner Jack Simmons has acted as an agent for overseas players looking to play club cricket in this country. Sitting in the committee room at Old Trafford, where he is now chairman, he reels off some of the great names of world cricket that he has organized clubs for: 'David Boon, Geoff Lawson, Courtney Walsh, Damien Fleming, Mark Taylor, Justin Langer, Roger Harper, Wasim Akram...' He could go on and on. All of them came here to play club cricket, mostly in the strong leagues of Lancashire.

'The traditions of the leagues in Lancashire are very widely known,' he says, looking out of the window as the ground is prepared for a new season. 'If you go back years and years, you have the likes of Everton Weekes, Clyde Walcott, Garfield Sobers, Wes Hall, Charlie Griffiths, plus some great Aussies as well as West Indians, and that was an outlet to earn money during their off-season. It also gave the supporters of league cricket in Lancashire a great chance to watch these great players.' Those players would generally play a greater role in the club and the community than just playing for the first team on a Saturday, coaching young players being one of them.

Around 1995 'Flat' Jack finally gave up being an agent, put off by the Sheffield suits and their red tape. 'They were getting more restrictive to bring people in,' he explains, 'and I didn't think that it was for the betterment of the game. It's nice to get a young up-and-coming player who wants to play and wants to get involved with the club and the youngsters and also knows it is going to benefit him as well. That player would not cost the club too much: just air fare, a bit of accommodation, maybe staying with one of the club members, and paying him spending money – and that's good for the club. Now the restrictions that they have now has put the cost up three or four times. You are not getting the same value, because that person who comes knows that there are not as many places available so he can say, "I want X amount and a posh car". So it places too much emphasis on the club having to find a lot more money, and maybe the development of the youngsters at the club is suffering from it.'

Gateshead Fell is one of the most famous clubs in the North-East. It includes among its past players Richie Richardson. The former West Indian skipper opened the batting with Doug Hudson, who is now the club chairman and who agrees with Jack Simmons about the overseas pro's role in a club: 'When you enter a league competition there's only one team that can win the league and hopefully we'd like to think it's going to be us – and perhaps cup competitions as well. I think our overseas player is the focal point of our season. He is there to stimulate the interest, perhaps to bring spectators in. You do find that members use the facilities more if you're a successful team, so your bar benefits, so in turn that's helping to pay his wages. If we offer a contract we expect him to be involved in coaching, because the youngsters of the club are the future and lifeblood.'

Hudson agrees that the OLS doesn't have a clue about what a club pro's role is: 'I think the biggest problem is that they assume that these people are coming in as hired assassins to score runs and take wickets, and the argument you get from them is, "Why haven't you signed an Englishman?" They don't appreciate that it's not just about Saturday afternoon or Sunday afternoon out on the middle, it's about what these people are doing on a Wednesday night or on a Sunday morning within the community.'

Like football and ice hockey, cricket has minimum criteria for any player wanting to come over for the summer, set in this case by the England and Wales Cricket Board:

A club wishing to employ an overseas national as a cricket player will need to ensure that the player has, during the 18 months immediately prior to the date of the work permit application, played in:

A) A minimum of one test match for his country (consisting of 5 days), or

B) At least three One-Day International matches for his country, or

C) A minimum of five first-class matches (not two-day).

These fairly strict rules are being broken in this country every single week of every single summer.

The small towns and villages nestling in the valleys of the Pennine hills make the area one of the strongholds of club cricket in the North of England. Derek Parker lives and works on the Yorkshire side and, like Jack Simmons, he has brought overseas players to Yorkshire to play cricket. He also has been forced to stop, due, he says, to the OLS.

'I think it's a peculiar situation,' he explains. 'We have criteria set out by the ECB [English Cricket Board] where they say if you are going to play professional cricket in the UK you have got to fulfil the criteria they demand. But I know from knowledge of the 1999 season that there were pros playing over here that do not have work permits, whether the DfEE or the OLS have been given the wrong information about them or the clubs had not bothered applying for a work permit, whatever the reason is.'

Jack Simmons agrees with Parker that players are coming here and earning a living illegally: 'I know for fact that does happen,' he concedes, 'and when you get the conditions that are restricting clubs and the amount of money they have to pay out then you are going to look for loopholes here and there. Unfortunately, the DfEE cannot go round 15,000 clubs in a year to find out if everything is legal, but yes, the system is abused.'

Neil Edwards is the secretary of the League Cricket Conference, the umbrella body of the league game. He acknowledges that a player who wants to play in this country must be a recognized first-class cricketer. If that had been introduced a few years ago it would have ruled out a few big names: 'When Shane Warne was a youngster he came over and played in the Lancashire League; he wouldn't be able to do that now under the current OLS regulations. If you look at the current Australian national side many of them played over here as youngsters in league cricket, but a lot of them now would be prevented because of that rule.'

The full extent of the abuse is, according to Edwards, amazing. The OLS handed out 352 work permits in the spring of 2000. Edwards conservatively estimates that around 3,000–4,000 foreign cricketers were playing club cricket by the summer.

'You have a situation,' he explained, 'where more clubs will seek to bypass the regulations by using working holidaymaker permits. The problem is that if you are raising the standard, saying that someone must have played five first-class fixtures, they are obviously a more experienced player than someone who has just played one, therefore his fee would be higher. So you're pricing the bona fide professional at a much higher level and at a level that probably clubs will not be able to afford. Because all of the clubs work to a very strict budget, the members raise the money to engage the player and there's a limit to how much they can raise, all clubs are suffering.'

Derek Parker now concentrates on his clients in Rugby League where they avoid arguments like these by having quotas, limiting each team to a set number of non-EU nationals. 'If you are going to have a system,' he explains, 'then let's have it run properly – and if it is not run properly then scrap the system and let every club who wants to get an overseas cricketer come in and get one. But to me you have got to have a defined way. To my knowledge a lot of clubs are getting players from overseas who do not fulfil the criteria and they are classed as pros.'

On The Line was sent a list of clubs and their pros for a recent season. After speaking to a number of club secretaries it became clear that cricketers and clubs are hoodwinking a system that has no real checks, a point made to the Employment Minister Margaret Hodge.

> MH: You say that. I think what I've got to say to you is give me the evidence that you have and I can assure you that I'll look at every case you raise and come back to you on it. From all the checks that we

do, and we do do checks, we think that on the whole the system works well.

OTL: The conservative estimate is that each summer there are between 3,000 and 4,000 professional cricketers over here, for each of the last 2 years. The OLS has issued 300 work permits for cricket; what are the remaining 3,000 doing?

MH: The others won't need a work permit. Now, they may be people who have come from elsewhere in Europe, or they may be people who have access to a British passport attached to their Commonwealth country of origin or something like that. The only ones where we have to give a work permit are where they don't have a British passport and they're non-European. Now, that's different from what you're saying to me, which is people fiddling the system, that's people working within the rules. If you're saying that we have a system where you have evidence that people are fiddling it, I want to know 'cos I will investigate and I will come back to you and talk about it.

If this is the case, then 90 per cent of all overseas cricketers in this country have some European antecedence, which is a little difficult to believe. What is easier to believe is that clubs faced with unrealistic regulations are bending the rules to attract the players they believe will benefit the game and their club.

In a letter passed between Margaret Hodge and the then Sports Minister, Tony Banks, and seen by *On The Line*, both claimed that the cricket authorities were happy with the current criteria. But in another letter, again seen by *On The Line*, sent by Neil Edwards to a cricket club secretary he wrote: 'The letters from the two government ministers, imply that the criteria now in place were supported by the ECB and the League Cricket Conference. This could not be further from the truth. It was quite clear that we were told what they were to be and negotiation was not on the agenda.' Margaret Hodge, however, maintains that the game is content with its work permit rules.

MH: Yes, again we negotiated with them. There may be one or two clubs that are unhappy but their governing bodies agreed with the criteria that are set. The issue there is whether we should have easier criteria for club cricket than for county cricket; that's a view taken by one or two clubs, it's not the view taken by the governing body.

OTL: It is the view taken by the governing body, they have told us that.

MH: No, it's not the view taken by the governing body because the governing bodies were asked specifically on that issue and wanted the same criteria for club and county cricket, I can assure you.

OTL: They say they were told, not asked.

MH: I know they were asked and I am told that's what they said.

Margaret Hodge claims they are never going to keep everyone happy all the time, but, she thinks, the OLS does make most people happy most of the time.

Yet ice hockey thinks the system is too lax; cricket thinks it is too restrictive; football thinks it's too muddled and open to abuse; and two government departments cannot agree on the details. Little wonder that the ambiguities, inconsistencies and anomalies of the Overseas Labour Service mean its rules are being made a mockery of right under its nose.

CHAPTER EIGHT

Keep On the Grass
The Systematic Culling of Road Running

Some of the oldest and most popular events on the sporting calendar are being struck off by men in blue uniforms with red tape. But what has that got to do with a French bike race, an eccentric English judge and street parties?

'Every year we see a number of races disappear from the fixture list,' bemoans Kevin Carr from the back room of his Sunderland semi. 'It's a worrying aspect and it has been like that for six or seven years. What's more, I can't see it ending.'

Mr Carr sits at a square table in front of the french windows. Outside, his garden looks a treat. Seedlings have been nurtured into blooms which boast every hue. He speaks with his back turned to the flowers; his mind is on his other passion: road running. 'We have the Great North Run here, which attracts 40,000 entries, and we have other races ranging from 5 kilometres to 10 miles, all of them draw anything from 50 to 2500 runners,' he says.

The North-East of England is the pounding heart of road running. As regional race secretary, Mr Carr keeps the diary of which event is held at what time. It's a busy job, but not nearly as busy as it was. 'Oh, it's a nationwide problem,' he warns. 'There are some areas suffering more than others and I think the North East is one of the worst.'

Road running is not so much the grassroots of athletics as the tarmac floor. The streets of Tyneside have produced a steady stream of world-class athletes. People like Brendan Foster, Steve Cram and Mike McLeod. McLeod's name doesn't spring to mind as readily as those of Cram and Foster, but that is more to do with his mild and modest manner than his race record. His Olympic bronze from Los Angeles was upgraded to silver after the man who finished second failed a drugs test. That makes McLeod the most successful distance runner ever produced in Britain. At a more local level he also holds the record for the Morpeth to Newcastle road race and a number of other similar events. 'Road racing was a benchmark for me and the majority of athletes in the area,' says the softly spoken Geordie, 'because it's difficult to get a good six miles or ten kilometres by yourself. With organized races you can have real competition. You might go in tired, or come out of it feeling great – you don't get any of these feelings if you've not been competing. Taking part in real races is the only way to see how you are progressing towards a big event.'

McLeod's enthusiasm is echoed by Kevin Carr: 'We're talking about events which are very necessary. Road racing is an arena where a lot of Olympians have served their apprenticeship and where a lot of times can be measured. They use it as preparation for the track season and so it's vitally important to athletics in this country that we maintain our quota of athletics on the highway.'

To understand why a sport that produces Olympic heroes and provides competitive athletics for thousands of club runners is under threat, it is necessary to discover what happened when the world's greatest bike race ran across the path of an eccentric old lord.

In the summer of 1994 the *Tour de France* took one of its regular detours into another country. Many times the race had veered into Belgium or Switzerland, but this was the first time the riders had been asked to haul their bikes onto a ferry and cross the Channel. The news of a Home Counties leg of the *Tour* was trumpeted loudly as a chance for cycling to build its support in the UK and for the south coast of England to show off its charms to the race's foreign legion of international hangers-on.

It went without saying that roads would need to be closed. It was common sense that hundreds of riders in one of the planet's top sporting events couldn't be expected to jostle with the regular combatants of the Chichester or Winchester rush hour. The officer in charge of keeping the *Tour* on the roads and the locals on the pavements was Andy Relf. When he looked into the legal measures employed to close public highways for such events he found that, in fact, no such laws existed. The Act that had been used across the nation to close roads for anything from marches of protest to marathon races only provided the powers to close roads for 'acts of public rejoicing'.

Road traffic authorities had, for years, been closing roads for sport by using a law which only permitted them to shut the highways for street parties and village fairs. If anybody had realized the error, they had kept quiet about it, and nobody seemed to mind. What concerned Mr Relf and the race organizers was that they didn't want their big moment disrupted by someone who *did* mind. There was a fear that the biggest bike race in the world might be the kind of event which would send keen objectors to scrutinize the contents of the legal library. They would have been particularly vulnerable to a legal bigwig with a point to prove. They might have got away with it – until somebody spotted a problem with the route: it went right past the garden gate of Lord Denning's palatial Hampshire home.

Lord Denning was, of course, the man who conducted the government report into the Profumo Affair – the biggest sex scandal of the sixties. As Master of the Rolls he had made his name as a staunch defender of the rights of the individual and as a man who was perfectly willing to take a controversial stand. On retiring in 1982 he had retreated to his Whitchurch home amid 35 acres of garden. In 1994, when the *Tour de France* came to town, he was 95 years old. Asked about the reason for his long life he said: 'By eating plain English food. I don't want any of that French stuff.'

If race organizers had tried their utmost to imagine the worst possible opponent to road closures, they could not have come up with anyone as problematic as Lord Denning. He was just the kind of chap who could quote chapter and verse on the difference between public rejoicing and a bike race. It was perfectly possible that, rather than have his garden path coned off while the riders whizzed past his gate, he would cause enough trouble to get the race stopped. Andy Relf knew that the elderly lord would have the law on his side.

With haste not commonly associated with the higher echelons of the legal community, the Road Traffic Regulation (Special Events) Act 1994 was rushed into operation just weeks before the cyclists arrived. The government documentation describes this as 'an Act to make provision, in connection with sporting or social events held on roads or entertainments so held, for the restriction of traffic on roads, and for connected purposes'. It might just have well have said 'an Act to allow us to close the roads for the *Tour de France*, just in case our old friend Lord Denning feels like getting prickly', as Andy Relf admits. The Special Events Act was introduced to allow sport to take place on the roads, because existing legislation was inadequate. The first beneficiary was the *Tour de France*. 'Ever since then the only real Act to close roads for a sporting event has been the Special Events Act, because all the other legislation is frankly inadequate,' says Andy, a former policeman.

In fact, Lord Denning did absolutely nothing. There was no legal objection from the famous old judge and the race organizers' fears were totally unfounded. It appears that the new law was completely unnecessary. Worse than that, it was counterproductive. The irony is that long after the cyclists have gone home, a law designed to make it easier to stage road-based sporting events has become the single biggest tool for closing events down. Kevin Carr in Sunderland says he has seen it happen: 'The police now say that they won't support your event, and if they won't support it then you'd be a fool to go ahead with it. They've used the Act from 1994, which was brought in for the cycle race, to clobber a lot of road races in the UK.'

While the law on road closures remained a grey area, race planners could take unwitting advantage of the uncertainty, and races were held freely. Many police forces probably didn't know that the law they were using was meant for public rejoicing, and nobody seemed to care. Then, after 1994, the unfounded fears of recrimination from an old judge caused the position to be clarified. But clarity worked against sport. Constabularies were told that the new Act was the correct, and only, law for dealing with road closures for sport. It transpired that this was an appalling blow to road running. The problem with the new act is right in the title: the *Special* Events Act.

Red-letter events such as the *Tour de France*, the London Marathon and the Great North Run are undeniably special. Can the ten-kilometre jogs in provincial towns that fill the spaces of the club runner's calendar really be classed in the same category? The interpretation by the Department of Transport is 'No'. Hundreds of these races are planned around the country every week, and it's their ubiquitous nature that is used against them. The conversation would appear to go something like this:

> RACE ORGANIZER: Hello, Officer. Please can I have some roads closed for my big race?
> POLICE OFFICER: That depends, sir. What's the event?
> RACE ORGANIZER: It's the annual town circular which has been held every year since 1846.
> POLICE OFFICER: So it's quite routine then?
> RACE ORGANIZER: (Thinking routine is good) That's right.
> POLICE OFFICER: Not really a very special event, is it?
> RACE ORGANIZER: No, it's not a very special event, really quite ordinary, nothing to worry about.
> POLICE OFFICER: And that's exactly why you can't stage it. Goodbye.

This made-up account might appear a little far-fetched, but compare it to the experience of Les Venmoor, who for many years arranged the Heaton Road Race in Newcastle, a race which lists Mike McLeod and Steve Cram amongst its former winners: 'Over the 80 years that it has been going, the Heaton Road Race has taken various routes, but the last one had been used for eleven years,' Mr Venmoor recalls. 'Then in 1997 the police came along and we got a letter.'

The letter said that the police had been monitoring the race and that the officers were not happy with the safety of the event and its effect on local traffic flow. It asked that the organizers find an alternative route for the next year, or the event would lose their backing.

'We followed the police advice, and found another course which was not very far away,' continues Mr Venmoor. 'It was mainly on roads, with a small section travelling along wide paths in a local park. It was completely traffic free. So we went back to the police and they said, "We can't support that because it's not an established event." The race had been held for 80 years under the same name. They asked us to change the course and because we did what they asked they said it was a different event and they would not grant us a road closure.' Les's opinion of his local constabulary has plummeted. 'I feel as if we've been cheated by the police,' he says.

What would appear to be needed is a Road Traffic Regulations (Not-Very-Special Events) Act. Andy Relf says even the Department of Transport recognizes that it has made a mistake: 'The department has been working on introducing a less onerous power so that local authorities could close roads for events – whether for a street party or a sporting event would be irrelevant. What they need is a simple and inexpensive power which is more flexible than the Special Events Act, and cheaper to enforce.' But whereas the legal process moved with haste when faced with the prospect of upsetting Lord Denning, it is dragging its heels with a vengeance when the beloved races of thousands of runners are at stake. While the statutes remain static the policy of the police is to push runners off the road.

The Association of Chief Police Officers (ACPO) has a clear recommendation which it passes to all constabularies. Their Operational Commanders' Conference in March 1996 concluded that: 'We should, wherever possible, continue to discourage organizers from conducting events on the highway in the interests of road safety.' The trickle down of this decision is that event planners all over the country receive stern letters from their local constabulary making it very plain that they ought to get off the road. Cars, it appears, are no risk to safety. It's pedestrians that are the problem. As George Orwell might have put it: 'Two legs good, four wheels better.'

The intolerant approach has won the police few friends, and many enemies. One critic is sports lawyer Nick Bitel, who is also chief executive of the London Marathon. He says: 'If Britain is to remain a leading force in distance running our athletes must have access to quality road races at home without having to travel half the way around the world to compete. Also the general public should have the chance to enjoy taking part in popular road races.'

Complaints like these reached the ears of those in the House of Commons and an all-party group of MPs came together to fight for the survival of road racing. Of course, it should be remembered that the single biggest threat to the sport is a hard-line implementation of a badly drafted law which was approved by these MPs and their colleagues. John Austin, the Labour MP for Woolwich and a keen runner, is furious: 'Road racing is a serious sport for serious athletes,' he reminds us. 'It is also a great mass participation sport for thousands of runners. It's nonsense to suggest that roads are only for cars. Driving races off the roads into parks would kill off the sport as well as the ability to raise thousands of pounds for charity.'

Events could ignore police advice and run on the open roads, dodging the traffic. Unsurprisingly, Mr Austin warns against that. He says it is the police who need to change course. 'If you're going to run a race safely, you are going to need the co-operation of the police and I am urging ACPO to tell their members to be a bit more sensible and compromising to race organizers. I think the dangers are exaggerated ... There is no evidence that there have been major accidents as a result of road running,' asserts the MP. 'With sensible management you can separate runners from traffic to minimize the dangers and I don't think there is evidence to show that there is a danger, but there does seem to be an attitude amongst some police officers that roads are only there for motorists to drive on.'

Just as the pressure from MPs like Mr Powers was growing, another legal change made the police even more entrenched in their opposition to road races. In June 1999 the Health and Safety at Work Act was extended to apply to the police force. As with the Special Events Act, it was well intentioned and seemed to make sense by giving police officers the same safety cover enjoyed by all other workers. In practice, however, it works against sport.

Part of the Health and Safety Act passes responsibility for safety onto local management. Police officers were told by their bosses that this meant that if there was an accident in a race that had received constabulary backing, then the individual officer who approved the race could be held responsible and sued. Police officers were faced with having to carry the can for an accident which occurred in a race, just because they said it could take place. They were also reminded that Sundays, the day when most road closures are sought, have become much busier since the growth of Sunday trading. Kevin Carr says that once this information was digested by local officers, race approvals became rarer than an endangered species: 'They give out a statutory letter now which goes to everyone in the country. It says that they're not giving you support because there is a stadium nearby and you could run there. If not, they recommend we run in the countryside. More or less they're saying, "We don't want you on the roads, you're too much bother."'

To state the patently obvious, road racing does not take place on a stadium track or in a field. Track racing and cross-country are totally different disciplines. While this point appears to be lost on ACPO and the Department of Transport, it is fully understood by Mike McLeod: 'Even the best parkland gets rutted in bad weather, and that means there's a chance of getting injured. Elite athletes can't afford that kind of risk so they steer clear of cross-country races, they prefer to race on roads where they can get long distances and smooth surfaces.' He says that if runners can't get road races in this country, they will move abroad: 'I used to go abroad for odd weekends over the winter and used to have some cracking races in places like Spain, France and Belgium where road running is a big thing. Elsewhere in Europe people accept this as an important sport and traffic adapts to it. I used to love going abroad because it was so much better than running here.' And while a run across a muddy field is undesirable for elite competitors like Mike McLeod, it is completely impossible for some of our best athletes, those who race in wheelchairs.

From his home near Nottingham, Rick Cassell, the chairman of the British Wheelchair Racing Association, plans his members' participation in races all over the country. He says most race organizers keep grass to a minimum for the wheelchair racers, but even a small amount is too much for some of his members. 'As an association I have to think about everyone who is a member of the organization being able to complete the course, so that includes the people who are weaker and therefore would find it harder to push over any surface other than road,' he explains.

But still the closures continue. One volunteer in Essex who had successfully and safely put on a race for many years was told by police that if he went ahead with the same event under the new laws he could be charged with involuntary manslaughter. If the intention of the officer was to scare the organizer with an exaggerated threat, it worked. In Manchester, organizers of races that had raised thousands of pounds in sponsorship for local hospitals were told in very blunt terms that the police wanted the races to stop. As one experienced runner lamented in an article in *Athletics Weekly*, 50 of the races he used to take part in had disappeared in the last two years.

Given that police policy is to refuse road closures and withdraw their backing from races sharing the highways with cars, organizers have three choices: launch a charm offensive on their local constabulary, ignore the police and take a chance on the roads, or scrap the race all together. In Littleborough, a market town in the moors above Rochdale, they have successfully adopted the first of these alternatives, though they did have a head start.

Andy O'Sullivan leans with one hand on a sturdy darkwood table in the Falcon pub; in his other hand is a ballpoint pen. To his right is a square cardboard box full of paired white sports socks, on the left is a round metal biscuit tin containing coins, and in the middle are various rectangles of white paper bearing lists of names. Snaking from the table to the door of the pub is a single-file line of runners in loose-fitting vests and leg-hugging tracksuits. As they wait their turn to register for a five-kilometre race around the town they chat quietly and limber up gently. The age range is wide and the bodies are slim. One by one they report their name, club and age category. They pay their money and collect their complimentary socks. They might not appreciate it, but these are some of the luckiest athletes in Britain. And it has nothing to do with getting free hosiery.

'I organize between 30 and 40 races a year,' says Andy O'Sullivan, once all the runners have checked in. 'They range from five to ten kilometres and include some that go over the moors.' Andy's enthusiasm is so infectious that an epidemic of road running has swept Littleborough. The town's car parks are full and athletes canter around the narrow streets as they keep warm before the off. He has been uncommonly successful in his dealings with the local police officers, but that's because he is one himself: 'Being a police officer I report every event as I stage it, explaining what the course will be and always making sure that I have already chosen the safest possible route.'

There's no suggestion that Andy gets special treatment because of his job. But he is in a position to be able to answer all the questions he knows will be asked by his fellow officers, and his answers are more likely to be accepted by them. 'I'm very fortunate in this area,' he continues, 'because in the Rochdale division I know of a number of special constables who want to join the force full time and I know that the officers who supervise these specials like it if they can have some experience of controlling traffic, so I get them to help me out with my races.'

There are similar pockets of tolerance around the country, but they are becoming rarer, as John Joyner of the British Association of Road Races concedes. 'It's very much down to the local officers,' he says. 'For reasons which I don't fully understand some of the police areas in the North are less keen to accept road racing than their counterparts in the South. Even in the South I can give you examples of some local officers who are very supportive and then stations where they are not.'

Stuart Pailor, a runner based in the North-East who fought unsuccessfully against his local council and constabulary to keep his beloved 'Hartlepool Ten' road race going is more bitter. ' It's a growing cancer, they seem to be picking off races one by one. Soon there will only be the big city marathons left,' he warns.

John Walker, a member of the road running committee of UK Athletics, concurs: 'The Midlands is not too bad, but when you get to the North they've been having tremendous problems.' Mr Walker has also seen a growing number of race organizers taking the third option – ignoring the police and staging events without the prior knowledge of the local constabulary. 'Unfortunately, this is happening quite a lot,' he says. 'There are a number of fun-runs over which we have no control, but equally there are many races which UK Athletics should be in control of, but which are put on by clubs without telling either us or the police. I'm not at all happy about it.'

While the athletics authorities are worried about races taking place behind the back of the police, or in complete defiance of police advice, there is nothing to stop this happening. Andy Relf, who left the police to form a consultancy offering guidance to road race organizers, says it is a myth that police approval is needed to stage a race on the public highway. 'The responsibility for authorizing races doesn't fall upon the police, and never has done,' he reveals. 'The police service would always be consulted by the highway authority if a road closure was sought, but the police could not authorize it themselves.'

If the event is small and no road closure is needed then anyone can run on a road; the only offence that it is possible to commit is that of causing an obstruction, but if the racers are well spread out then this is unlikely to happen. Mr Relf says that what race organizers have interpreted as a refusal by the police to allow events has been more a case of the local force telling runners, 'It's your risk.' He explains: 'In the past, officers have always tried to help people, especially people who have no specialist knowledge of the rules for road closure, but in latter years they have decided to encourage organizers to take responsibility themselves and have made sure that they put this in writing. They have basically told the people who arrange the races that they are responsible for safety, and that is absolutely true under the health and safety regulations.'

To the officers, and informed people like Andy Relf and Andy O'Sullivan, it is simply a statement of fact. To everyone else it appears as a passing of the buck and, in practice, a refusal to allow a race to take place. Since an organizer's insurance cover is likely to be invalidated if the race takes place without police backing, the constabulary is in a position to cancel races. Andy Relf agrees that race organizers are being scared by the police into cancelling their events: 'Yes, if people are not versed in these matters then a letter from the police saying, "Don't do it," is going to put them off. Now, the police might be doing that for very good reasons, such as the planned route is too busy, but the reality is that you are perfectly within your rights to use the road all of the time.'

And that's what some people are doing. It might be dangerous and the race is quite possibly not insured because any cover is dependent on police knowledge and approval. But race organizers who are unlucky enough to live on the patch of an uncooperative copper are having to choose between cancelling their race or running a risk.

'I think you should have the police involved,' says John Walker, 'because if you don't and there is an accident then you're asking for trouble. My personal belief would be that if the police did not support an event, then you should not stage it.'

Andy Relf is now working with the Department of Transport to draw up new guidelines for allowing sporting events to happen on public highways, with approval and the insurance cover which police support brings. But while those discussions are held, races are disappearing because of an inappropriate law being misapplied by police officers scared of being sued for allowing a race to take place. When a solution is found, many people will have been lost to a sport which has provided health and fitness for the masses and medals for the elite.

CHAPTER NINE

The Noble Art of Brain Damage
The Legal Knockout Which Has Boxing on Its Knees

Boxing's bosses have been caught short by a court ruling which says they are to blame if a boxer is injured with anything less than gold-standard medical care on hand. But they still don't get it. Hundreds of fights still take place every year with second-class medical cover.

Even by boxing standards it was a brutal fight. Paul Ingle, the scrawny scrapper from Scunthorpe, had invested too much pain and effort to submit his International Boxing Federation (IBF) featherweight world title to South Africa's Mbuelo Botile while he could still stand. But that night of 13 December 2000 the Yorkshireman, exhausted and battered, went at least one round too far for his own good.

Knocked down twice, Ingle stayed on his feet, just about, till the twelfth round of the fight. But to no avail. His 13-month reign as champ was over when referee Dave Parris ended the fight. But it wasn't the end of the drama.

As Botile celebrated, Ingle collapsed and slipped into unconsciousness. Doctors and paramedics piled into the ring as the auditorium in Sheffield fell silent. Fans on their feet craned their necks and stared intently at the fight for life, as they must surely have known it to be – just as minutes earlier they had noisily focused on the contest.

Ingle was rushed to hospital, where surgeons operated to remove a clot from his brain. In the run-up to Christmas, sports and news bulletins were punctuated with reports of his slow journey back from the most serious, often fatal, boxing injury, a bleeding brain.

A week after Ingle hit the canvas, another boxer, who had

suffered similar injuries to the Yorkshireman, was nearing the end of his long courtroom battle for compensation and justice. Michael Watson was certainly not the man he had been when, nearly ten years before, he stepped into the ring to face Chris Eubank. For a start he was in a wheelchair, paralysed down his left side and had difficulty with speech. But his spirits were high after he emerged triumphant from the Court of Appeal in London with his million-pound suit for damages against the British Boxing Board of Control (BBBC) confirmed. Although Watson was the first boxer to seek damages on the grounds of injury from the people who control the sport in this country, he is unlikely to be the last.

The casual observer might assume that he had a cheek to take any action at all, given that he was a willing participant in a sport where the aim is to batter an opponent senseless. But the whole point of an officially sanctioned fight, as opposed to an unlicensed scrap behind closed doors, is that it is specifically organized to reduce the risk of injury. That is why there are rules over the length of a fight and duration of rounds, why there is a referee in the ring and why there are 'seconds' ringside. It is also why there are doctors ringside.

The trouble from the British Boxing Board of Control's point of view is the Michael Watson case proved that these measures, designed to protect the boxer, amounted to a duty of care. His case demonstrated that, in that duty, the BBBC was not providing the best care available and appropriate to a boxing injury.

It still doesn't. Already bankrupt, the BBBC could now be sued out of existence by a queue of boxers waiting to follow Watson into the courtroom on similar grounds. And all because of what amounts to an 'amateur' ethic that dominates medicine in boxing.

You are about to read the words of two boxers. Both of them collapsed in the ring after ferocious bouts and later underwent emergency brain surgery. One of them has made a complete recovery.

BOXER ONE: I don't remember anything. Just travelling to the Albert Hall on 2 May 1998, then waking up in a hospital bed with people leaning over me saying, 'You're never going to box again.' I thought six months out and I'll be back. Only three or four days afterwards, my wife walked me to a toilet and I looked in a mirror and realized how bad it was and that I would never box again.

BOXER TWO: My girlfriend said I came round after six or seven days but when they tried to help me I started to panic. Maybe I thought I was back in the ring. I started to fight them all, anyway, they had to put me to sleep. I came round eventually 12 days after the fight. Even then, all I wanted to do was get out of bed. I kept trying to stand up and kept falling down. They decided to tie me down to the bed because I would not give up trying to get up.

BOXER ONE: They kept me sedated for about five days. First day they got me up to walk, it felt weird, you know, just like when you have been out for a good drink the night before. After a few hours I had got it together and that was it. A lot of fighters are weaker down one side or something like that. When I was sedated my wife told me they were shining a torch in my eyes and they weren't reacting. They thought I was blind and paralysed down my left-hand side. I was fortunate that I came out and everything was the same.

BOXER TWO: I couldn't move my right hand and my right foot. I had and still have problems with eyesight and talking. The speech is improving and the eyesight is too. I still go for regular physio sessions.

BOXER ONE: I ran the Marathon the following year for the hospital, ran the Great North Run. I train a couple of guys, Adrian Dobson and Dean Pithie. I have been kept pretty busy really. I also work for Sky TV as a boxing pundit.

> BOXER TWO: I can't really do much because I can't
> really walk very well and I have had spasm attacks,
> the last one in September. I can't walk. I just sit there
> and my mum has to do everything for me.
> BOXER ONE: I still love the sport as much. As long as
> boxers know the risks involved and they want to do
> it and they have got the right medics there I think
> boxing should carry on. Great sport, great discipline.
> BOXER TWO: I think boxing should be banned.

The boxer who can't walk very well, who has spasm attacks and thinks boxing should be banned, is Chris Henry from Tottenham, north London. In 1997 he was stopped in the final round of a bruising bout for the southern area cruiserweight title. He was rushed to hospital: 'They operated on me straight away because I had a blood clot on the side of the head from where I had been punched repeatedly. They had to operate and I have got a scar there from where they removed the blood clot.'

The other boxer was Spencer Oliver, his friend, who, as it happened, boxed for the same club: 'I used to go and see Chris in hospital. I used to think it was a shame that it happened to him. I was quite shocked to look at him, he was very weak down his left side, he can't train, he has put on a lot of weight. Even so, I did not think it would ever happen to me.'

And he was right. Spencer Oliver would never suffer brain damage quite like Chris Henry, even though a year later he received almost exactly the same type of injury. There was a crucial difference, however. A consultant anaesthetist was at the ringside and was able to work with Spencer almost immediately.

'I was fortunate to have Eddie Carter in my corner. He works as a cuts man but he is also a nurse and he had done all the research in case anything happened.' It was Carter who noticed that Spencer was fitting a little bit after he was knocked down and slipping in and out of consciousness. He knew immediately that something was wrong. 'He told the anaesthetist to put a line in me and sedated me there and then in the ring. That stopped the swelling in the brain, which saved my life. If they had just packed me off to hospital, all the time from the ring and during the journey, the swelling would have been going on in my brain and I would probably have come out brain damaged, if I survived at all.'

Having a trained anaesthetist ringside may seem a strange addition to a boxer's or promoter's backroom. Although not unheard of, they are a rare presence at a boxing bout. After all, as the title suggests, their expertise is in doing, certainly more subtly and a great deal more safely, what a boxer hopes his fist will do. But of course the massive advantage of having an anaesthetist on hand is that they daily deal with people who are unconscious. They do not just put people out – they maintain them while they are in that state and then bring them around.

Dr Peter Farling is chairman of the Neuro-Anaesthesia Society of Great Britain. 'People can be trained to resuscitate but that is more a skill you might need in dealing with an acute cardiac arrest,' he explains. 'What we are talking about is trying to maintain someone in order to get them to surgery. Bleeding may be going on, there might be fitting, you need to gain control of the body and the only way to do that is to give drugs intravenously to sedate them, in effect to paralyse the body so you can control breathing.'

Failure to control the breathing in such a situation can mean that the brain is starved of oxygen and becomes damaged. Being able to stick a tube in correctly to clear airways or administer drugs is vital. And, what to a general medic could be a difficult and chance affair, is a matter of routine to the trained anaesthetist. 'Anaesthetists deal with people who are unconscious daily,' notes Peter Farley, 'they are putting tubes into people at the start of operations all the time. I think it is interesting that Jackie Stewart, when he was racing in Formula One, employed an anaesthetist to travel with him to all the circuits so, in the event of crash, he would have the proper medical management there and then.'

Repeatedly over the past decade the British Boxing Board of Control has been given clear warning of the need for anaesthetists ringside and, as the Spencer Oliver incident illustrated, clear evidence of how effective they can be. But boxing has consistently rejected this advice. It may be that as a result the legal floodgates could now open and engulf the sport, especially as the Michael Watson case so completely demolished the BBBC in court.

Michael Watson suffered a sub-dural haemorrhage, or a bleed in the brain, in his fight with Chris Eubank. If this sounds serious, it is. His injuries were severe. It has taken years of intensive therapy just to get back some power of speech and he will never walk unaided again.

The nub of the legal argument between Watson and the BBBC was that the ringside medical care was not up to providing what was regarded as the standard response to such an injury and that this failure was the BBBC's fault. As Watson's lawyer, Michael Toohig, put it: 'The board had a duty to provide better medical care. The inappropriate response ringside and the time it took to get him to hospital meant a redeemable situation became irredeemable.'

Crucial to the outcome of the Watson case, upheld on appeal, is that the courts found that the BBBC does have a legal duty of care. In other words, the liability is not with the guy who presents his head for a beating but with the body that sanctions the fight. Incidentally, this ruling is believed to apply to all sport.

The BBBC has governed British boxing for over 70 years and, as already noted, organizing medical care for fighters is one of its most important functions. There is no doubt that great strides have been made in this direction. There are now fairly stringent pre-fight and post-fight checks on all competitors. Every year boxers must have a head-to-toe physical check-up, a full eye test, an MRI scan to check for brain abnormalities and tests for hepatitis B and the AIDS-causing HIV virus. Any fighter stopped inside the distance three times in a row can't fight again for a year, and then only after passing a full medical. All this is designed to spot not only acute injuries but also damage that may be suffered in training or even outside the ring. Where the Watson case caught out the BBBC is that it showed this thoroughness did not extend to medical provision on fight night itself.

From when Watson began showing signs of brain injury in

the wake of his savage encounter with Eubank, it was seven minutes before a doctor got to him. The doctor concerned was a GP. It was found he had neither the expertise, drugs or resuscitation equipment to be of much use to the stricken boxer. It took more than an hour before Watson was operated on and this in part was because neither the board nor the promoter was aware which local hospital had neuro-surgical capability.

Mr Justice Ian Kennedy (and then the Appeal Court) found all these factors contributed to the fighter's subsequent brain damage which left him physically and mentally impaired; and, crucially, the court decided the BBBC was liable.

Huge public interest in Michael Watson led to meetings between the Minister for Sport and Michael Watson's neurosurgeon, Peter Hamlyn. As a result, new regulations were brought in. Whereas before the BBBC had merely required the presence of two doctors ringside, the new regulations insisted that appropriate resuscitation equipment and drugs be available ringside and that a team of neurosurgeons be on standby less than an hour's drive from ringside.

For those who in the sport who have hailed the 'Hamlyn Protocol' as it became known as a breakthrough in medical care for boxers and proof that the BBBC and promoters really do care about the welfare of the fighters, then it is as well to point out that Peter Hamlyn himself is less impressed.

'While no doubt it has made it safer for fighters, I should point out that Formula One racing and horse racing have had even more stringent provisions in operation for decades now. A Formula One race could not even get off the grid without an anaesthetist at the track and before the sport's chief medical officer had inspected the neurosurgical, orthopaedic and other medical facilities at the hospital designated to deal with any injury. As far as horse racing is concerned, there is an anaesthetist in attendance at every race meeting. If a jockey falls off a horse there is someone minutes away capable of getting a line into the injured person to administer the vital drugs.'

And for those who argue that, for all this, serious and calamitous injuries are part and parcel of a dangerous sport,

Formula One again provides evidence of the extent to which properly applied health and safety procedures can drastically reduce death and serious injury.

Ironically, by adopting the Hamlyn Protocol, the board left itself open to Watson's claim that its previous procedures had been inadequate. But, as *On The Line* discovered, not everyone involved in the care of boxers felt that the new post-Watson protocols went far enough.

In Wales, boxing doctor Ray Monsall reasons that as only an anaesthetist has the skills and the experience to care properly for a boxer in the immediate aftermath of a brain injury, there should be one at every fight. With the help of a consultant, the late Colin Wise, he drew up a protocol insisting on it. As a result, since 1993 an anaesthetist has been on hand at every professional fight in Wales. However, the BBBC refused to implement this policy in the rest of the United Kingdom.

In 1994 Dr Wise wrote to the board to complain: 'I would point out it is only a matter of time before such an incident, as occurred with Michael Watson, is repeated. If death or, perhaps worse, survival with neurological damage ensues, the question will always be raised as to whether adequate precautions might have mitigated or prevented such an adverse outcome. Morally we and the BBBC would be guilty of negligence if we had not done our utmost to minimize the degree of damage or prevent the death of a boxer.' Those words were to prove sadly prophetic.

There stands in the former mining village of Newmains, just outside Motherwell, a bronze statue of a gloved boxer poised and ready for action. The sculpture was paid for by local people and it is a tribute to one of their own. A short distance away in the front room of a neat semi-detached house there is a more personal shrine. Kenny Murray keeps it. A collection of photographs and trophies which marks his son Jimmy's boxing career.

'He was a natural fighter,' recalls Kenny. 'Since he was a wee boy. He was always sticking up for himself. Anyone who wanted to fight Jim, he would fight them.'

It may be something of a cliché but life can be tough for

slight children in rough, tough mining communities. Jimmy became handy with his fists. 'I think it was to calm his aggression that Jimmy took up boxing because he was going off the rails a wee bit. He loved the training, six o'clock in the morning he was away, four, five, six miles, back and away. He just loved the sport.'

Jimmy had won 16 of his 17 fights as a professional when tragedy struck in 1995 in a contest for the British bantamweight title against Scottish rival Drew Docherty. The nature of a brain injury sustained in boxing can be insidious. It is not immediately obvious. The fighter can stagger on for a couple of rounds literally with his life draining away inside his head – and only a trained eye would notice the critical nature of the injury.

And so it proved. Jimmy collapsed in the final moments of the final round of his fight with Drew Docherty. If that wasn't bad enough matters took a tragic and squalid turn. As his trainer and medical staff rushed to him a riot broke out among spectators.

His father recalls, 'I can't remember much of the fight but I know it was a rabble afterwards. There were people under tables. I don't know where the doctor was but by the time I got to the ring there were tables and chairs flying everywhere. I looked about but I could not see anyone with medical machinery at all.'

As the Master of Ceremonies appealed for calm the contents of the medical trolley were hijacked by the rioters and used as weapons. 'I couldn't tell how long it was before they took him away in an ambulance,' recalls Kenny. 'No one could tell us even to which hospital he had been taken. When we found out, we had to take a taxi.'

The surgeons removed the blood clot from Jimmy Murray's brain but it was too late. He died. A fatal accident inquiry was later held and the presiding Sheriff ruled that there was no one to blame. At the time Kenny Murray was still distraught and said he did not seek a further inquiry. But a combination of the final outcome of the Michael Watson case and what he regarded as a low insurance payout – £60,000 – has brought about a change of mind.

'Well, £60,000 does not even make a dent in the trauma we

have been through in the last five years. Every time there is an article there is invariably a picture, the last one of him on his knees. It is horrendous for myself, my wife and my other sons and daughters. I still have to go out to work. Jimmy had said he intended to set us up in business.' It is a lack of cash that has prevented Kenny Murray going to the law but he says he is on the look-out for a no win, no fee lawyer to take the case on.

It is uncertain whether Jimmy Murray would have survived had there been an anaesthetist on duty at the fight. All we know is that there was not and Jimmy Murray died. The board responded by introducing compulsory annual brain scans for all boxers, but still no anaesthetists. The Welsh were left to go it alone.

In 1997, so pleased were the Welsh doctors with their experiment in having anaesthetists ringside, they felt moved to spread the word and two Welsh Area doctors attended the first medical congress of the World Boxing Council (WBC), the most influential of boxing's global governing bodies. Anaesthetist Peter FitzGerald explained the Welsh system to a gathering of 200 delegates, who had travelled to the event held on the idyllic Caribbean island of Aruba. The conclusion to the speech ran, 'We believe the Welsh Area protocol for the ringside management of the acutely head-injured boxer provides for a cost-effective and logistically simple set of guidelines allowing for immediate intervention by doctors who are skilled in controlled intubation and the management of raised intra-cranial pressure. We would ask the WBC to accept it as a mandatory safety requirement that anaesthetists should be present ringside worldwide.'

If the Welsh delegation had expected crashing applause and enthusiasm for their plea, they were severely disappointed. The speech was met in stunned silence, followed by a barrage of hostile questions from the floor. The recommendation was not adopted.

One month after the Aruba conference Chris Henry was brain damaged. Again it cannot be proved that an anaesthetist would have made any difference. We just do not know. After the fight the BBBC instituted an immediate inquiry. Three years later

Chris Henry had still not seen it, and his solicitor has contacted Michael Watson's, Michael Toohig. Toohig says it may be difficult but not impossible to prove a claim.

'The claim might succeed if a boxer who is injured in England could show that it would have made a difference if the additional steps taken in Wales had been implemented at the fight where he sustained his injury. He would also have to show that the board had no good reason for failing to implement the Welsh protocol in England.'

In 1998 the BBBC finally decided to have anaesthetists at ringside – but only for championship fights. This saved Spencer Oliver but came too late for Jimmy Murray and would have been no use to Chris Henry, who was not contesting a British title.

In the absence of an anaesthetist, training in the arts of intubation and maintaining an unconscious person for the GPs that typically attend fights would be handy. *On The Line* asked the BBBC if it offers this. They would not tell us.

Dr Ian McNeil is chairman of the British Association of Immediate Care or BASICS. 'If they hope to improve care then training is essential,' says Dr McNeil. 'I think you would have to have appropriate skills to do the job, like maintaining an unconscious person. If you don't then not only are you letting the patient down but probably laying yourself open to legal challenge and sanction from the General Medical Council.'

BASICS runs a pre-hospital emergency course to equip doctors to deal with the majority of life-threatening illnesses and injuries, particularly in sport. Unless reimbursed by the governing body, the doctors have to pay for themselves to attend such courses. It does not come cheap. A three-day course will set you back £500, a five-day one £1,000 – an expensive undertaking for a GP who would also have to underwrite the cost of a locum in his or her practice while away.

Dr McNeil could not say how many ringside doctors have taken a pre-emergency hospital course, but given that there are at least 350 title fights a year of one description or another, certainly not enough. 'Having to pay out of their own pocket is probably an issue,' says McNeil. 'A ringside doctor would have to attend a number of fights just to get back the cost of the course as the remuneration they get for attending boxing matches would appear to be token but, really, how much for a human life or a brain damaged one?'

Quite. Any claim that boxing cannot afford £500 for a medical course that can help prevent brain damage or death to competitors has to be treated with scepticism. The huge monies generated by the bigger promotions alone could easily afford to ensure that there was a cadre of appropriately trained doctors.

The BBBC has somehow boxed itself into a corner now. If it installs anaesthetists at every fight, or even appropriately trained doctors, the lawyers of injured boxers will rightly ask why it was not done years ago. If it maintains the status quo, it is open to charges of continuing a two-tier medical system, with the five-star standard available only in title fights or in Wales.

So what is the difficulty with having appropriately trained GPs or consultants ringside? The most likely explanation probably lies with an ancient turf war that extends way beyond sport. It is this: In the medical profession, consultants have been known to be at odds with GPs. Specialists sometimes resent generalists meddling with what they see as their patch and the generalists are understandably annoyed when a specialist insists that they are not up to the job. These are old battle lines. Some orthopaedic consultants for example have little time for GPs with sports medicine qualifications, arguing that as most sports injuries relate to the skeleton, that is their business. A broken bone is a broken bone be it sustained on a football pitch or paving stone. GPs argue that an empathy for and knowledge of sport is worth any number of letters after a name.

Michael Watson has been awarded £1million by the courts. It is an award that has bankrupted the BBBC. If the board finds a way back from financial oblivion on this one, it may find several other litigants itching to take it back through the courts.

Then there is the future. Many believe that the BBBC will go out of business and then reform, like thousands of businesses bankrupted each year. But the High Court and Court of Appeal judgments on the Watson case mean that whoever takes over boxing will have to get to grips with the duty of care imposed on them by the law. Medical expertise is going to make it difficult for them to ignore the need for an anaesthetist or a doctor sufficiently equipped with such skills to be present at all boxing promotions.

Indeed, Peter Hamlyn, the author of the eponymous protocol, highlighted the fact in the media the very next morning that there did not seem to be an anaesthetist on duty for Paul Ingle's fight. The fight, at the time of writing, is the subject of a BBBC inquiry. Hamlyn says there are key questions that must be addressed.

Ingle was first taken to a district hospital and then transferred to the neurological ward at the Royal Hallamshire Hospital. Now the question that needs to be answered is: if he needed to be resuscitated, why was that not done at ringside? And if it was, why was he taken to the district hospital first and not straight to the neurological unit, as agreed under the Hamlyn Protocol?

It is hoped that the BBBC inquiry will answer these questions. If it does not, then the board could be staring at serious problems. There was not just one world title fight on the bill that night in Sheffield but four. Given that the BBBC introduced the requirement for anaesthetists or appropriately trained GPs three years ago, the medical coverage at Sheffield should not just have been adequate but gold standard.

The number of fighters who suffer blood clots on the brain is mercifully very low but it would seem that when it does happen in this country, as sadly it will again at some point in the future, the presence or otherwise of an anaesthetist is bound to be on the media checklist.

Spencer Oliver, whose quality of life was saved by an anaesthetist on the scene in his hour of need, believes there is no option: 'It is a very dangerous sport and every time a boxer gets in the ring he is putting his life on the line. Boxing is a licence to kill really. If someone dies, the opponent does not get sent to jail. It is down to the promoters and the boxing board to make sure they have got anaesthetists or similar ringside, whether it is a small or big title fight because the risk is always there.'

And that is the issue: getting together with risk. Boxing is lambasted for being barbaric, for being a killer and for being exploitative. The powers that be, like the boxers they nurture, have tended to come out fighting when faced with fundamental criticism. But as Formula One, horse racing, climbing and other sports where people die have shown, it is possible to neutralize such criticism by taking sensible steps that reduce risk to a minimum. It is a lesson boxing must learn if it is to survive the implications of the Michael Watson case.

CHAPTER TEN

Course for Concern
Three-Quarters of a Million Golfers Are Paying for a Course They'll
Never Play On

*English golfers have one of the best courses in the world at their
disposal. However, this is news to the majority of them. Bought in
their name, the National Golf Centre at Woodhall Spa is the result of
an extraordinary deal signed by those at the very top of the sport.*

As famous sporting names of the world go, Woodhall Spa doesn't
normally make the definitive list. Surrounded by acres of flat
arable farmland, located halfway between Lincoln and Skegness,
and boasting a population of around three thousand people, the
town became popular in the nineteenth century for its mineral-
rich waters and its country air. But leave its small, quiet centre,
head out and up the wide tree-lined boulevard, and hidden
among the large houses you will find the entrance to the town's
real gem – its championship golf course.

   Just calling it a golf course, however, fails to do it real justice. Step past the ornate fountains and around the modern,
clean, glass-fronted buildings, and there are not one, but two
championship courses beautifully crafted onto the flat
Lincolnshire countryside. The original course is, according to
those in the know, one of the great courses in the world. The
influential Golf Magazine of America voted it the thirty-third
best inland course in the world. Its owner boasts on the website:

*'This outstanding masterpiece of golf architecture is renowned
for its 18 individual holes with cavernous bunkers.'* It continues,
*'The natural beauty of this Lincolnshire oasis serves only to
emphasize the majesty of this famous course.'*

The gushing owner of Woodhall Spa golf course is the English Golf Union (EGU); established in 1924, it is the governing body of men's golf in England. Through a network of county associations, it looks after the interests of the country's three-quarters of a million amateur players, ranging from the scratch player to the humble weekend hacker. It also credits itself with producing golf's famous names like Faldo, Westwood and Rose.

In 1995 the EGU decided to buy the Woodhall Spa course from Neil Hotchkin, an ex-stockbroker whose father, Stafford Hotchkin MP, had co-built it in the 1920s. In order to do so it needed an awful lot of money, money it didn't have, so it tapped the massive source of funds at its ready disposal – the membership. Each member of a golf club, as part of the annual membership fee, contributes a levy to the EGU. This has been a token sum of one or two pounds, nothing to the average golfer; in fact it is questionable whether the majority of golfers actually know they pay it. The Union decided that it would have to go up to fund the proposed purchase of Woodhall Spa.

However, far from being the jewel in the EGU's crown, Woodhall Spa has proved to be a millstone round its members' necks. Through the levy they are now footing the bill for a course many have no prospect of playing. Each of the counties that make up the EGU has representatives on its committee. Retired policeman Jim Barbour is a former secretary and president of the Essex County Golf Union he recalls the idea of buying Woodhall Spa being raised when he was in office. 'We knew sometime before the January 1995 council meeting that they were looking to buy a golf course and premises,' he says. 'There was no indication where that was until a couple of months before the council meeting in that year and we were informed that Woodhall Spa was something they were looking at. They said it was something that would be raised at the council meeting in that January.'

The plans were raised and passed at that January meeting, but owning a golf course was against the EGU's own rules, and if it was to buy Woodhall Spa or any other golf course it would have to make major alterations to its own constitution. As its former secretary, Keith Wright knows the constitution well, and is well aware of how difficult it would have been to make the necessary changes. 'Well, in my day it would have been a tortuous process,' he says, leafing through the Union handbook. 'I know when we changed the constitution when I was there it was a fairly major job and caused one or two of us headaches. What they have done very quickly is change the constitution to facilitate the buying of Woodhall Spa I suppose. Buying it was just a dream at that time and as we went on through the years there was more and more argument that we should have a base where we had our own golf and that was very sensible.'

He explained how important, in his experience, the constitution was in the day-to-day running of the Union. 'I remember while I was there it took us two years to change the constitution,' he says. 'It went to solicitors, back to us, back to solicitors again and was finally adopted by the council, and that is why I am a bit surprised that when I look at the handbook of 1996 that the objects 2.2 (e), (f) and (g), because they were certainly not in there when I was secretary.'

The changes to 2.2 (e), (f) and (g), referred to by Keith Wright, basically allowed the Union to buy Woodhall Spa:

2.2 (e) To purchase, or by other means acquire freehold, leasehold or other property for any estate or interest whatever movable or immovable or any interest in such property including the purchase of shares in any company owning such property and to sell, lease, develop or manage such property or otherwise turn the same advantage to the Union.

(f) To subscribe for, take purchase or otherwise acquire any company or business which in the opinion of the council may be carried on so as to directly or indirectly benefit the Union.

(g) To borrow or raise money in such a manner as the council think fit and secure the repayment thereof by the creation and issue of debentures, debenture stock mortgages or in any other way.

Wright believes the changes were brought in very quickly to allow the purchase.

OTL: Can you remember when was the first time
that Woodhall Spa was mentioned?'
KW: It wasn't really when I was there, but I do
remember it was mentioned and I understand subsequently that there were moves that I was not made
aware of about them negotiating to go there.
OTL: You say you weren't aware of the plans, even
though you were the secretary, was that something
that concerned you?
KW: Yes it did, I felt that the costs of going to Woodhall Spa were beyond our means at the time, if any
discussion had happened I would have been very sceptical about whether the EGU could have afforded it
without going to the golfer and saying put your hand
in your pocket we need a lot of money from you.
OTL: You were party to the EGU's accounts, and how
much money they had in the bank and how much
money they could afford to spend on something like
that?
KW: Yes I was, and it was nowhere near the kind of
price that has been mentioned to me that they paid
for Woodhall Spa. I think the general feeling was
that it wasn't a very good location for what they
were calling a centre of excellence for English golf.

Wright now works as a football coach, having left the English
Golf Union before it relocated itself to Woodhall Spa.

Back in Essex Jim Barbour and his colleagues were concerned. 'We were unhappy with it,' he remembers. 'When the
crunch came we didn't have the courage of our convictions to
vote against it, we abstained at the council meeting in January;
the only people I remember voting against it were Yorkshire.'
The Yorkshire County Union, the biggest in the country, admits
it did vote against the move, the only Union to do so, but that
was as much information as it was prepared to give.

Woodhall Spa is slap-bang in the middle of rural Lincolnshire; to be cruel it's in the middle of nowhere. As Keith Wright

pointed out, not an obvious place to have a national Centre of Excellence. Sources within the Union have said that courses did become available in the Midlands, closer to major motorways, but they were quickly rejected by the EGU, whose heart was obviously in Lincolnshire.

Three-quarters of all clubs in the UK, including Woodhall Spa, are Members' Courses, (the remainder are called Proprietary Courses), owned by individuals or companies rather than the members who play them. Their executive director is Bob Simmons. Sitting in the luxurious grounds of a private course in Kent he explained why, after the levy was raised, he started to take a keener interest in EGU affairs. The location of Woodhall Spa, he says, baffled him: 'I find it very difficult to get there from my office in Kent, it takes me about five hours to drive and I am told that for people in the West Country, you could actually get to Holland quicker.' Whether that's geographically true or not, it makes a point felt by many golfers who feel disenfranchised by the Lincolnshire location of Woodhall Spa, which is served only by minor roads.

Now retired but still keeping a watchful eye on the way the sport is run from his home on the Devon coast, Jim Arthur is one of the world's leading builders of golf courses and has been for over 50 years. The key, he says, to a successful golf course is simple: 'It's the old, old story. Location, location, location; put it in the wrong place and it is never going to survive. If they had asked me, which they didn't, I would have told them not to go there.'

He agrees with Keith Wright and Bob Simmons about Woodhall Spa's claim to be a National Centre for Golf. 'Well, it's extreme arrogance on their part to call it a National Centre, because a National Centre surely means a UK centre and if you set up a centre that deals with England you are diluting the resources available on a national scale. They were not qualified in my view to make jurisdiction over all the other aspects of golf they say they thought they could make decisions about.'

Bob Simmons, who sits on the EGU Executive Committee, felt so strongly that his members were asked to consider withholding the levy they paid to the Union, which would have made a major dent in their income, when they obviously needed it most. He says he felt that his members were kept in the dark about day-to-day issues: 'Firstly the levy was too high and being used for the wrong reason, secondly there was no management structure in place to run the golf club, and thirdly there were no accounts produced. When you have an investment in a golf centre as the EGU has on behalf of its members, one would expect that as in any normal business they should produce monthly accounts at least to see what the situation is in terms of finances. This obviously wasn't done and something that has caught up with them, and caught up with them very quickly and something they weren't expecting, hence the levy being introduced.'

From his Essex home Jim Barbour says it takes him over three hours to drive the 140 miles to Woodhall Spa – not a journey he would like to make every day. As he recalls, the Union didn't waste too much time in sealing the deal: 'I certainly don't think that it was any more than three or four months from the time we first heard about Woodhall Spa until we had the meeting in January 1995 and they were going ahead with the development. I think they went to planning in April and got the authority to go ahead in June with the construction. What they were talking about was purchasing enough land to build another 18-hole golf course plus building the management block to go with it, and we all know what the development costs of a golf course are. If you buy the original course at Woodhall Spa you have got to be looking at several million to develop that one. So you are looking at eight million or thereabouts.'

So why was it so important to the EGU that it bought Woodhall Spa, changing their own constitution and taxing their own members along the way? The answer lies five hundred yards up the road from the entrance to the club, in one of the town's large, and largely hidden, houses. It is the home of Neil Hotchkin, the man who provided the EGU with its prestigious new base, ensuring the course his father built was left in safe hands – but his role was far more than that.

As a former president of the Union and a long-serving member of its most powerful committees, Hotchkin's shadow looms large over many areas of the EGU. He is also a very good friend of the 2001 president and long-term chairman, John Flanders. This relationship at the very top was extremely important, according to former secretary Keith Wright: 'The way that the organization operates, you have got to work from a friendship basis and a lot of people were friends. In some respect it was a good job they were, because things got done, so from that point of view it was essential there was somebody who could push it on.'

Next to the original course, which they named The Hotchkin, after its seemingly generous benefactor, the EGU built a second course called The Bracken. But as the Union's own constitution didn't allow it to own or build a golf course, it was forced to set up a separate company, Woodhall Spa, 1995. That particular hitch over, the deal quickly went through.

The amount it paid its former president, Mr Hotchkin, for Woodhall Spa golf course was never made public, leaving senior officers like Mr Barbour and his fellow members guessing. *On The Line* enlisted a concerned golfer, experienced in interpreting company accounts, to examine those of the EGU. He found them very interesting reading. 'With regards to the purchase of Woodhall Spa golf course,' he told us, 'we know that Lloyds Bank agreed to advance £5 million, this to be repaid at £500,000 per annum for each of the next 10 years and at a fixed rate of interest but at a rate unspecified. The accounts also show a second loan of £1.5 million to be repaid at £187,500 per annum, logically an 8-year loan but again no term specified. Lastly an equipment loan of £300,000 to be repaid over 4 years in equal instalments of £75,000 also at terms unknown.' With added interest, that meant the EGU was committed to paying back at least £1.3 million a year, an awful lot of money for an amateur organization. Our expert, who didn't want to identify himself, carried on poring over the balance sheets laid out in front of him.

'The capital outlay here therefore is £6.8 million, to which can be added the £2 million that Lloyds Bank have made available by way of overdraft facilities which has no specified repayment terms. We therefore arrive at a total commitment of £8.8 million, which suggests that Woodhall Spa was sold for around that figure.'

The EGU had set up separate companies to operate the golf course; in effect it was paying itself nearly half a million pounds a year in rent for the privilege of basing itself in the middle of Lincolnshire at its own course. And, if they weren't paying rent to another of their own companies, Woodhall Spa golf course, it would have been in serious financial trouble.

'A service charge of £385,000 for the 11 months and £420,000 for the full year is shown to be paid to Woodhall Spa Golf Management Ltd. This is rent paid by the EGU for premises it occupies at Woodhall Spa.' Our financial expert continued his examination: 'One would question whether any offices in a situation such as a golf course warrant a rent of £35,000 a month. We must conclude that had the EGU not taken premises at Woodhall Spa and paid £35,000 per month rent then the Woodhall Spa golf course would not show a trading surplus before capital expenditure.' Prior to taking up residence in Lincolnshire, the Union was based in Leicester city centre, in a property they still owned in 1999 and were offering for rent at just £18,500 – a big difference from the rent they were now paying themselves for the privilege of using Woodhall Spa.

And here we come back to Neil Hotchkin and John Flanders. An accountant from Derby-shire, Flanders had risen up the ranks of golf administration in his home county, finally being able to sew the EGU badge to his well-worn blazer in 1989. When *On The Line* attempted to speak to the EGU, we were informed that Mr Flanders was the only person who did interviews on their behalf. On ringing his office we were told that Mr Flanders would not agree to speak to us, and that he hadn't done any interviews for 38 years! Speaking elsewhere, however, John Flanders has said that buying Woodhall Spa 'is the greatest thing I've done for English golf. I was chairman for 11 years and during that time the game exploded dramatically. Something had to be done and now it gives me a thrill to see what has been achieved at Woodhall Spa.' As a golf course, it is certainly a fine legacy for any official to leave, but surely it is Neil Hotchkin who has gained the most from this extraordinary deal rather than the three-quarters of a million English amateur golfers, near but *mainly* far who have paid for it.

Such selfless altruism from the octogenarian ex-stockbroker Neil Hotchkin couldn't of course go unrecognized, and as well as the several million pounds he was given for the course, he also received a rare and remarkable veto allowing him a say in how it was run. This veto came in the form of a 'Golden Share', allowing him one vote, which superseded all the rest of the shares put together.

The documents were shown to Lancaster University's Mark Armstrong, an expert in company law; he was surprised at what he saw, to say the least. 'Golden Shares became popular,' he explained, 'during the last Conservative government when they started privatizing the old nationalized companies. In order to retain control of those industries it was decided that the Secretary of State would take a share in the newly privatized company, which basically gives them veto over certain actions of the company in terms of management and future plans, etc.'

To have veto over the rest of the directors of a company, 51 per cent of the shares are required, but Hotchkin had all that power just in one solitary share. Although the Union didn't exactly shout it from the rooftops, at a meeting on 8 December 1998, John Flanders stood boldly in front of county union secretaries and tried to assure them that the Golden Share was a good deal. 'Mr and Mrs Hotchkin were concerned that the EGU might at some time consider selling the golf course or even dispose of some of the land for housing, etc. To allay their fears and respect their wishes, the solicitors for all parties agreed to the issue of a Golden Share in both Woodhall Spa Golf Management Company Limited and Woodhall Spa Golf Club Limited.'

But why would the Hotchkin family need any reassurances that the course was not going to be sold when the EGU was so obviously proud of its new base? And why would John Flanders think of selling it, when as he said himself it was the greatest thing he had done for English golf?

What the Golden Share actually meant, according to official EGU documents obtained by *On The Line*, was that it provided Mr and Mrs Hotchkin with the power to bring:

1) Any special resolution to amend the Memorandum and Articles of Association.
2) Any ordinary resolution to remove a director.

What wasn't explained to the county union secretaries at that December 1998 meeting was that the Golden Share in the two companies gave Neil Hotchkin the power to stop any major changes to the Union, the final say about who could be a director and an unassailable position as a director himself – all news to a shocked Jim Barbour: 'It was explained several times that the Golden Share was only there for Mr Hotchkin's lifetime, and it is not to do with the sale or purchase but the general management of the course, rather than whether it is sold or anything else. That was always my understanding about the Golden Share, that Woodhall Spa didn't pass from the EGU to someone else.'

Until *On The Line* informed Mr Barbour of the true implications of the Golden Share, he claims he and his county union were totally in the dark about how far-reaching it actually was. 'It certainly isn't a deal you would get anywhere else,' he continued ruefully. 'If you are going to sell something you sell it, you certainly don't retain an interest unless you don't sell the whole thing. If you sell the whole thing then you relinquish interest, it doesn't matter what you buy. If you buy a motor car, once you have paid the full price for it, it becomes yours and the other guy should have no attachment.'

Such is the rarity of Golden Shares in normal business that Mark Armstrong says he was forced to consult colleagues at Lancaster University: 'These things are very rare indeed in the ordinary day-to-day commerce of private limited companies. When you think of a normal commercial sale, or when one company sells to another, part of the contract is that there should be a clean break between two companies, so if you sell the company its legal shell plus its assets you want to make a clean break, because the new buyer of the business may have different ideas of how the company is to be run and managed. So they won't necessarily want the old directors or the old management involved in the running of the new business.'

Sources within the Union backed up the fact that, despite banking millions of pounds, Neil Hotchkin did indeed still have a huge influence over how the course was run, a clear case of Mr Hotchkin having his cake and also the final say on who else could eat it. All the more remarkable a deal in the eyes of Mark Armstrong, who confirmed the worth of the Golden Share. 'It's obviously very attractive for the person who has the Golden Share and has made a huge amount of money out of the sale,' he explained, staring at the documents' complex paperwork. 'For example, if he or she is the majority shareholder, or if he or she is the owner or founder of the company, or it has been held in the company for generations and it has passed on, if it is a particularly profitable company, or it has certain assets that are extremely valuable, then that individual has the right through the Golden Share to effectively have veto over certain decisions that are made.' Valuable to the party that has the all-important share, but surely a disincentive for the buyer, or at least Armstrong would have thought.

'I would have expected it may have been a stumbling block for a potential purchaser to find that the managing director wants to retain an effective veto over the new company's management decisions, depending, I would suspect, on how desperate they are for this company and assets.'

How the actual purchase price was worked out isn't clear, but what is clear is that Mr Hotchkin sold his course to the EGU, of which the chairman, who proudly boasted of brokering the deal, is a long-time friend. But there is more. As well as being a past president, Hotchkin crucially was also a member of the Presidents Advisory Committee (PAC), one of the Union's most powerful bodies, according to former secretary Keith Wright.

'It is selected by the president and it was initially brought in to help the president in his year of office,' he carefully explained. 'They would guide him through his year but because the

Executive is so big and almost unwieldy, over the years the Presidents Advisory Committee very often shortcuts things. They would discuss things and strategies would be put into place to get things through. At that time it was the best thing to do, because the most frustrating thing was if you have a project on the go and you take it to the Executive Committee and they say, "No, we'll shelve it", then your work stops and that was in many ways unacceptable. So in many ways the PAC was in fact a steering committee to get things through.'

On The Line put it to Keith Wright that the PAC, although an advisory committee, is actually a bit more than that. 'Most certainly, there is no question about that, it was certainly a very, very powerful committee,' he replied.

On The Line asked: 'The most powerful within the EGU?'

'Certainly the most influential: the Executive Committee's decision was final but the PAC laid the foundations and sometimes built the wall before things went through with the executive.'

From the evidence of Keith Wright a major decision such as the one to buy Woodhall Spa golf course wouldn't have been made without the PAC's involvement. Neil Hotchkin hadn't sat on the fence during the sale of Woodhall Spa; he vaulted backwards and forwards over it, taking a major interest in both sides. Rumours about PAC member Hotchkin's exact role were rife in golf circles, but they were never proved according to Essex man Jim Barbour: 'I think this was felt by quite a lot of people. It was never voiced very much, and it was one of those things that there was never any evidence that this was going on and without evidence you can't really make comment. I would think you will find that very difficult to substantiate anywhere because of the way the thing was dealt with. I think it's painfully obvious that Mr Hotchkin had a great deal to do with the sale and purchase of Woodhall Spa on behalf of the EGU.'

The English Golf Union has stayed at Woodhall Spa golf club and John Flanders, its long-term chairman, has accepted the honorary position once held by his friend Neil Hotchkin, the presidency. The ordinary members will be required to fund the project through the levy for a good few years yet. In fact, after the initial rise in subsidies they went up for a second time on 1 January 2000, as the realities of the deal hit home. Bob Simmons of the Association of Private Golf Course Owners has a privileged view from his position on the top table of the Union on whether the investment is being looked after properly. 'From the accounts we have looked at,' he says, 'I certainly think, and it's the opinion of the golf operators that have also seen the accounts, that Woodhall Spa needs very close management and tender care to see it through to fruition. We have expressed our doubts that the projections that have been put forward are not achievable in the not too distant future.'

The EGU refused to talk to *On The Line* and a stern letter from its secretary, Paul Baxter, was dispatched, barring its members from doing the same. But in an article in one prominent golf publication, the EGU protested its innocence of any wrongdoing under a headline proclaiming 'We Are Not Corrupt'. It was never actually claimed that they were corrupt – but what they did do was strike a unique and extraordinary deal with one of, if not *the*, most important members to build a National Golf Centre on one of the least accessible sites in England. There is no doubting that Woodhall Spa is an impressive golf course. It probably also deserves the accolade bestowed upon it by *Golf Magazine* of America that it is one of the best in the world. The problem remains, however, that the vast majority of the three-quarters of a million golfers in England who are bankrolling it will just have to take the magazine's word for it.

CHAPTER ELEVEN

No Limits
It's Violent, It's Dangerous and It's in Milton Keynes

The American Medical Association has called it 'human cockfighting'. The press have labelled it 'more violent than the most brutal boxing match or street brawl'. It is ultimate or extreme fighting – and it may be here to stay.

'If we want to step into the ring and beat each other up then that's up to us, we have the choice and that's what we want to do.' So says Justin Gray, a courteous and unassuming man who lives with his young family in a modest semi on a housing estate in Coventry. Despite his cropped hair, Justin looks nothing like the common perception of the hard man. He has no bulging steroid muscles and doesn't swagger when he walks. But when he goes to war, he means business.

'I think there's a certain amount of mutual respect, but at the same time I'm out to hurt the person. I'm not there to mess around. If I can knock him out I will knock him out and if I can break his arm with an arm bar that's what I intend to do. But there's a mutual respect knowing that he has had to go through the same as you to get into that ring. Once you're in the ring, that's all out of the window. You know, I want to do damage. That's what I've been preparing for and that's what I'll do.'

Justin is a fighter, and a good one. He trains daily in a bewildering array of dangerous martial arts: judo, boxing, *ju-jitsu*, *muay thai*, *tae kwon do* and wrestling. He has his own web page and offers personal tuition and seminars in submission fighting and self-defence. He has won British and European titles at his weight in *vale tudo* – the Portuguese for 'anything goes'.

Justin is one of a growing number of participants in a sport that has swept the martial arts community. *Vale tudo*, otherwise known as no-holds-barred or limited-rules fighting, pitches fighters of different disciplines against each other. Some even see it as a serious rival to boxing, a sport declining in popularity in the West. Yet it remains a quasi-underground activity, condemned by legal experts as outside the law and by medical experts as 'human cockfighting'. It has provoked a storm of protest.

'No-holds-barred contests are probably as old as man himself,' says martial arts historian Peter Lewis, editorial consultant for the British *Fighters* magazine. 'From when we came out of the caves into villages, there would be a no-holds-barred contest between warriors for supremacy: who was going to be the chief, who was going to be the leader.'

The Ancient Olympics had *pankration*, a form of wrestling with few restraints. The Romans, of course, had their gladiators. With the fall of the Roman Empire such contests largely died out in Europe. But in Asia they flourished. 'In the martial arts there is a long history in the various south-east Asian countries of challenge matches, a bit like duelling in the West, where one would be insulted by another and they would take out the pistols at dawn or out came the rapiers, the foils, and they would fight to the death,' says Lewis. 'Just so in the East. In Hong Kong, for instance, they had what are termed *kong sau*, the secret bouts, where two champions from two different schools would fight, quite often with no rules at all. The one left standing was the winner. Quite often deaths would result.'

The difference from duelling was that the *kong sau* contestants were unarmed. The closest equivalent in Europe and America was bareknuckle prize-fighting, which appeared in the eighteenth century and lasted for a couple of hundred years before it was outlawed and replaced by modern boxing. In the meantime, the Eastern martial arts continued to develop but – according to Peter Lewis – they made little impact in the West until the 1950s, when America soldiers went to fight in the Korean War.

'They were exposed to the Korean martial arts, *tae kwon do*, *hapkido* and some other indigenous martial arts of Korea. Most of the soldiers that fought in Korea then did their "R'n'R" in Japan. So they were further exposed to the Japanese martial arts. The Korean War ended, they all went back home but they took with them these new forms of fighting.'

Hollywood and TV did the rest. By the early 1970s the movies of Bruce Lee and the television series *Kung Fu*, starring the dancer David Carradine, caused an explosion of interest in the martial arts. Today they are among the most popular of all participation sports, with clubs in every town. But there were also disturbing whispers that the old and highly dangerous challenge matches were still going on

'There was scant information because it was rumoured that deaths often occurred and where deaths are occurring in fighting you've got manslaughter, maybe even murder, so secrecy is [a necessity]. So little is known, but around the early seventies invitations were sent out whereby top people from martial arts disciplines, even streetfighters, would all converge on a location – it was rumoured that it was somewhere in the Bahamas – and they would fight for a purse of $20,000.'

Such contests, if indeed they ever existed, may have remained a minor sporting dead end had it not been for the phenomenon of subscription television in the United States. This allowed minority interest sports to reach an audience and show a profit. Enter Bob Meyrowitz, boss of the New York-based Semaphore Entertainment Group (SEG). Meyrowitz, a producer who had worked with stars like Whoopi Goldberg, Billy Connolly and Bette Midler, was looking for pay-per-view and cable opportunities. He was interested in the martial arts and, on his travels, noticed how popular the likes of karate and judo were around the world: 'It became apparent to me that actually martial arts was the international language. It also was of interest to me that they never competed against each other to the best of my knowledge,' he says.

Then, crucially, Meyrowitz discovered they *did* compete against each other. In Japan mixed martial arts matches had survived. And in Brazil a remarkable family called the Gracies had pioneered their own brand of no-holds-barred combat in front of big crowds. Here was something Meyrowitz thought might work, particularly for the redneck end of the US television audience.

In 1993 SEG staged the Ultimate Fighting Championship (UFC), a tournament featuring eight opponents including a boxer, a kickboxer and a Sumo wrestler slugging it out in an octagonal pit devised by John Milius, the Hollywood director. Royce Gracie, a *ju jitsu* stylist from Brazil, dominated three straight matches to win the tournament. He was tall, handsome and athletic. A sport was born.

Soon others followed, sensing an untapped TV and video market. Battlecade Inc, backed by the publishers of porn magazine *Penthouse*, started the rival Extreme Fighting Championship, with muscled competitors fighting in a caged ring. Stars emerged, extraordinary athletes like the Gracies, Frank and Ken Shamrock, Dan 'the Beast' Severn and 'Tank' Abbott. Marquee names could earn up to £50,000 a fight. Viewing figures of up to one million were claimed, excellent by pay-per-view standards. But the raised profile brought public opposition from groups appalled at the sight of one muscular man straddling another and pounding him in the face, or choking him unconscious. The early bouts had no judges, no scoring system and no time limits. A fight could end three ways: by knockout, surrender or by intervention of the referee. You weren't allowed to gouge eyes or 'fishhook' (tear an opponent's mouth with your fingers) but you could choke, pull hair and kick a prone opponent in the face.

The most vocal group in its dissent was the powerful American Medical Association (AMA), which issued a strongly worded statement:

The American Medical Association strongly opposes the new ultimate or extreme fighting contests and actively supports efforts to ban these brutal and repugnant contests as posing an imminent danger to the health and lives of the participants. Far from being legitimate sporting events, ultimate fighting contests are little more than human cockfights. The rules are designed to increase the danger to fighters and to promote injury rather than prevent it.

The phrase 'human cockfights' stuck. The AMA called for a

national ban on the sport. Dr George Lundberg, the editor of its journal, remarked, 'Someone's spinal cord could be fractured, an arm could be broken and choking could result in brain damage. The possibility of injury is very high.' Politicians jumped on the bandwagon, men like Senator John McCain, a later candidate for the Republican presidential nomination, who described it as 'a brutal and repugnant blood sport'. Suddenly state legislatures started to ban the contests.

But the biggest blow to the sport was the 1997 decision by the main US cable distributor to discontinue its feed of the Ultimate Fighting Championship, citing public concern and an overly violent content level. It instantly killed off most of the sport's revenue. Battlecade folded. Bob Meyrowitz was caught completely off-guard: 'In all honesty, we never anticipated any criticism. We were looking at this as a martial arts event. We were not thinking at that point that it would be such a big event or that it would cause so much stir. We were amazed when all the criticism came in. It makes absolutely no sense when you see states allowing things that are far more dangerous to take place.'

The UFC limped on, slashing its budgets and running shows via small satellite dish providers. It also changed its rules to gain greater acceptance, forcing competitors to use martial arts gloves – like boxing gloves but with cut-away fingers – and prohibiting kicking an opponent who is down, pressure point strikes, small joint manipulations, hair pulling and groin strikes.

'We had to change a lot of rules not for safety purposes but to make it acceptable to people who don't understand it,' said Meyrowitz. 'Bareknuckle fighting doesn't look pretty but it is actually safer than with gloves. With bareknuckles, they really can't punch very effectively or very hard, with gloves they can. But states want gloves and so we have agreed to put gloves on the fighters.'

Meyrowitz also denied the AMA charges against the sport: 'They admit they have no statistics that would in any way indicate that this is a dangerous sport. It's a sport that somebody doesn't like. Certainly in a democracy it is anyone's right not to like it but to say that no one can see it because *they* don't like it is quite another thing. If there's one person who's innocent and one person who's attacking him, that would be violence. When two competitors get into an arena to compete against each other with a known set of rules, that is not violence. What happens in the soccer and football stands in the UK, that is violence, what happens on the field is not violence.'

Events elsewhere gave further fuel to the critics. In April 1998 American father-of-five Douglas Dedge died from severe brain injuries after a bout in Kiev, Ukraine. His opponent was allowed to punch him repeatedly on the ground as 4,000 spectators screamed, 'Kill the Yankee' and 'Finish him! Finish him!'

Things were looking very bleak. 'There's one of the difficulties we have to deal with every day,' said Meyrowitz. 'God only knows what that event was in the Ukraine. The event was nothing to do with us and was totally unregulated. I would love to see a set of rules that everyone has to abide by.'

A Sunday night in the Sanctuary Arena in Milton Keynes, Buckinghamshire, and more than 2,000 people have bought tickets to watch Night of the Samurai II, a tournament in the British version of ultimate fighting. It goes by the name Total Fighting and contestants can punch, kick, throw and grapple. The event is the third by a British fighter-promoter who is trying to get the sport off the ground and build on its success.

Lee Hasdell, a muscular, shaven-headed, former kickboxer, describes himself as the UK's top fighter in this field. He competed in events in Japan before starting the TotalFight Forum in Britain. He is well aware that the rules will have to be seen to be strict if he is to be allowed to continue promoting. 'We don't allow bareknuckle fighting or punching to the head,' says Hasdell. 'If we allow punching to the head, they have to wear specially designed grappling gloves. If they don't want to wear the gloves then you're only allowed to use a palm, similar to Sumo wrestling or rugby, they use palm-offs or hand-offs. We're very, very strict on the rules. Things like striking to the groin, striking to the joints, eye-gouging and certain locks aren't allowed.' Elbow strikes and head butts are also out.

Even so, Hasdell admits he has concerns about the legality of his events and does his best to ensure compliance: 'We're very careful. We negotiate with the local councils and the environmental health officers. We have a solicitor that deals with any legal problems. We've got very, very strict guidelines, probably one of the strictest in the martial art industry at the moment. All the fighters have to have medicals, all the fighters have licences, they're all insured, we have paramedics who are specially trained in this style of fighting, we have a ringside doctor, ringside solicitor, you name it, we've got it.'

If audience response is anything to go by, Night of the Samurai II was a roaring success. Two competitors needed oxygen in the ring after being knocked unconscious, while others were forced to 'tap out' of particularly painful holds. The crowd of mainly young men was vociferous in its approval.

'It's rough, it's ready, it's tough,' enthused one.

'Outstanding,' said another. 'Well organized, the fighters are good, the techniques are good, everyone's enjoying themselves, it's a good night.'

And the knockouts? 'I close me eyes then,' giggled his girlfriend.

The British press was less impressed. 'TOTAL MADNESS' headlined the *Daily Mail*. 'STOP THESE DEATH FIGHTS' ordered the *Daily Star*. Editorials called for immediate bans. The British Medical Association echoed its US counterpart and joined in the condemnation.

Yet at the same time, in clubs and gyms and *dojos* around the country, there were signs that no-holds-barred styles of fighting were catching on. Suddenly any martial artist worth his salt was cross-training − blending different combat and self-defence styles − and copying the techniques they watched on imported videotapes of the UFC and other events.

'When I first started watching the videos from the States, there were a lot of fighters who I thought shouldn't have been there in the first place, unconditioned, some of them very overweight, and with only one form of fighting experience, perhaps just wrestling,' says martial arts instructor John Boyle. 'Some of the videos I've seen from the early days of the UFC were very barbaric, brutal and hardly epitomized any form of martial art. It was just like something you see outside a pub or in the street. But the quality of the fighters is getting better all the time.'

Boyle, a fourth dan in karate, introduced mixed martial arts training at his gym in north Manchester. Practitioners learned to develop their skills at all ranges: long distance (kicking), middle distance (boxing/punching), in close (elbow strikes, throws) and on the ground (grappling). The idea, he says, is to try to be proficient in all of those fighting systems.

'It is becoming very popular,' says Boyle. 'Any martial artist worth his salt will be cross-training. That means they are not just training in one system, you've got to diversify a bit to become a more all-round martial artist. Many of the techniques trained can be seen in no-holds-barred contests, but the difference is that the latter is full-on combat for pay. It is a professional sport – well, whether it's been classed as a sport or not I don't know, because it is quite barbaric. But I've got a keen interest in it. I think it's quite positive. I think it's taking the martial arts to a completely different realm which we've never encountered before.

'A lot of people do think it's barbaric, brutal, but there are rules. Although people think there aren't, there are. There's no gouging, you can't bite. A lot of people don't think it is as dangerous as boxing. The fighting range is broken down very rapidly, sometimes within a couple of seconds, and then they're grappling and wrestling. Then the fight might finish on a submission or a choke or possibly unconsciousness through a choking technique. But the fighters have got the option to tap out and submit when they want.' Boyle acknowledges the dangers but feels it could take off in Britain. 'It could operate as long as everything is done professionally, as long as fighters are thoroughly conditioned, thoroughly trained, they're medically sound, I think it would be okay. I don't see a problem with that.'

Lee Hasdell has undoubtedly been helped by the liberal attitude of Milton Keynes Council. Its chief environmental health officer is Phil Winsor. 'I don't concern myself with what goes on in the ring,' he says. 'The sport has its own built-in checks and balances which we are satisfied with. These include having a proper referee, an MC to coordinate all the bouts along with a doctor at ringside, paramedics and full medical equipment.'

To allay the concerns of some councillors, a minimum age limit of 18 was imposed on spectators. But generally they have taken a *laissez faire* approach. 'The view of the elected members of Milton Keynes Council licensing committee is that they endeavour not to pass judgment. They work on the basis of live and let live. But if things were to go to the extreme where people were getting seriously hurt, I would have no hesitation in recommending that these events cease to take place.'

Critics would argue that waiting until someone is badly hurt or even killed would be too late. But Lee Hasdell defends it: 'There's always going to be pros and cons to everything that you do, especially in the fighting business. We just try to make it as safe as possible and we try and explain and educate the spectators and the media as to what it is that's going on. There is a fine art to it; although it might look a bit basic it is very, very highly skilled.'

But isn't it brutal?

'I don't think so. I've been involved in the martial arts for 15 years and I consider myself to be in perfect condition as an athlete.'

Another athlete in top condition is Justin Gray, who was one of those competing – successfully – at the Milton Keynes show. He is refreshingly candid about what it takes to be a top limited-rules fighter and admits that he trains in the techniques that will do the most damage – within the rules: 'Definitely, yeah. I don't want to be in there for ten minutes. If I can do it in a minute [I will] but you have to prepare for ten minutes.'

He also says he would happily fight in contests where there were no rules at all: 'Definitely, yeah, if the money was right. There's no problem there, especially if people were paying for it. If the money was right, I'd fight under any rules: bareknuckle, gouging, everything, because I'm confident in what I do. A lot of people are probably thinking that I'm a thug and all the rest of it but definitely not, we're all good people – people who train hard and dedicate their life to it, the majority of them are good people. We pray to God and he looks after us. So definitely I'd do that.' His family, he says, have not opposed what he does: 'They love it. It gives me something to do, that's the main thing, and they're happy for me to do that if I'm happy doing it. They don't like seeing me getting hit but that's part of life. Them streets are bad out there. You'd do a lot worse going outside and fighting than going into *vale tudo*.'

There are three main arguments against limited-rules fighting: medical, ethical and legal. The medical case has been made strongly by the AMA and others. People can argue over whether or not the sport is as dangerous as, for example, boxing, but there are undeniably inherent risks. But pointing out that an activity carries health dangers is not in itself an argument for abolition. Many sports carry risks.

The ethical argument poses the question: are those risks acceptable in a civilized society? Some say yes, many say no. Even within the combat sports fraternity, there are influential figures who oppose full-contact fighting on ethical grounds. Dr Eugene Da Silva, president of the UK-based Society of Martial Arts, which promotes academic study, believes the ancient values of the Eastern arts, tied up as they are with pacifistic philosophies such as Taoism and Buddhism, reject the fight-for-pay ethos of the sport: 'We promote the authentic values of martial arts, the original values, the philosophy and way of life. Fighting of that nature wouldn't fit into our purpose. Martial arts originated as a way to defend yourself. Offence was used as the last resort. This no-holds-barred is purely offensive.'

But it is the legal case against the sport that, in the UK at least, may be the greatest threat to its survival. This takes the ethical argument one step further and asks: can one participant legally consent to being assaulted by another? In the context of limited-rules fighting, it appears the answer may be 'No'.

In 1882, in a legal landmark known as the Coney case, 11 British judges held that bareknuckle prize-fighting was illegal and that consent to the interchange of blows during the fight did not afford any answer to the criminal charge of assault. The fact that they consented was irrelevant, said Lord Coleridge: 'The combatants in a prize fight [cannot] give consent to one another to commit that which the law has repeatedly held to be a breach of the peace. An individual cannot by such consent destroy the right of the Crown to protect the public and keep the peace.'

It was, however, decided that sparring and exhibitions with gloves were exempt. And so boxing was recognized as legal almost by default because it was not prize-fighting. Does this same dispensation apply to the martial arts? Nobody really knows, because to date it has not been tested in the British courts. In the 1990s the Law Commission examined this thorny question. In looking at violent martial arts such as *muay thai*, it found that 'under the present law ... serious injuries deliberately inflicted during such contests would appear, in the absence of an express exemption such as is enjoyed by boxing, to be plainly criminal'.

'At the moment I think the probability is that some of the so-called martial arts may fall within the dispensation which was recognized by Coney and some may not, because the intentional infliction of injury is a criminal offence regardless of the circumstances of its being inflicted,' says Dr Ray Farrell, secretary of the British Association for Sport and the Law. 'As far as boxing is concerned, it is the noble art of self-defence. I think too many of the martial arts, particularly kickboxing, involve the deliberate infliction of injury and I think that raises a serious question mark. At the moment the police authorities don't know what to do [but] serious injury or even death occurring could be the problem which might provoke a case in a court of law, and then we would get a more definite ruling.

'The question of consent to injury is one which has bedev-illed the law for a number of years. Consultation papers have tried to address this issue. I simply cannot imagine that the law will ever countenance the deliberate infliction of injury in the sporting context whether it be in the *muay thai* boxing ring or on the rugby field. My own view is that several of the martial arts practitioners could well find themselves in a court of law in the future if serious injury is inflicted which the police will have to take notice of.'

So where does this leave limited-rules fighting?

'I would regard it as no different than a fight outside a pub on a Friday night that the police would be expected to break up and charge the assailants with a variety of offences against the person,' says Dr Farrell. 'Never mind whether there are gloves covering the hands, if people are using feet and heads and other parts of the anatomy and elbows to inflict possibly life-threatening injuries on other participants I think the fact that gloves may be used is incidental. I don't think there's the slightest prospect that this all-out fighting will ever be legal in this country.'

Outside of Milton Keynes the rest of the UK seems to agree. Limited-rules tournaments have been refused permission in several towns and cities. And in November 2000 three fighters from the north-east of England flew to Russia to compete after councillors in Houghton-le-Spring, Wearside, refused to grant a licence for them to fight at their local leisure centre. 'We are having to travel to St Petersburg to make our professional debuts,' said Carl Simpson from Sunderland. 'If people came to see total fighting they would see you are not sustaining constant blows to the head or body, like you are in boxing, but it is mainly wrestling. If it was that bad, we wouldn't do it.'

In January 2001 Bob Meyrowitz sold the Ultimate Fighting Championship to Lorenzo Fertitta's Zuffa Entertainment. Fertitta, aged 31, is based in Las Vegas and is a former Nevada State Athletic Commission member and the owner of the Station Casinos chain. Vegas is the mecca of boxing, and holding a mixed-style event in that influential state could turn around the fortunes of the sport. Meyrowitz said it would mean the UFC returning to cable pay-per-view within six months.

'I just felt that it was a once-in-a-lifetime opportunity,' said Fertitta. 'I felt that it had a ton of potential as a sport in the future. My brother and I decided to go forward and buy it. Hopefully, what we can do is be successful at educating the public on what mixed martial arts is. It is a safe sport, safe certainly relative to some of the other sports that are out there. When it was on cable, it was widely distributed and that's what people remember. If we can get back in their minds and convince them that it's a sport with rules and regulations, weight classes ... that's really where we want to take it.'

His main concern will be to try to get mainstream cable access once more. It was the loss of major distribution that forced the UFC to cut its cloth and skimp on the advertising budget. Few fighters were ever highlighted or sold to the public. Fertitta talks about making UFC the Super Bowl of mixed martial arts. Industry insiders believe he does have the necessary connections and long-term goals to make the UFC a viable company. He wants to expand the sport aggressively and the next two years will be crucial: 'We look at this as a great opportunity. We're going to try to do things that will hopefully make the UFC bigger and better. We just don't know exactly what those things are yet.'

Whether or not men like Fertitta and Lee Hasdell succeed, there seems little doubt that such contests are here to stay. Ban them in one country and the fighters will simply travel to another. The question is not whether the sport will survive but how big it will be. Pioneer Bob Meyrowitz has no doubts about its potential: 'There is no question that this sport has not reached its peak. Sooner or later the truth has to come out that this is a legitimate sport, that it is a safe sport and that there's absolutely no reason that this shouldn't be seen. I think with the popularity of martial arts in America and the world there's no reason why these shouldn't be the most popular athletes in the world.'

CHAPTER TWELVE

Guns on the Green
Arson and Shooting in the Gentle Sport of Bowling

Players of one of our oldest and most successful sports are being forced to quit because of a plague of hooliganism which reaches from one end of the country to the other. Those who remain face abuse and violence on an unprecedented scale.

Bowling and arson go back a long way. It was 1588 when Sir Francis Drake famously rolled his woods across the greensward of Plymouth Hoe as he plotted to torch the advancing Spanish Armada. Firestarters still inhabit the greens of Britain, but nowadays they burn down the pavilions, dig up the grass and terrorize the players. Bowls suffers like no other sport from burning, looting, vandalism and even shooting.

Half a million people play bowls in the United Kingdom. Indoor and outdoor, flat green and crown green. Players come in all shapes, sizes and ages. It is one of very few sports where men and women, young and old can compete on equal terms. At the highest level bowls delivers medals at major events like the Commonwealth Games and wins creditable audience figures for televised tournaments. An official policy of the Health Education Authority is to encourage more of us to bowl on health grounds: plenty of gentle exercise and fresh air, little chance of injury. It is well organized, largely free from controversy and attracts sponsors. It also attracts thugs and is uniquely vulnerable to their antics.

Barry Durrans turns the shiny key in the fist-sized padlock. He tugs on the weighty chain and it snakes through the steel fence around the reinforced gate and coils onto the floor at his feet. Bending easily, he scoops up the links and carries them into the compound. Another key opens the metal-cased door of the windowless box that serves as a clubhouse to the bowlers of Bradford Moor.

When Barry first started playing here it was the pride of Yorkshire's thriving crown green community. A Victorian park on the city's ring road, its four manicured rinks allowed for as many as 24 games to be played simultaneously and ensured Bradford Moor became the venue for many championship finals. Three gloriously steep-roofed pavilions with white walls over-looked perfectly square greens with crowned tops as smooth and gently risen as lovingly baked sponge cakes. Knee-high privet hedges and evenly spaced benches completed the picture.

Now the pavilions have been burned to the ground and eight-foot fences with steel spiked tops guard the two remaining greens. Small knots of dedicated bowlers timidly cower over their woods inside reinforced grey compounds. Less like a public sports ground, more like a prison exercise yard.

'Well, we've had the cafe burnt down, we've had the veterans' hut burnt down and the Saturday hut, that was burnt down,' recalls Mr Durrans, as he checks the amenity for signs of fresh damage. 'We've had horses galloping around, we've had motorbikes flying around. One of the biggest things to affect the state of the green was the fact that when the kids come home from school instead of walking around they walk straight across the green. Players have had stones thrown at them, followed by swearing from kids when you tell them off. And that's just the mundane end of spectrum. One lady was shot with an air pistol,' he continues in surprising understatement. Nursing a painful leg-wound, the woman was taken to hospital. She was deeply shaken, as anyone would be: no one expects to be shot at while playing bowls. 'One of our bowlers chased some young kids off, he didn't touch them, just chased them off and within half an hour there were 30 more, rather larger ones came, so the bowler had to leave for his own safety. We've even had cyclists on the greens when we were playing a match. They were weaving in and out of the players and kicking the woods about.'

Jean Naylor, another member at Bradford Moor, says she is

in fear every time she goes to the club: 'Well, it's just not safe. Before, there used to be people about. There always used to be someone you could have a game with but you don't come down to this park on your own now. Even some of the men won't come down on their own, never mind the women.'

Verbal abuse and the fear of violence is a high price to pay for a hobby, why does she bother? 'Well, we all enjoy our bowling, we all get together and we're all friends, it's a way of meeting up. At one time you could come down during the week, or just two of you could come down in an evening, which you couldn't do any more,' she says, looking across the bare clubhouse table to Barry Durrans. 'Two years ago we had a membership of 65,' he responds, 'now we're down to just about 30 if we're lucky and some of those don't play.'

They could go elsewhere and play, but private clubs have waiting lists – such is the popularity of bowls – and anyway most of them have only one green and so cannot stage championship finals where many ends have to be played at once. Other municipal greens in Bradford suffer the same way as the Moor. Barry Durrans's son Mark is on the regional organizing committee. He says things are getting worse all the time: 'Every time you go to a delegates' meeting there are more and more teams having to drop out because they haven't got enough bowlers that want to stay.' The prognosis from Mark's dad is grim: 'It will eventually – I won't say die out because the clubs will always be there with at least one or two teams, but I can see people saying it's just not worth it. It's not helping and there's a lot of theory going round that all the municipal greens will go.'

No sport relies on municipal facilities more than bowling, and no sport is more vulnerable to vandalism. A football pitch which has been churned up by a motorbike can be returned to playing standard in a matter of hours, a bowling green takes a year to recover. Bradford is not the only place where greens are under attack – a short drive along the M62 finds a similarly depressing story of blighted sport.

In Manchester, clubs have closed down completely as sportsmen and women have been driven out of the game by thugs. Stories abound of gangs running across greens during matches, stealing the woods and throwing the jacks at the players. At one club, where John Parry is secretary, the youths were confronted. The next day the bowlers' hut was covered in obscene graffiti and there were bullet holes in the windows. And that was just the start. 'The old pavilion had to be pulled down because it was set on fire so many times and there were so many people using it at night for sex and drugs that it was deemed a health hazard and had to be pulled down,' says Mr Parry.

The replacement building – the one with the bullet holes in it – is a tin box with grilled windows. John Parry says extra fortifications had to be added to stop the youths breaking in and looting it. 'It's been robbed and broken into on approximately ten occasions in the ten years that I've been here,' he says. 'Both the darts boards that should be in those cupboards have been stolen. A wall there was knocked down where they tried to get the fridge out. All the doors have been smashed on repeated occasions. All the cards that they use for whist drives, the dominoes, the chess sets, the draughts sets have just been stolen. We used to keep the jacks and woods locked up in the hut, they've all been stolen and that's taken place on two occasions. People steal dominoes, biscuits, tea bags, cups, saucers, plates, knives and forks. Anything that can be stolen. They've even stolen the clock off the wall three times.'

On one occasion the bowlers locked themselves inside the metal box as stones rained down on the roof. Another time a stolen car was crashed into the front of the building and set on fire. The heat melted the wire-reinforced plastic windows and the looters climbed over the molten goo to pillage once more. The burn marks still stain the walls.

'I don't think it's isolated. I think it's general across the country,' says Nick Pratt, who speaks for local authorities on issues to do with parks. 'I think most probably you'll find it [vandalism] in areas of high-density population. So obviously within the city areas. I'm situated in the west area of London but I'm sure it's true of Birmingham and Manchester and places like that where you'll find problems of vandalism. I think bowling greens will tend to suffer because they are easy targets and look inviting. I think they tend to be more attractive to people who want to cause that kind of damage because they're a much finer turf and the amount of work that goes into them is far greater and therefore damage to them takes far greater work and longer to repair. Indeed, the damage can be seen by people who can actually make a visual impact on them.'

Back in 1982 the Sports Council wrote the wittily titled report *A New Bias: A Report into the Future Provision for Bowls*. It concluded that not only did bowls depend on local councils for its facilities, but that those councils were letting the sport down. It said, 'The sport has at least 8,600 greens which require intensive maintenance. Evidence from the survey indicates many local authorities could no longer afford to send employees on fine-quality turf maintenance training programmes.' Since then no further study has been performed, but the consensus, even amongst councils themselves, is that the situation has worsened a great deal.

Nick Pratt lays the blame on compulsory competitive tendering which forced many authorities to abandon their policy of permanent staff in parks in favour of cheaper alternatives which provided less protection. 'I think this has happened over the last 15 to 20 years and I think that's related to the reduction in budgets that are available for this type of service,' he says. 'Park maintenance is a discretionary service for councils, not like things such as education or refuse collection which have to be provided at a set level. That means when we've had to find ways of reducing costs we've looked at what is discretionary. One of the ways of doing that is a gradual withdrawal of the traditional park keepers and the general movement away from having static workers in parks and onto a more mobile basis. So, you don't have that relationship and continuity of people in parks working and being recognized by the local community.'

Back in Bradford, Jean Naylor has seen the consequences. 'At one time you had people looking after the greens for you, you had greenmen that looked after the greens and saw to everything but now they just don't set them on,' she laments. Although thousands of people rely on councils for the provision of sporting facilities, the councils have no obligation to make pitches and greens available. As a result, parks are in decline across the country, and, of all sports, bowls suffers most.

'If there's any cost cutting to be done, bowls appears to be the first to suffer,' says Ron Hails of the English Bowling Federation (EBF). The EBF is one of seven bodies which run the sport. Its patron is the Queen and it represents around 30,000 players, mainly in the eastern counties of England. Mr Hails says his members feel neglected: 'They feel they're the poor relations of sport and they feel that they aren't getting a fair crack of the whip.'

Sitting in the tidy living room of his North-East home, Ron tells a story of decline that will sound familiar to bowlers everywhere. 'Here in Hartlepool we have 116 teams that play in our area and in the last 5 or 6 years we've had 5 bowling pavilions burnt down. It's accepted as being par for the course that bowling greens are fair play to the idiots that hang round them in the summer particularly. As soon as the game finishes in some areas, they're on playing football. You need to provide facilities for bowlers to change in inclement weather and you do need a reasonable bowling surface to play on, and they don't just happen,' Mr Hails explains. 'Our greens need cutting at least twice a week and of course they need feeding and fertilizing before the season starts, it's quite a fair amount of cost.'

One of Ron's friends and colleagues is Mal Hughes. In his pomp he was 'The Durham Dancer', forever chasing his woods just like Nobby Stiles skipped around Wembley in 1966. Now he is the manager of the English national team and a TV commentator. He's not so much dancing Nobby Stiles, more whispering Ted Lowe. 'Any bowling, private or park, is good. Once people get playing, they're hooked,' he gleefully announces. But even Mal's enthusiasm is dampened by the vandals: 'All the councils are being strapped for cash and they look at the various things and they think, "Well, it's only bowls." So they cut the costs down or raise the price for people to play. It's sad because we're looking to get more people, especially older people, involved in the sport. You can't attract people if the greens have gone.'

The English Bowling Federation is a flat green association, but crown green players are suffering in the same way. Ray Angus is the chief executive of the British Parks Crown Green Bowls Association. 'Public park greens, there's not many what I would call excellent greens because they just don't get the personal attention that they used to get way back in the fifties and sixties when each bowling green had its own personal attendant and greenkeeper,' he says. 'That's all gone now I'm afraid. All these chaps from the local corporation do now is throw three or four lawnmowers and several other bits of equipment onto a truck at nine o'clock in the morning and go round all the greens and by three o'clock they've finished.' And one game of football, especially if the players wear studs, can take a bowling green out of action for a year.

In Hartlepool, Bradford and Manchester no one has been caught and prosecuted for damage caused. 'In terms of prosecutions through the courts – it's been absolutely minimal,' admits Jeff Stanniforth, Manchester's parks manager. 'More often than not we're just appealing to the better nature of the youngsters and asking them to leave the greens alone. We need to look at strengthening the bylaws so we can make the regular offenders pay the penalty. People get away with too much.'

Ray Angus insists that the bowlers could identify the culprits – if they dared: 'The clubs know who they are, they're not strangers. They aren't coming from one area 20 miles away to go cycling on another bowling green, they're the local youths. And they're not little children and they're not adults, they're the youths, probably from about 11 to 20 years old – boys and girls.'

No one knows for sure, but the people who raided a bowling club in Somerset were probably a bit older, and a little bit more organized. Wedmore Bowls Club near Cheddar would appear to have been the victim of a run-of-the-mill theft. Intruders took a safe, seven bottles of spirits, a lawnmower and a heating boiler. What makes this event an attack on the sport is the nine separate holes dug in the green. The craters, each measuring roughly one-foot across, were spread around the playing surface in a way which caused maximum disruption to play. One night of deliberate destruction had destroyed the playing surface for a year. The loss of the green was felt more deeply than the theft from the club-house. Once more, the culprits got away scot-free.

One place where the spoilsports got their come-uppance was Halifax. Shroggs Park is a council-run facility just to the north of Halifax town centre. It still has an old pavilion, but the windows are grilled and the doors metal plated. It was broken into five times in a two-week period and fire extinguishers were sprayed around inside. Jim Crossley, a tall and fit ex-policeman, is a member here, and together with a few other bowlers he has struck a blow for the sport.

'There are three incidents I can relate to you,' explains Jim as he looks out over the two greens of Shroggs Park. 'One involv-ing myself where I was hit on the head by a stone, thrown by a youth who was in a group on the football pitch which is adjacent to the bowling green. Another occasion, bowlers were playing on the bowling green and missiles were thrown onto the green from the playground – one of the veteran bowlers went round to remonstrate with them and was punched in the mouth. And on one occasion a group of young girls were congregating around the number two green and started to pull the coping stones off the wall. They threw them onto the green. The bowlers remon-strated with them thinking they might go away. However, they didn't, they walked across to the number one green and started throwing stones at the bowlers there. One of the bowlers, who incidentally is a policeman, chased after them and caught a four-teen-year-old girl. This girl was arrested and subsequently appeared at the juvenile court at Halifax.' The stone thrower was bound over to keep the peace for a year, as was her mother. But Mr Crossley admits that if the bowler who caught her had not been a policeman, no arrest would have been made.

Set in parkland between two wooded golf courses in Bingley, the Sports Turf Research Institute (STRI) houses the nation's expertise in greenkeeping. Everything from the science of soil to the grading of grass is studied here. It might surprise you to know that their publication *Bowling Greens, Their History, Construction and Maintenance* was so popular that it had to be reprinted. It's the sod-loving researchers from here who come to the rescue of beleaguered bowlers.

STRI regional officers give advice on the preparation and repair of golf courses, tennis courts, cricket squares and bowling greens. Emma Kirby, responsible for the north-west of England, has had to deal with bowling greens that have suffered from motorbikes, burnt-out cars, fireworks displays and petrol. She says that no matter how small the renovation is, it can only be carried out at one time of the year – spring: 'Any renovation if it's going to be done correctly is going to take a long time, especially if the damage occurs at the end of the growing season when you haven't got good growth and you've got cold, perhaps frost. Grass isn't growing and it may not recover in time for the following playing season so it does depend on what time of year the damage occurs as to how you can repair it.' Ms Kirby goes on to say that given the pressure to get surfaces playable again, councils will cut corners. 'Many people will use ready-prepared turf because it produces a quick result, you get a green surface back with grass on very quickly, but problems will always follow with turf,' she continues. 'Bowls is a summer sport and trying to keep that turf wet and growing can be a problem. You can also have problems when you turf because it doesn't always produce uniform surface levels. Turf can sink slightly, or if it's standing a bit proud you can cut too close and scalp it. So there are lots of problems with turfing. The alternative is seeding. Some people may avoid this because it's not such a quick fix to the problem but it will give you a better result long term.'

In the short term, the greens get worse and many are closed down. Bowlers get disillusioned and some are driven indoors to a place where the carpet is always greener.

It's a bright spring day in the Midlands, still and fresh and warmer than might be expected for early April. The bowling greens of this Leicester suburb look reasonable to the untrained eye, but they are empty. A short walk down the road and the car park of a leisure centre is nearly full of sensible, modest cars. Inside, dozens of men in tan slip-on shoes, white shirts and the kind of trousers that their women call 'slacks' play alongside women in calf-length skirts, pastel-shaded blouses and flat shoes. Like all people who take their sport seriously they have a language of their own. 'Shot bowl, Brian,' one bellows across the hall. 'You're a bit heavy, Maureen,' calls another, without appearing to offend anyone.

Six thousand people play indoor bowls in Leicestershire alone, back and forth along the narrow carpet lanes from breakfast until suppertime. And being indoors it is free from vandalism. Or perhaps not. 'We got the problem of people doing silly things like dropping food and drink over the balcony, one pence pieces, two pence pieces and they were potentially dangerous,' reports Terry Green, a committee member at the Carlton Bowling Club. It appears that when the bowlers took shelter, the vandals took aim, and players soon got tired of being rapped on the head with remnants of fast food and items of loose change. 'Because it's a leisure centre there's a lot of other activities going on,' explains Mr Green. 'The balcony was an eating area where mothers came with their young children and other people came, so we suffered from a lot of noise. And then the throwing started. In the end the bowlers clubbed together and paid for a screen to protect them.'

The screen, a plastic, riot-shield type construction, cost £3,500. It seems a lot, but it costs more than twice that amount to fence an outdoor bowling green securely. In Manchester they've chosen to sacrifice some greens to raise the money to fortify the ones that remain. This pragmatic but unsightly decision is the result of a forum established between the council officers and the bowlers themselves. 'We all got together and looked at the greens and decided that we would fence as many as we could, as soon as the money became available,' explains John Parry. 'We've now done 14 greens altogether and it gives us a chance to repair the surfaces without people destroying them again.'

Jeff Stanniforth says the economics are quite straightforward: 'We've diverted funds from pavilions, litter bins, benches and what you might call the add-on facilities. The money saved is spent on securing the playing areas. The cost of returning a wrecked green to a usable form is about the same as fencing it off, that's between eight and ten thousand pounds.'

'We still get some vandalism,' Mr Parry interjects. 'We still get them breaking through the fences or climbing over, but nowhere near as much as they used to.'

The fortress approach has proved successful in Manchester, Bradford and Hartlepool, but Nick Pratt from Hounslow council in west London remains unconvinced: 'I think there's an attraction towards them, but you're creating barriers which in themselves are an attraction to people who want to carry out vandalism. It feels like a reaction to the problem rather than a solution to it. Plus there's the expense of the fences which also need maintaining. I also think that public places ought to be aesthetically pleasing, and an eight-foot high fence is just ugly.'

A less harsh approach has been tried in Bolton. They're called interpretative rangers, which is modern civil servant speak for what most of us would call the park keeper. But these aren't doddery old growlers in blue suits and pseudo-military caps. These are the park keepers of the new millennium. They have jeeps.

Gerald Riley is Bolton's chairman of leisure. 'For economic reasons a few years ago we decided to dispense with the normal park keepers, and soon we found that vandalism increased. Since then we've reorganized the system by making mobile park rangers who go around in jeeps and Land Rovers. So we've got a presence – it's just that it's not stuck in one place all the time,' says the councillor. 'They do make a difference. Very often they spot vandalism at the beginning and can sort the problem out.' There are an impressive 14 rangers to cover all the parks in Bolton.

Of course it doesn't work all the time. Bolton's interpretative rangers only work from dawn until dusk, whereas the average teenage vandal has no problem working evenings and weekends. This realization has caused one group of battle-hardened bowlers to set up their own 24-hour greenwatch. The Clarence Park Bowling Association in Western-super-Mare is home to three separate bowling clubs with a combined membership of about 250. The members tell familiar, if deflating, stories of flying stones, churned up grass and vandalized buildings. In the spring of 2000 they were building an extension to their clubhouse at a cost of £140,000. A building site to a young vandal is like a distillery to an old soak, and as soon as the first wall was built it was destroyed. With hats, coats and flasks the doughty bowlers took shifts to brick-sit the building work. Their presence was enough to deter the vandals and now the Clarence has a brand new facility with a new set of changing rooms.

The overall picture remains bleak. As one bowler complained, 'You tell me of another gold-medal-winning sport where the playing surfaces are wrecked, the changing facilities burnt down and the sportsmen and women terrorized.' Public parks bowling, a skilful, graceful and successful sport, is being driven behind the barricades.

Back in the sixteenth century, 47 years before Sir Francis Drake's game was the preamble to a naval engagement, Henry VIII banned bowls. He decided that it was the pastime of 'mainly subtle, inventive and crafty persons'. The sport rose above such prejudice. Bowlers might need all those skills, plus a bit of Drake's grit, if their pastime is to overcome its latest, less noble, opponents.

CHAPTER THIRTEEN

Good and Bad at Games
Why We Have the Fattest Kids in the World

*We have the fattest, least active kids in Europe. Our schools
spend less time on physical activities and our teachers are less able to
teach them than in any country with which we might reasonably be
compared. We are breeding sick generations. Despite this, alone
in Europe, we have championed competitive school sports where
resources are focused on the talented few at the expense of the
physical education of the many.*

On a quiet news day in February 2001 the media busied itself
digesting the results of a wide-ranging study into child health.
The top line certainly pushed all the right buttons from a head-
line writer's point of view. 'Tellytubby Generation', thundered
The Times, 'Expanding Toddlers', warned the *Mail*, 'Burger
Bellies', screamed the *Sun*.

The University of Liverpool study was indeed an eye-opener.
Researchers analysed data from 64,000 youngsters under the age
of 4 and found that a quarter were overweight and one in ten clin-
ically obese. Both headline statistics were sharply up on a similar
study that had been carried out at the university 15 years before.
Professor Peter Bundred, who headed both projects warned,
'There is evidence that obesity is likely to persist into adult life
and to increase the likelihood of morbidity and mortality.'

If this sounds reassuringly academic, consider it this way: It
is a time bomb that is not only a personal tragedy for the blub-
berous kids that will die young of any number of illnesses associated with obesity but also of concern to the rest of us because
the cumulative cost of treatment will clog up and in some cases
cripple our health services.

As terrible as these findings are, unfortunately they lack the immediacy of an earthquake, flood or train crash and consequently tend to slip from the news agenda. The newspapers for the most part blame computer games, fast food and their favourite whipping boy, TV, but it is more fundamental than that. All the above are available in equal abundance elsewhere in the world but it's our kids in the UK, right up to 16 years of age, who are among the least active in the world.

With an election approaching, Sports Minister Kate Hoey was able to announce a billion pounds' worth of measures to combat the slothfulness that afflicts so many of our children. The range of initiatives certainly goes far beyond anything any government has managed in the past but combating this crisis is not just a matter of resources. The nation that likes to think it invented sport has a severe cultural problem with exercise and anyone hoping to get to grips with that has to realize they are in for a long haul. It is a disaster that was born in our schools.

It says something about the understanding of a subject in school when no one can quite agree on what to call it. At my primary school it was PT but at my secondary we called it PE. Either way it meant larking about in a sports hall, between proper lessons. Why did we do it? Well, that was a mystery few cared to address and no one ever asked.

At other schools, what was called PE was in fact Games – rugby, soccer, athletics or cricket, depending on the season. But what everyone knew, be it PE or Games, was that there was little worry your parents would come down on you like a ton of bricks because of a bad report from the Games teacher. To some it was blessed relief, to others a misery without parallel but in the context of what you were at school for, Games or PE could not be taken seriously and wasn't – except perhaps by the Games master and the school jocks.

Government has taken pretty much the same view. While no minister would ever deny that a society that was fit and healthy and played plenty of sport was a good thing, this has at best been a vague hope rather than clear aim. Sport equates to play and play is a luxury when there is the prospect of unem-

ployment, inflation or any of the other crises that afflict governments, to worry about. But the clear impact of relegating the
importance of physical exercise in the school curriculum is that
in millennium Britain our children are among the least active
and fattest in the world. The Liverpool University report was
merely one more which confirmed this.

In 1997 Neil Armstrong, a professor at Exeter University,
looked over the latest findings from a rolling survey on child
activity he had been conducting for the previous decade. He
could not claim to be shocked because he was all too familiar with
the data and the direction it had been taking. 'We have done work
where we have monitored children for a minimum of three week,
days and a weekend day,' explains Professor Armstrong. 'What we
have found is that half the girls and about a third of the boys
don't even experience the equivalent of a ten-minute brisk walk
in a normal school week, and that to us is worrying.'

Although this is perhaps not as dramatic as Professor
Bundred's findings at Liverpool it is just as serious. Neither
Bundred nor Armstrong speaks about fitness in children, because
you can't measure it. The growing process masks 'crucial indica-
tors', so it is more useful to speak in terms of weight and activity.
In this sense the Exeter survey complements the Liverpool one
perfectly. Hard evidence of low levels of child activity in one, and
child obesity in the other.

Neil Armstrong spells out the implications: 'We know that
low levels of activity in adult life are manifested with things like
heart disease, obesity, osteoporosis, and unless we can make our
children more active these kinds of disease will strike at a
younger and younger age.'

In the Netherlands, where levels of activity are much
higher than in this country, the problem of sedentary children is
treated with the same seriousness as another well-known killer.
'Physical inactivity is a major public health issue which we think
is comparable in scale and seriousness to smoking. This is what
drives our government to do something about it,' says Professor
Willem van Mechlen, a professor of physical education at
Amsterdam University. Unfortunately for us, the peculiar history

of sport and recreation in the UK means we are less capable than our European neighbours of responding to this crisis. In Britain when we think of children and physical activity, we think of school sports. Elsewhere, with the exception of the United States, almost no one plays sport at school, never mind for the school team, which largely does not exist.

As Professor van Mechlen explains, 'Children have PE lessons at school where they learn about physical exercise, coordination and movement, where their physical development is tracked; but outside school, if they want to play games, they go to a local sports club where qualified coaches teach them and organize games.' It is a feature of European culture that most communities possess a single superclub that runs dozens of teams in a variety of sports. The European school day starts and finishes earlier than in Britain to allow for extracurricular activity. We may think of Barcelona FC as a football club, but actually it is a members' sports club, running teams from juniors to pensioners in a variety of sports, as do many famous brands generally associated with soccer clubs on the continent.

While there is nothing intrinsically wrong with team sports or sport at school – quite the opposite – it has tended to dominate the UK government response to 'fat kid' reports or surveys. The truth is the very people that an increase in school sport is supposed to help are the very children for whom traditional team sports hold no attraction whatsoever.

The persistent calls for increased resources for school sport spring from a mistaken perception that the education system is capable of delivering sport that can make a difference to the majority of the school population. But because our education system is a two-tier affair, mostly, it can't. When government ministers or journalists on the posh papers talk about school sports they are thinking, perhaps, of the five-star facilities they enjoyed in their own schooldays. The chances are they went to a boarding school or at the very least a well-heeled Grammar: schools which bear a passing resemblance, at least as far as this argument is concerned, to one you might come across if you took a walk in the Pennine foothills that rise above Burnley in Lancashire.

At first sight Stonyhurst looks more like a stately home, set as it is in verdant and dramatic scenery. In fact it is a Catholic public school founded in the middle of the nineteenth century. At Stonyhurst sport is big. From the Games teachers' lodge just inside the main gates you can look out as far as the eye can see on playing fields. Cricket up the hill to the left, rugby fields stretching up either side of the half-mile long drive and even a river well stocked with fish where pupils so inclined can while away their free time catching them. Out of sight there's a gym, squash courts and a swimming pool.

Among its old boys Stonyhurst counts Kieran Bracken, the sometime England Rugby Union scrum half; but all the pupils get the opportunity to spread their wings at sport. The Games master is Simon Charles. 'The games curriculum runs for four afternoons a week. On Saturday afternoons we have block fixtures with schools which are able to offer us fixtures in depth (three or four senior teams as well as at colts and junior levels). We obviously value the place of sport within the daily and weekly routine of the boys at the school and sport is a traditional part of college life.

'We will obviously strive for excellence with our senior teams but will also try and get all pupils, or as many as we can, involved with competitive sport but at a level commensurate with their ability.

'All teachers have to help out with games when required – it is written into their contracts – there are the resources, physical, financial and human, to ensure every pupil can take part in sport at almost any level of expertise.' At Stonyhurst school sports make sense. Team games, organized in such depth, are the most efficient way to keep the 400 youngsters at the school fit and healthy.

Twenty or so miles south in Bury, near Manchester, there are very different games arrangements. Prestwich High School is well regarded and, in the context of a local education authority bordering the inner city, is also a well-resourced school. Barry Williams is directing a PE lesson for 13-year-olds.

Some 60 boys and girls are pounding around a running

circuit in the pouring rain that takes them from the car park in the front, out onto the road, through a gap in the semi-detached homes opposite, and down into a playing field. It is a large all-purpose sports field with a confusion of white markings in various states of fade. It does not look too impressive, but then several days of persistent rain have turned it into a quagmire. But it is the only quagmire the school has.

To help address the physical education and sports requirements of more than 800 pupils Barry Williams has the help of a Games teacher, Caroline Leng: two full-time staff to deal with double the number of pupils at Stonyhurst. Other teachers do help out, but they do it for free and it is always a matter of negotiation.

Barry is a busy chap: 'Basically I stay behind every night. We do lunchtime practices, we have fixtures pretty much every night of the week, bar a cancellation, so we have something for them every evening and there is demand for me to come in early and open up the sports hall for basketball practice.'

Despite considerable investment of time beyond the call of duty, both Barry and Caroline admit their efforts tend to be directed towards those sports and teams in which the school competes with others. 'I have to be honest, if we had a teacher who was an expert in gymnastics they would not get the opportunity to teach it very often because there are no fixtures against other schools in gymnastics. We do play other schools at football, rugby, basketball and cricket, so that is where we invest our time.'

An understandable reaction. Barry Williams and thousands of PE and Games teachers at state schools up and down the land have very little alternative. But Neil Armstrong at Exeter University believes focusing on team sports contributes little towards creating a healthier nation.

'Schools have always been keen to win things,' says Professor Armstrong. 'So you find kids that are active in the school soccer team are often the same children involved in the school rugby and cricket teams and so on. I think this leads to the lion's share of resources being focused on a small elite of talented children. A consequence of this is other children become quickly alienated from sport and develop negative attitudes towards exercise.'

The impact of all this focus on school sport is that the proper role of PE in a school curriculum is not widely under-stood. It is seen as a branch of Games when in fact Games are, or should be, a branch of PE. This perverse perception is rooted in the very particular history of the evolution of schools and sport in this country.

Dr Martin Lee, a former PE teacher and lecturer in psychol-ogy at the University of Sussex, has researched the matter, 'The English school's obsession with games was inspired by the Greeks. Greek was a key subject at the public schools of the nine-teenth century and Plato's book *The Republic* was well read. *The Republic* propounded the theory that physical exercise was an aid to academic excellence. In nineteenth-century Britain the English public school developed this philosophy further.'

Dr Arnold, the headmaster of Rugby School in the middle of the nineteenth century, took Plato's theory of the aesthetic value intrinsic in physical exercise and gave it a religious spin. In Dr Arnold's view physical exercise amounted to prayer and thanksgiving to God. Underpinned by this 'Muscular Christ-ianity' movement, as it became known, the English public schools either invented or codified many of the sports that remain popular in the world today.

Sport was championed in Britain's public schools princi-pally for the character that it was perceived to bestow and because it gave pupils something to do between lessons, meals and bed. The physical benefit was almost incidental. But any pupil banged up in boarding school had little chance of avoiding games and, by default, was physically robust by the time he or she emerged into adulthood.

Fast forward to the 1950s and universal secondary educa-tion more or less imported its curriculum from the public schools. Games presented a problem, however, because there was not the room in the school day, the facilities, resources or even the vibrant ideology behind the maintained school's attempts to inculcate pupils with a love of sport and physical recreation –

as the contrast between Stonyhurst and Prestwich High illustrates. PE, although not compulsory until the national curriculum was revised in the 1980s, was introduced into most schools after the war. It was an opportunity to weigh and measure pupils if nothing else. But in many schools there was little purpose to it beyond such minimal tracking of physical development. It frequently became 'indoor games' with little or no instruction. It too often became a subject that provoked apathy from teachers and pupils alike. Although there were exceptions, PE was the subject that tended to be cut back when there was pressure on the timetable.

In 1992 the then Prime Minister, John Major, in an attempt to stem the decline of PE, announced that every school should deliver at least two hours of PE every week. Three years later Professor Len Almond of Loughborough University's PE project reported that the subject was still in decline. 'In 1995 the average time was 106 minutes, not the 120 that John Major told us was the minimum required in the UK. Only a minority of children actually experience two hours a week.' And that was the good news!

Very often time is taken away for wet weather, Christmas activities and so on, so the real time pupils spend actually engaged in PE becomes exceptionally small. By the time you factor in changing time and possibly the time it takes to get to the gym or whatever you are looking at, it may be less than a hour.

So what exactly is good PE? What have millions of children in the past 50 years been missing out on? The national curriculum outlines five elements: games, gym, dance, outdoor and adventure activity and swimming. But that is only part of it.

'PE is looking at the whole child,' says Professor Neil Armstrong. 'It is looking at developing aspects of the child's health and wellbeing. It may well be that these objectives can be championed though school sports but it may be that other activities are important too, such as aerobics, or dance. People tend to think that PE is sport. It is not, it is much more than that.'

An important difference between PE and sport is that sport is usually conducted on behalf of someone else – the team, the coach, the school, the trophy cabinet – whereas PE is concerned with the individual's physical wellbeing. In this sense it is a subject where there should be no 'first or 'last' in the class. Good PE is whatever suits the individual – be they spotty Herbert, athletic Adonis or fat lad.

As Dr Martin Lee puts it, 'I think there is a difference between having a fit and healthy population and producing athletes and that is something that needs to be faced.'

Organized sport is only one path to fitness for children and it can be a hit and miss affair. An individual will, in all likelihood, take to some sports and not others. If a child is confronted with a team sport he or she does not care for early in life, and worse, then compelled to play it, it tends to give that child a negative attitude towards physical activity.

Howard Wilkinson, now the Football Association's technical director, once worked as a PE teacher before embarking on his career as a football manager at Sheffield Wednesday, Leeds and elsewhere. He does not have fond memories of teaching PE. 'I felt that the atmosphere that existed in, let us say, the maths group was such that the relative ability between the best and the worst was much, much narrower than was the case in the PE class. You almost had "PE drop-outs", for whom it was not only a chore but it was positively painful, which is a terrible, terrible shame.'

Professor Margaret Talbot was part of the team that drew up the national curriculum for PE and is desperately worried by the apparent inability of schools to deliver effective PE: 'We are talking here of the only opportunity that every single child has to develop the skills necessary for participation in sports and dance. It is not about sport, although it can be if that is what appeals: PE's principal purpose is to improve young children's appreciation of exercise and health as a whole.'

And, just as in order to do maths, one needs to be numerate, and to read, one needs to be literate, so to be successful at sport and exercise, one needs to master certain basic skills, a physical vocabulary if you like. How to catch, how to strike a ball, how to balance, run and string different physical activities together, these are all elements required to play sport effectively. None of which are difficult to teach in principle but it is important that children learn them when very young if they are to absorb a positive attitude toward exercise.

Children vary in their physical capabilities as in their mental ones and whereas the point of sport is to win, either as an individual or team, the point of PE is to find your own level and progress from there. There is strong evidence that even the most physically impaired can make massive improvement if taught properly.

Leeds University's Professor David Sugden is an expert at treating dyspraxia, the physical equivalent of dyslexia. You might recognize it as clumsiness, something that afflicts to a debilitating extent one child in ten: 'We have conducted a project in Singapore where we identified 18 children with fairly severe difficulties between the age of six and nine. We then worked on lessons with teachers for them to do every week. We prepared a different programme of activity for each child. After six weeks, of the 36 measures we had taken 34 were significantly improved.'

Less scientific but just as impressive is the case of a Salford mum and son. 'Robert had terrible coordination difficulties as a child,' his mum, Anne, recalls. 'He was so poor at coordination that he had to come down stairs on his bottom. We spent hours in the garden throwing balls, catching, rolling, bowling, aiming for targets, to get him to use his hand and eye together, his feet and eyes together so he could approximate to normal children.'

He did better than that. Today he plays for his school lacrosse team and enjoys a whole range of sports. He is not a natural but neither does he stick out like a sore thumb. Sport and exercise form a key part of his life and are his main interest. 'He can do things now that a few years ago I would never have thought possible because he has done exercises and he's practised and done things to make his hand and eyes work together,' says Anne.

It hardly needs the authority of peer-reviewed research to point out that we tend to like doing things we are good at or have skill in. This is especially true of children. A child who can master catching, striking a ball, running and balance, is a child who will take to sport and exercise. But for a child to learn about such things you first need teachers capable of instructing them and infusing them with the necessary enthusiasm for physical activity. All of the people who will be teaching our youngsters the basics of PE in the future are either at teacher training college now or will be.

All the surveys on the levels of child inactivity highlight that as bad as the problem is in general it is worse among girls than boys. Girls are twice as likely to classify themselves as sports failures as boys. In primary schools, where the delivery of good PE is vital for creating a positive attitude towards sport and physical exercise, the majority of teachers are women. Statistically many of them are likely to have had negative PE experience when they were at school.

However, it would appear that the training on offer to teach PE is as poor as the provision for it in the schools that they will be going out to teach in. The time devoted to PE teacher training has been declining steadily over the years to the point now where some courses insist only on a health and safety course. In 1998 Her Majesty's Inspectors surveyed the 77 teacher training colleges in England and found that the average time spent training a primary school teacher on PE was 34 hours over four years. The figure was only that high because a couple of the colleges made sport a specialism and spent over 90 hours. Take them out of the equation and you are more likely to get a figure of around 22. PE professionals recommend 60 hours. In the one-year graduate conversion course, or PGCE, in some cases the time allocated was just eight hours.

Ivor Morgan is the PE inspector for Wales and he is a worried man. 'You are talking about a very complex subject. By the time teachers come to teach nine- or ten-year-olds they are having to deliver quite technical and specialist knowledge. Quite simply you need to spend the time acquiring that knowledge before you can even begin to think about teaching it,' he says.

Peter Warburton, head of sport at Durham University, is similarly in despair: 'We are finding it very difficult to get teachers up to a standard in an area like PE where in some cases hours have been cut to 15. The bottom line is that it is not possible to train a non-specialist teacher to teach pupils in five areas of PE given that sort of time.'

Once in post the teacher is likely to come up against the culture of a particular school. If they are lucky they might end up with a head who is keen on the subject, someone like Wendy Zaidi in Hulme in Manchester. Hulme used to be a byword for all the demons of the inner city. Matters have improved dramatically but throughout the period Royce County Primary has been a model of PE practice.

'There are so many pressures on newly qualified teachers,' says Mrs Zaidi. 'PE is not foremost in their minds, but that is where I come in as PE coordinator. In our school none of the teachers are PE specialists but I have acquired skills over the years and in turn I pass them onto my colleagues.'

Mrs Zaidi is keen on PE as a mainstream subject because she can see the tangible benefits good PE can confer on children. So does Elizabeth Knight, a PE adviser and academic: 'If a child cannot read or write, it is not good but they can hide the fact. If a child is clumsy and physically awkward they can't hide from that. I would say being able to move about and feel good about yourself is the most important skill from a child's point of view and physical education helps them achieve that.'

In very young children the basics of PE can help coordination which can lead to benefits such as improving handwriting, self-esteem and the confidence to 'have a go'. It is for these reasons that Wendy Zaidi is keen on PE and has gone out of her way to protect it in her school week, even though she would never describe herself as remotely 'sporty': 'With the core subjects of maths, english and science there was always a danger that some subjects, like PE, might be squeezed out and it was a danger I have been keen to avoid. We have made it clear that we would fight for PE in our timetable.'

For other schools, ensuring PE standards are maintained and improved falls to the Ofsted inspection team – and here there is more bad news for PE. Few Ofsted teams have the technical knowledge to assess a PE programme well enough to make constructive comment or ring alarm bells.

'The vast number of reports regarding PE are positive,' notes Professor Margaret Talbot. 'My worry about that is that so few Ofsted inspectors are themselves physical educationalists and therefore may well see lessons that are enjoyable and fun and to their eyes purposeful but they actually do not have the technical knowledge to make a reasoned judgment.'

On The Line has seen two reports by inspectors in Lancashire on two schools 30 miles apart where the PE assessment was almost word for word the same. They were almost entirely general in comment on the activities taking place at the school and had not one criticism that could be described as specific regarding the schools concerned – hardly indicative of anything but the most cursory assessment of what was actually going on.

For Len Almond this lack of accountability is a major issue. Such flimsy inspection and drastic decline in standards simply would not be tolerated in any academic subject. 'The gap between the rhetoric and practice is extremely wide and until accountability is introduced then there is no way we will introduce major changes to improve the entitlement of all children to an appropriate and adequate PE programme.'

In among all this gloom, there are, however, some beacons of hope – and one of the most effective to date was generated from a most unexpected source. With the crisis in PE overlooked to a terrible degree by government, local authorities and school inspectors, five years ago a private initiative began which, against all odds, has proved itself to be something of a platform for a fightback for PE: it is called the Youth Sport Trust (YST).

Ultimately many of the initiatives announced by Kate Hoey as sports minister can be traced back to lobbying by the Youth Sport Trust. The YST was the brainchild of Tory businessman and philanthropist, John Beckwith. Beckwith enjoyed his schooldays and especially school sports. When he stumbled across the poverty of PE and sports provision in state schools he was shocked to the core and boldly decided to try and do something about it.

That was in 1995.

Sue Campbell, erstwhile boss of the National Coaching Foundation, was recruited to help turn Beckwith's dream and his money into something more concrete. 'Six years and several millions of pounds later the Youth Sport Trust,' says Campbell, 'has offered physical education and sports resources and training to teachers in every special school and nearly every primary school. We are also taking programmes into every secondary school by 2005. We are all extremely proud of what we have achieved.' And rightly so. The Youth Sport Trust – and Sue Campbell, in particular – enjoys respect from and access to most of the sports establishment but that is no substitute for a long-term commitment to funding and training and educating our young generations in the value of PE.

Peter Warburton of Durham University sounds a cautionary note: 'There has never been so much money available for young people and sport, the lottery and the Youth Sport Trust, which is a magnificent initiative, are two examples – and it is money well spent in many ways, except one. You really need teachers to control PE because they are the ones that have been trained to work with children. They are the ones who are in the classroom week in and week out, who know their pupils.'

Certainly the dangers of handing over physical exercise duties from teachers to coaches promoting specific sports are clear to Ivor Morgan: 'We have come across sports development officers from various sports coming into school brandishing an almost messianic belief in the importance of their sport but for children to be physically educated we need to talk about exposing them to a wide experience of physical activity such as dance, gymnastics, athletics and all the rest. You cannot forget that ultimately the objective of a coach or a development officer is to harvest talent for the sport concerned. Ultimately they are not interested in failures, they are not interested in an individual child's physical exercise needs or progress, they are interested in the health of their own particular sport.'

Nonetheless, the happy accident of both the Education Minister, Estelle Morris, and the Sports Minister, Kate Hoey, being old contacts of Sue Campbell led to an exercise in joined-up government that in turn resulted in a number of PE and sports initiatives being rolled out at the end of the year 2000 and the beginning of 2001. Sue Campbell has been working with civil servants in both departments to tackle the problem. She has also roped some big commercial guns like Nike into the project. So 'Girls in Sport' is focusing on helping schools fund trendier sportswear for girls, recognizing that young girls are fashion conscious and that too often sports kits from the past have been a complete turn-off.

Other government initiatives are more ambitious and long term. The New Opportunities programme will see a total of £780 million over the next three years spent on improving school PE and sports facilities. Primary schools in 65 of the most economically deprived local education authorities are to share a further £130 million under the Spaces for Sports and Arts initiative. Money is to be invested in people too. The number of secondary schools designated as specialist sports colleges is to be expanded from a few dozen to over 200. There is funding for 1,000 school sports coordinators, intended to improve the quality and quantity of after-school sports opportunities for young people, whatever their ability. And there will be funding made available in the education budget to increase training opportunities for 6,000 primary school teachers to develop their knowledge and skills in physical education and become PE coordinators in their schools. All in all £980 million has been earmarked for all these projects and schemes.

All this may be the start of clawing back ground so scandalously given up by a succession of governments whose attitude to sport and exercise can be summed up as indifferent at best. But as noted at the beginning, the purpose and provision of sport and physical exercise in this country has never been well understood and thus is a battle for minds as much as anything else.

Our curious tendency to see PE as a dispensable offshoot of Games has meant that, as finances have tightened, so PE has tended to disappear from the curriculum. The ability to take up the slack outside in the community has been cruelly exposed as inadequate. As a result millions of children have grown up with little understanding of the benefits of exercise. We are at a desperately low level. The stated aim of two hours a week of physical education for youngsters is hardly ambitious, but such is the depth of the crisis in resources, both human and physical, that PE has available to it, it will be something of a miracle if we achieve even this bare minimum any time soon.

CHAPTER FOURTEEN

Cover Tackle
Crippled Rugby Players Discover They Have Never Been Insured Properly

Each week players from both rugby's codes are taking to the field without adequate insurance and finding that if they get injured their governing bodies just aren't there when they need them – even in the most serious of cases.

Dewi Coates should be in a wheelchair, with no prospect of ever walking again, relying on other people to care for him 24 hours a day. Luckily, he isn't. Dewi is only too aware how fortunate he is to be on his feet, five years after breaking his neck, playing against the All Blacks in the famous crimson-red jersey of his country.

Enjoying a welcome break from supervising the local schoolchildren at the swimming baths where he works in Pontardawe near Swansea, he takes a long, deep breath and recalls how the best day of his life quickly turned into the worst. 'It was open play and my opposite number made a break, he was tackled, but I didn't come in from the wrong side, I was onside. I picked the ball up, their blindside flanker hit me in the backside with his shoulder, driving my head into the ground.' Dewi continues, his frankness belying the gruesome scenario he is replaying: 'This made my nose touch my chest, there was one hell of a crack – I knew there was something wrong. I couldn't feel any part of my body, I shouted to the referee and he brought on the stretcher and I was carried off and was taken to Cardiff Royal Infirmary where I was told that I had dislocated my C5 and C6 vertebrae in my neck.'

He lay in traction in his hospital bed, scared and in excruciating pain, but then a few hours later he heard a click from his neck; he hoped it was a good sign. 'I told the doctors,' he says. 'They x-rayed me again and said, "we are going to have to fuse you." That was on the Saturday. On the Sunday they didn't do anything but on the Monday they operated. They operate by cutting you down the front, and then they took my disc out, which was completely shattered. They took some bone from my hip, putting that in place of the disc. Then they inserted a metal box with two screws and then came round the back and cut me round the back. They wired all my vertebrae up and that was it then, recovery time.'

Staring into the middle distance oblivious to the excited screams of the children in the pool next door, Dewi, obviously still upset at the memory of that weekend, explains how he never gave up hope, even when the doctors told him he was paralysed. 'I always knew I was going to be fine, the Saturday and Sunday when I was completely paralysed from the neck down I knew I was going to be OK. During this time they were telling my parents I was never going to walk again, but I always knew I was going to be fine.'

A couple of days later Dewi started to regain some feeling: 'I woke up and it all came back. I had so much hypersensitivity, you couldn't touch my hand; the slightest touch was like you had stuck a knife into it, the nerves were in ribbons, there was so much pain in my body.'

The pain was a good sign, according to the doctors, he could now get on with his rehabilitation; and after months of intense and painful physiotherapy he was walking and back home. But Dewi had to face the reality that he wouldn't be able to play rugby again. His goal had been to play for the full Welsh side, but now he wouldn't be able to train, as he had also hoped, to become a PE teacher. His career was over before it had started.

'Working in a swimming pool is not what I wanted to do,' he explains, looking around him, the familiar smell of chlorine thick in the overly warm air. 'OK, we do teach children to swim, but I wanted to teach PE and I don't know what to do really. I don't know where my life is going. I can't be here all my life. I don't know what to do – it's so hard. I wake up on a Monday morning and I think, "What am I going to do now?" because your mind is on rugby. Wales is a rugby nation and it's all around you, it's all I think about. There are boys who I work with now who play rugby, they come in on a Monday and they talk about the rugby and I think, well, it's not everything, but to me at that time it was.'

Far from being the caring, supportive organization he had hoped, the Welsh Rugby Union (WRU) was conspicuous by its absence. He assumed that he would be eligible for insurance to reimburse his parents for the daily journeys to the hospital, and some alterations to his house, as well as compensation for the suffering of the past months. The WRU sent forms to fill in, but, as he examined them, he realized that he wouldn't get a penny. He contacted solicitor Spencer Collier.

'The arguments were fairly polarized,' Collier admits in the Swansea offices where he is a partner. 'The Welsh Rugby Union were saying that even though Dewi couldn't carry on in his intended occupation he could work in some capacity. We took a different view and from an early stage it was clear that we would-n't get a payment unless we litigated. I think Dewi was aware from the word go that if he wanted his money it wasn't going to come in a cheque with a letter. It would have to be fought in court.'

The case did go to court, as the WRU argued that Dewi was still able to work. Spencer Collier agreed he could – but not in his chosen career of teaching. 'He is not unemployed and he is not permanently disabled from attending to his usual occupation,' Collier continued. 'Now we have all come across cases where people have had horrific injuries from an accident where they might have tetraplegia, and they are totally dependent on others for care and assistance, but because they can move their right index finger then potentially they could input data into a computer and therefore are employable. It wasn't as absurd as that in this case, but the principle was the same: as long as Dewi could do some work, however poorly paid or however menial it was, then he didn't qualify.'

Also called to give evidence was Dewi's schoolboy coach,

who told the court that, in his opinion, Dewi would have gone on to play at the highest level. The WRU defended their line doggedly. Peter Owens of the Union explained their position: 'I was present when Dewi was injured and it was a very distressing time for his parents and for the young man himself. The Union was very conscious of the injury from day one and spoke to the insurers throughout. The claim by insurers was that he was playing for Welsh Schools at that time. The claim was under the senior policy, and they offer slightly different benefits and less money to the senior policy and the issue was: should the claim go ahead under schoolboy or on the basis of the senior policy?'

Dewi injured his neck in January 1995; it was to be five years nearly to the day until he walked out of the court, having won his case. The judge at Swansea County Court decided that the WRU and their insurers should, in fact, have to pay compensation.

Naturally Dewi is still bitter: 'I gave everything for Wales and could have easily have ended up looking at a ceiling for 24 hours a day needing constant care. As it was I had to have five serious operations to allow me to walk again. I got nothing from the WRU, no telephone calls or letters. Basically the Union did not want to know me once I could not play for them any more. I went through a lot of pain and trauma and just a few indications that they were behind me would have helped a lot but there was nothing.'

Dewi received £100,000, which is roughly five or six years' salary as a teacher, but not a great deal to a top rugby player, which Dewi was to become in the professional era. In the Union's defence Peter Owens says that they weren't entirely to blame: 'Can I just stress that it wasn't the Union that was stopping the payment. The insurance company determined it should not be settled under the claim policy and we did make recommendations on behalf of Dewi to the insurers over a long period of time.'

Not the answer Spencer Collier was looking for, he believes that the Union has a duty to ensure its players are properly looked after: 'Dewi was a very good player who must have pleased his family and his parents immensely to get to the level he did, and to play at the Arms Park against the All Blacks was a schoolboy dream. I am sure that insurance was the last thing on his parents' mind but regardless of the legal arguments it is quite unsavoury that the Welsh Rugby Union should take such a stand and do so when he really needed them. They were not interested.'

Every weekend nearly 300,000 players take to the Rugby Union field. A fair assessment would be that the vast majority of them have given very little thought to insurance or any sort of provision if they suffer an injury. Whilst captaining England Sevens in Hong Kong, Damian Hopley injured his ankle, an injury which eventually ended his career. When he looked to the English rugby authorities for insurance he found he didn't have any – a situation that, he admits, has left him bitter. Labelled 'rugby's Arthur Scargill', in this case as a compliment, he is now the chief executive of the Professional Rugby Players' Association, and insurance takes up much of his time.

'I went to the RFU [Rugby Football Union] for compensation, but the treatment they gave me was appalling. It is a new wave of administrators in now but these people told me to stop writing begging letters, and you think, hang on, here am I out there captaining my country and all of a sudden I get short shrift and head in the sand. And it's very much the case of: "It doesn't matter very much about Damian, let's get someone to fill his place" in the terms of the team. One of the motivating factors for the Players' Association being set up was that it's a very lonely existence. Mine was just a minor injury compared to a full-scale neck injury, but it can be a fairly lonely existence when you have no one to turn to. There are very few people to whom you can say, "How does this work and who do I turn to?" Unfortunately, given the nature of sportsmen, people do not want to know anything about you until they need you and when they need you they cannot get to you quickly enough.'

Currently, Hopley says, clubs insure the majority of the players at club level so they have a basic level of cover and if they get permanently injured they would get a payout of just £25,000.

'At international level the players obviously have an awful lot more to lose,' he explains, 'so we have worked to improve their levels, which is around £150,000 to £200,000 if they get injured – but if you are a budding international like Jonny Wilkinson or Mike Tindall and you get injured early in your career, that could be a year's earnings. It's imperative that players understand the fragile nature of sport.'

Martin Bayfield agrees with his former England team-mate; the six-foot-ten Northampton second-rower was also forced to retire prematurely due to injury. 'At Northampton at the time we had Ian McGeechan in charge of the club,' he says. 'He forced all the players to go to a presentation with an insurance company and like all typical rugby players we think it is never going to happen to us and it will be fine. I was looking to renew my insurance and I never got round to it but he said, "No, go to this meeting and listen to what they have got to say." I went along, liked what I heard, took out insurance and then a matter of five days later I injured my neck. It's ridiculous!'

A good example of Damian Hopley's point about the fragile nature of sport, the imposing ex-policeman was looking to force his way back into the England team and add to his 31 caps, when he suffered his freak injury. He was told he couldn't play again, nor could he go back on the beat. He looks back at Ian McGeechan's advice, knowing it could have been a whole different story: 'I think there are the basic insurance packages which pay out a sum of money,' he says. 'On the face of it if someone was to give you that money now, you'd think great. But if you are disabled and you cannot work any more, it doesn't go a long way. I think the authorities should insist on examining every player's insurance to make sure that he is always adequately covered.'

Bayfield recognizes that players must take their share of responsibility. He also knows, though, that the future isn't the top of the priority list when the present means trophies, caps and reaping the benefits of professionalism: 'The Union mustn't shy away from their duties if a player is injured on international duty. The national set-up must pay out and unfortunately it means that players do not take out adequate insurance because they just can't afford it. If you ask a player for £5,000 to £7,000 in premiums to cover themselves adequately, a young player will say, "No, I am not going to do that."'

A broken neck in Rugby Union Premiership or the Six Nations is no different an injury to a broken neck in Division Five of the Yorkshire League. It's not just players at the top, according to Damian Hopley, who need to be aware of life after injury: 'We are dealing with a very difficult culture from an amateur era. The administrators see players getting paid a lot of money and say, "Why should we insure them for any more money?" So, fortunately or unfortunately, it always has to come back to the individual to make sure they have correct cover. I deal mostly with the professional end of the game, but across the board it would be far more fitting if we didn't have so many charity dinners, if we knew that this player if he got injured would have sufficient level of care for the rest of his life, not for the next five years.'

In one high-profile case, Ben Smolden was involved in a collapsed scrum, leaving him with a broken neck. He was forced to sue the referee, Michael Nolan, for failing to keep proper control of the game. Smolden, who will spend the rest of his life in a wheelchair, received £90,000 from the RFU, but this was nowhere near enough to cover the care he would need. Eventually he received a £1 million payout after taking the case to the High Court.

Players, of course, cannot be nannied by the Union or their clubs, they are grown men after all, but the Players' Association's Damian Hopley says that the game is paying lip-service to the players' welfare: 'You take a builder who breaks his arm, for instance. He is out of work for say four to six months, the current RFU insurance can cater for that player if he is amateur. But it is when we get to the tetraplegic or paraplegic, the horrific neck injuries that do happen in rugby, let's not turn away from it. Those players need the right sort of payout because £370,000 is the para- or tetraplegic payout. I would suggest that figure is derisory when you consider you have got to live the rest of your life off that.'

One estimate is that a young man paralysed in an accident needs around £6 million to care and provide for himself for the rest of his life. In the 1999–2000 season in English rugby there were 12 serious neck injuries; Irish Rugby Union has in the 1990s seen 15 of its players paralysed, most of them from teams in the lower leagues. The picture isn't much better in Rugby League, in fact it may be worse. The 13-a-side game is poorer than Union as it has neither the annual money-spinning internationals nor high-profile sugar daddies to bankroll it. The vast majority of clubs even at the top exist on a hand-to-mouth basis. Money is swallowed up before such luxuries as insurance can get a look-in.

Andy Goodway spends a large part of his days ploughing along the trans-Pennine M62 in his sponsored car, attempting to educate the game's young players about the importance of covering themselves. As a player, Goodway won multiple honours and was part of the Wigan team that dominated the sport in the eighties and nineties. After coaching Wigan, Oldham, Paris St Germain and then the full Great Britain side he became the chairman of the Rugby League Players' Association. He admits to a good deal of frustration when he speaks to players, saying the last thing a youngster clutching his first win bonus thinks of is, 'What happens if I can't play again?'

'I think that the League has got to insist that the players are educated on a good insurance policy,' he says. 'And then the players will see the benefits and see the realities of being insured, but also the realities of being uninsured. I think it is up to us to sit with the people in charge of the game and say, "This is what we require." If we can get a minimum requirement out of them and everyone is covered for a career-ending injury and has some sort of medical cover, then we will have been relatively successful.'

Like Dewi Coates, Phil Hardwick finds it difficult to sit and watch a game of rugby. Hardwick was also injured playing in a match and went through a series of horrifying operations and was told he would never play again. A builder by trade, he is a big, solid bear of a man, typical prop forward material, ideally suited you would think to the rigours of professional Rugby League. Again, like Dewi, he remembers his incident vividly.

'It was about the third or fourth minute,' he recalls, his deep Yorkshire vowels slightly quivering. 'I was just taking the ball on, the defence was very compact and everybody was very hyped up. I more or less met the bloke who tackled me head on and I could feel my head concertina back into my shoulders. My shoulders just felt like two weights, my arms were dead as I went to the floor. I wasn't concussed but I felt groggy, so I got up, fell down and got up again because in the first five minutes after you get injuries you try and shake them off.'

Phil was playing for Batley in the traditional Good Friday Derby against Dewsbury. Local pride, if not national glory, was at stake; he didn't want to come off but was persuaded to by the physio who sent him for treatment. In the hospital he was told that he had crushed two vertebrae.

'The next day they moved me to the Leeds General Infirmary to see a better surgeon,' he continues. 'He told me what I had done and that there were two courses. They could put me in traction where they could screw things in to your head and immobilize it or they could operate on me; and he did tell me there was a one in five chance of being paralysed and the operation not being successful. I wasn't happy at all.'

As Phil lay helpless in the hospital bed, with his damaged vertebrae encased in a metal box, he knew that his career was over and, having just bought a new house, he knew that the future looked bleak. Three weeks after the accident he was told that he wouldn't be eligible for any insurance payout from the Rugby Football League, who told *On The Line* that they 'didn't discuss individual cases'.

Phil was declared 40 per cent disabled and was off work for three months, putting a tremendous strain on his savings and the income of his partner, Gail. He took his case to Andy Goodway, who knew immediately that Phil was not being treated correctly. 'He thinks, and rightly so, that he should get some recompense for the risks he has taken,' Goodway says, 'and I think we will be looking for changes so that it is not going to happen to other people like Phil. If he is a builder and he has plates in his neck, he won't be able to do the same amount of work he has done before, and his earnings are obviously hit. So we have got say to the insurers that you have got look at this case as it is.'

Batley, Phil's club, did hold several charity evenings for him but according to the their chairman, Kevin Nicholas, the simple fact is that clubs like his cannot afford to insure players: 'I agree that that there should be increased benefits for people in Phil's position to obtain any cover. There is a premium to pay and someone has to pay the premium and the problem at the moment is that there is not sufficient money to pay the premiums. I would have thought over a season we have 60 to 70 players who play the first and second teams and obviously the cover has to be for all those players and not just the first-team players.'

Andy Goodway deals not only with players who are as high profile as he once was, but the level of player who earns a meagre living in the less glamorous outposts of the game such as Batley, Whitehaven and Doncaster. 'There are demands on clubs to survive,' he concedes. 'We have got to say to them, "OK, we appreciate that this is low down on your list of priorities so how can we help to increase it?" Well, this is a certain amount of your income you pay on insurance cover, we will try and find the rest through levies, through profit-sharing schemes, through the Rugby League and Super League and the biggest companies sponsoring.'

Matters nearly came to a head during the last Rugby League World Cup. *On The Line* was told by several Super League chief executives in the lead up to the competition that they seriously considered withdrawing their players due to their lack of insurance.

Back in the Rugby Union stronghold of South Wales, Jabez Matthews has been relentlessly banging the insurance drum for years. He is the manager of Blaenavon, who play in the seventh division of the Welsh League: 'I believe monetary rewards are great for any lad and if they can get paid for playing, at any level, then fine, no problem. But at the end of the day, I believe that as a club we have a responsibility to the lads. If I had a young lad coming into the game at 16 or 17, he is very impressionable and money is thrown under his nose, even if it is only say £30 a win at lower level. Let's say the boy plays three or four matches and gets a serious injury. Then the money dries up straight away. So I believe that irrelevant of what the boy earns, get the welfare system set up and then look at wages later.'

On a summer's evening looking over the rolling Gwent countryside, Matthews, universally known as 'Curly', passionately puts the case for insurance for all players as a matter of course. He doesn't mix with the big earners of the Welsh game but part-timers who earn their living as steelworkers, miners and farmers. Using an empty pint glass, a beer mat and a salt cellar he explains the realities of life in grassroots rugby.

'If you have got three players playing in the front row,' he begins, raising the pint glass to represent player number one, 'the loosehead, say for example, is unemployed. The hooker, who is a student, and then the third member, who works at the steel works. If those three boys were unfortunate to run into each other and were carried off with neck injuries, you then have to send in a form. As the system stands now, the first boy won't get paid as he is not earning, because it's all about loss of earnings, so therefore he will not get paid. The student is in the same position as the third member. If the club has insured him for £50 a week and his company pays him £80 he will not get paid; if he gets £40 a week from his company, then they make the insurance up to that difference, in that case £10.' In other words, the system doesn't help those who need it most.

The Welsh Rugby Union's Peter Owens disagrees. 'Well, I think the argument has been that our policy provides for players who have suffered a loss as a result of playing rugby football,' he says. 'That loss is shown by a loss of earnings. Now I think that Mr Matthews is looking for a policy that provides compensation where there is no loss there. It is effectively a pain and suffering loss, not a financial loss.'

On The Line examined insurance across the sport closely, and it revealed some startling anomalies. For instance, the Welsh Rugby Union policy compensates as follows:

A loss of right thumb (where right-handed) Sixteen thousand pounds
A loss of left thumb (where left-handed) Twelve thousand pounds

Whether the left-handed players in Welsh rugby are aware of this 'sinister' discrimination by their Union is unclear. Equally, amateur players in Rugby League are covered for injury for up to £50,000, but officers of their governing body, BARLA (the British Amateur Rugby League Association), are insured for double that amount for travelling to and from games.

Prioritizing money is an obvious problem for Rugby League and Peter Owens of the WRU also maintains that his sport cannot spare funds for its prize assets. The maximum payout for a player in Wales who is disabled is just £110,000. 'Well, it is a great deal of money,' he claims. 'But put it into context of a man who won't work for the rest of his life, it still isn't a very large sum. We are restricted, though, on a financial level to what we can do; we do all that is reasonable within the resources that are available to us to make sure that players are looked after as well as we can make them.'

In an ideal world, players from both codes would take to the field every weekend knowing that in the worst-case scenario, the sport would look after them. But the rugby world is far from an ideal one. Phil Hardwick was declared 40 per cent disabled and received a cheque as a 'full and final settlement' for a paltry £200 less tax; Dewi Coates had to battle for five years for what he was entitled to; and Damian Hopley had a similar struggle.

Player wages in Union and League have shot through the roof. Full-time contracts at the very top are commonplace, unfortunately so are the career-ending injuries. Those players at the top can afford to think about cover – at the bottom end it's a lottery. If a player is injured he not only has to give up rugby but his job as well. Jabez Matthews says he could put together a half-decent team from the valleys around Blaenavon of good players who have given up rugby because they cannot afford to live on the payouts if they get injured. Meanwhile, in England, Damian Hopley gladly helps with the charity fundraising dinners and collections at grounds for the latest young player to end up in a wheelchair; he would, though, rather all that effort went into making sure they didn't need to hold them at all.

CHAPTER FIFTEEN

The Heavyweight Champion of Sleaze
British Amateur Boxing's Demise at the Hands of Big Frank

He's presided over the crumbling wreckage of British amateur boxing.
Fighters went uninsured, medal hopes were denied their chance, inter-
national squads were asked to smuggle booze, and power was secured
by mystery votes. Welcome to the crazy world of Frank Hendry.

The horrid realization struck Alex Arthur halfway through his
futile, baggage-laden sprint across Brussels airport: his Olympic
dream was in the hands of a buffoon. Alex had been given seven
minutes to get from one end of the terminal to the other in order
to catch a flight to Istanbul. All through the brightly lit, winding
corridors he side-stepped trolleys and skipped around weary pas-
sengers. He might have made it, if he wasn't struggling with the
bags of Frank Hendry, the overweight head of British boxing who
had arranged the improbable itinerary. 'We ventured over to
Turkey, me, the national coach Tom Brown and Frank Hendry,'
recalls Alex, a tiny and uncommonly gifted boxer. 'And when we
actually set off we found that our connecting flight was so close
to the flight that we got off it was a time-span of about seven
minutes. It was in Brussels, which is quite a large airport, and we
had to try and get from one end of the airport to the other and
we just never had the time.'

   The Istanbul Olympic qualifying tournament was to be
Alex Arthur's stepping stone to Sydney where, as the 1999 world
champion, the Edinburgh-based bantamweight had a realistic
chance of a medal. 'Everything was really geared towards Sydney
from the day that I turned senior, every competition that I went
to was like a training thing, its only purpose was to get me more
experience to get me to go to Sydney and achieve my goal of win-

ning an Olympic gold medal,' says Alex, who took the gold medal at the Commonwealth Games in 1998.

But his arrangements were in the hands of a man who for years has been at the top of amateur boxing in Britain and whose reign has been characterized by a series of blunders, divisions, court battles and a bogus election. It is an empire of crisis and calamity in which the victims have been the boxers.

For years Frank Hendry has been the most powerful man in amateur boxing in Britain, and has been so for many years. Over the years he has been president and executive director of the Scottish Amateur Boxing Association (SABA), boxing's representative on the British Olympic Association, secretary of the British Amateur Boxing Association and president of the Commonwealth Amateur Boxing Association. Scarcely a jab or a hook is thrown by an amateur boxer in Great Britain without the puncher being in some way accountable to 'Big Frank'. His weighty influence also extends overseas where he is vice-president of the European Amateur Boxing Association (EABA) and an executive member of the World Amateur Boxing Association (AIBA). It's quite a list of honours for a Dundee publican.

Round of figure, red of face and rich of voice, Frank Hendry likes to paint himself as the boxer's friend, but he is not. Alex Arthur says the Istanbul fiasco was symptomatic of the way fighters suffered as a result of schoolboy errors: 'I would have said that it was fairly typical, it wasn't the only occasion that things didn't seem to have been organized right. These guys are famous for it.'

The seven-minute dash predictably resulted in a young boxing hopeful, and two ageing officials, missing their connection. The consequence was a seven-hour wait for the next flight, which would get Alex to Istanbul just in time to fight. Seven hours kicking his heels in an airport terminal just before the biggest contest of his life was not on the tiny fighter's Olympic schedule. There was no opportunity for training or exercise and the only food was junk. The delay burdened Alex Arthur with a few unwanted, scale-tipping pounds; it was enough to take him over the limit for a bantamweight.

The trio arrived in Turkey the night before Alex's first bout, for which he had an early morning weigh-in. 'I was up most of the night training, to try and get my weight down so that I wouldn't be disqualified,' he recalls angrily. 'I went to sleep at about five in the morning and Tom Brown woke me a couple of hours later for the weigh-in. I weighed-in OK and then I went back to the hotel, got some breakfast and by this time I was really exhausted because I'd been up all night in the gym, training to get my weight down.' So Alex announced that he intended to squeeze in another nap before his opening contest. Tom Brown, the national coach, was to wake him later. Once more the boxer was let down by his officials.

'He calls me 15 minutes before the bell is due to go for the start of round one, and tells me that I'm fighting,' says Alex, still struggling to believe the way he was treated. 'I have just opened my eyes. I'm shocked, I haven't even had time to wash my face or anything like that. I have to grab my bag and run downstairs, literally exhausted, and jump on a bus. We get to the venue with two minutes to spare.'

The hall used for the Olympic qualifier was cavernous and freezing, but Alex's opponent was already glistening with sweat. Unlike the Scotsman, this fighter had been given plenty of time to warm up and get his muscles loose. All the preparation the British bantamweight enjoyed was a panic-stricken ride on a bus.

Making matters worse, Alex had been given strict pre-fight-instructions by his physiotherapist. In order to stop the recurrence of a shoulder injury it was essential that he warm up his body thoroughly with a series of carefully planned exercises. But there was no time for that. With his body still waking up, the gloves were strapped on his fists and the headguard wrapped around his skull. Seconds out, round one.

The three-round contest was all there was to Alex Arthur's Istanbul campaign. Unsurprisingly, he was beaten on points by the man who had been prepared properly. Disgusted, he sought to escape as soon as possible. 'After that I paid £350 of my own money to come straight home that night. I didn't want to wait and travel with Hendry and Brown again, I was too depressed. I felt terrible so I just decided to come home,' he says.

Following a dose of encouragement from his father, the young fighter was persuaded to try once more, at a later qualifying event in Halle, Germany. This time Mr Hendry arranged an itinerary which got his fighters to the venue in plenty of time, and Alex looked forward to the luxury of a full night's sleep before climbing through the ropes. Frank Hendry had other plans.

'When I was getting ready to qualify for the Olympics in Germany they started to have some kind of party in one of the hotel bedrooms, and I'm in the room next door trying to get some sleep.' Once more Alex splutters through an explanation of how boxing officials appeared to forget that the reason for qualifying tournaments is to qualify, not an excuse for the officials to have a party. 'I had to get up the next day for a fight that would get me to the Olympic Games, and they're having a party and drinking bottles of whisky. It was crazy. At about 2.30 in the morning I actually had to ask my father, who had come to watch me, to go along and ask them to be quiet,' he says.

Once the officials had been asked to keep quiet so that their best medal hope might get some pre-fight rest, Alex says they changed their behaviour: 'They started singing and put the television on. I had to be up at half past six for a seven o'clock weigh-in and these idiots were getting drunk in the room next door. It was a nightmare. We're the boxers, we're the guys who are dedicating ourselves, watching our weight and not drinking too many fluids, and these guys are up all night drinking whisky.' Mr Arthur Snr made a further, more strenuous request for peace and quiet, which was finally heeded. The party was over. It seems that even time-served boxing officials have to rest some time.

Halle was another failure for a tired and increasingly disillusioned Alex. Before Sydney he was as realistic a medal hope as Audley Harrison had been. Whereas the games became a springboard to fame and fortune for the heavyweight, the bantamweight watched it all on television at home in Edinburgh. Within weeks he had turned professional, his career starting with four impressive wins and much speculation in the boxing press about Alex being the most promising young professional in Britain.

Also in Halle was the five-times Scottish middleweight

champion, Colin McNeil. A medal would have been less likely for McNeil, but qualification for the final stages in Sydney was not beyond the experienced fighter's reach. He too has stories to tell of how the head of the Scottish Amateur Boxing Association handles his boxers: 'I have been away on trips when I have thought that Frank is all right, and I've even argued his case on occasions, but in Germany I saw his true colours. I've seen for myself what he is really like and he only cares about himself, he doesn't really care about Scottish boxing in my eyes.'

McNeil's disillusionment had started a year before Germany, at the World Championships in Houston, Texas. He and Alex Arthur had made their way to the tournament in plenty of time for their fights. The hard-working Mr Hendry had already settled in his plush American hotel a few days earlier. The fighters bumped into their leader by accident in the lobby. He greeted them, not with a 'Good luck boys, how was your flight?' but with a terse 'What the f**k are you doing here?' Colin McNeil says that Mr Hendry's greeting was definitely not a joke: 'No, the man was really depressed to see us because to his eyes it was going to cost him money. He wasn't interested in who we were going to fight and how we would do when we represented Scotland in the World Championships, all he was interested in was the money.'

When it came to the ill-fated Olympic qualifier in Halle, Mr Hendry was again only concerned with money, but for very different reasons. Frank Hendry cares for his boxers so much that he takes the worry of international travel out of their hands, as any sport's governing body should do. Using a travel agent close to his Dundee home, Mr Hendry has sent boxers (and himself of course) all over the globe. When he dispatched tickets for the Halle event to Colin McNeil and the middleweight's manager, John Clare, they were shocked at the price they were being charged. The pair went to their nearest high-street travel agent and were astonished to find flights that were not only more convenient, but £200 each cheaper. Expecting Mr Hendry to be pleased that they had saved the Association a lot of money, Mr Clare informed Mr Hendry of the bargains. His news was met with a warning that he was *never* to try and organize his own flights. Frank and the Dundee firm would see to everything.

Puzzled at this profligacy McNeil and Clare flew to Germany where they ran into another cash crisis. Amateur boxing events charge a set rate for board and lodging to competitors who then claim any expenses back from their national association. In Germany the rate for fighters was US $50 per day. But, thanks to an error in registration by Mr Hendry's SABA, McNeil had to pay the US $90 rate charged to visitors. He says he is disgusted: 'I have seen first hand what he really thinks of the boxers who spend days training and whose families are committed to them doing well in boxing. He's in charge and he just doesn't care, he only cares about himself really, and that hurts.' Other people had come to the same conclusion years before.

Glasgow-based Andy Grant was coach to two young Scottish boxers who went to Puerto Rico for the World Junior Championships in 1987. When they arrived in the Caribbean they found Frank Hendry was there too, acting as their team manager. Unlike most other team managers at the event, Mr Hendry wasn't staying with the fighters in their dormitory accommodation 40 miles from the tournament venue. He was tucked up in a swish hotel just yards from ringside. Andy Grant was furious with what he interpreted as Mr Hendry's indifference to the plight of the boxers he was there to represent: 'In the period of time that we were at the championships he only ever came to the camp where the team was based on two occasions. How can you be a team manager and only visit the camp twice?

'We were also told,' continues the Glaswegian, 'by the SABA before we left Scotland that because this was a Junior Championship there would be no subsistence money paid to the boxers. But then I found out that every other country's fighters were getting money, except for our boys. If we hadn't taken the so-called team manager with us we could have afforded at least another two boxers. Now, what's more important: taking on someone who is completely superfluous or taking two more boxers? It's that type of thing that you looked at and said, "This is crazy!"'

Hendry fiercely defends himself against any accusation that he behaved improperly and denies that he has ever put the needs of himself above those of the boxers, but Andy Grant says he has seen it happen many times: 'When you went abroad with a team you were instructed to see who was not bringing back their full allowance of duty-free whisky and cigarettes, then you had to give them extra to take through customs so that Mr Hendry could collect it on the other side, and sometimes it was quite a large amount of alcohol and cigarettes.' The non-smoking, bar-owning globetrotter insisted to *On The Line* that the booze and fags his boxers hauled across the border for him were not for sale in The Sporting Lounge in Dundee, which he owns. It was all for his personal consumption.

The last time light-heavyweight Lee Ramsey went abroad he didn't bring back duty free for Mr Hendry. He wasn't fit enough to bring anything at all following a brutal knockout in a fight in Dublin. 'In my opinion Ramsey was cruising the bout in the final round,' says former SABA official George Brown, who was ringside in Dublin on that night in February 1998. 'Suddenly there was a right cross and Ramsey was down. It was a blow to the head, but he recovered well. Then, out of nowhere, the Irish boxer connected again and I knew that Lee wasn't going to get up that time.'

Ramsey lay motionless on the canvas for around three minutes before being helped to a car and taken to hospital, accompanied by George Brown. At the hospital he was quizzed by doctors who wanted to be sure that his memory was returning, but he was given no x-ray and no brain scan. Within a couple hours of being knocked cold he was back in his Dublin digs. After an incident like that a fighter is banned from sparring or boxing in a competition for at least 21 days and even then he should have to pass a strict medical, including a brain scan, to ensure there are no long-term effects from the knockout. But two weeks later the SABA entered Lee Ramsey into the draw to fight in the Scottish National Championships. The boxer was spared when he received a bye, but George Brown was livid: 'Lee didn't have a scan, or an x-ray. The welfare of the boxer should always come first and I know that Lee Ramsey received a raw deal.'

As well as failing to ensure that boxers were never entered for fights unless they were medically fit, the SABA under Frank

Hendry failed to provide Scottish fighters with adequate insurance cover. Seventy-seven boxing clubs made up the SABA, but the total insurance premium paid was only enough to cover 24 of them. Frank Hendry insists that he had an arrangement with the insurance company that he could pay for insurance for the members of 24 clubs, and that he didn't have to stipulate which clubs were covered. He tries to argue that the insurance company allowed him to cover only a third of the boxers in his care, knowing that wherever a claim came from, he could nominate that club as one of the ones which was covered. *On The Line* asked him to clarify if it was true that he insured 24 clubs and gambled that he would get fewer than 24 claims from boxers each year. His answer was, 'More or less, yes.'

It is hard to imagine any insurance company knowingly permitting such a practice. It would be like a haulage firm only insuring half of its vehicles and whenever one crashed nominating it as one of the few with cover. The SABA accounts show that the following year insurance premiums had trebled. Either Mr Hendry's fantastic deal was withdrawn as soon as it was exposed, or it had never existed.

The case against Mr Hendry was mounting, and people like Andy Grant were sick of his reign. But he had an iron grip over every official body for amateur boxing in Great Britain. The disgruntled ranks had only one option – a breakaway. Nearly half the amateur boxers in Scotland left the SABA and formed the rebel Scottish Amateur Boxing Federation (SABF). Being rebels meant they could not fight internationally and they gave up all their claims to funding from the Sports Council, but even those sacrifices were worth making to get away from what they had suffered under Frank Hendry.

The split forced the Sports Council, by now renamed Sportscotland, to act. An inquiry was launched into both bodies, chaired by Barry McGuigan. Andy Grant claims the findings of the report were a vindication for the splitters: 'When the report came out there were about 13 pages of condemnation of the SABA and their incompetence. In particular the finger was pointed at the man who was the main cause.' The report concluded that Big Frank 'had a responsibility in respect of many aspects which are alleged to have led to the decline of the sport. The main problem is that the powers of his office are all embracing and consequently he is held accountable for the successes and failures of the organization.' Those failures included poor safety for fighters, bad administration, inaccurate information about clubs and members, fractured relations with the Sports Council, lack of democracy, failure to secure funds and a lack of planning. It was a mess.

Sportscotland and the UK Sports Council, launched inquiries into the finances of the SABA. UK Sport demanded the return of more than £7,000 in expenses paid to Mr Hendry, and Sportscotland insisted on seeing the accounts for £20,000 in grant aid given during the 1990s. On one occasion Mr Hendry was berated by a senior UK official for having the highest expenses of any British sporting administrator. In 1998 the public purse shelled out £8,000 towards his jet-setting. Within a fortnight of assuring *On The Line* that he paid for every trip himself, and had subsidized Scottish boxing with £14,000 of his own money, Mr Hendry was writing to the Sports Council pleading for his phone bills to be reimbursed.

After reading this catalogue of ineptitude, Sportscotland stopped pumping public money into boxing in Scotland and recommended that both Mr Hendry's SABA and Mr Grant's breakaway Federation be disbanded and a new unity be built from the wreckage. Eight months after that was announced, the SABA was still limping along. By now many of the officials who had stayed loyal to Big Frank had become fed up with the way the organization was being run. John Clare, the head of the Fauldhouse Club where Colin McNeil is based, proposed a vote of no confidence in Hendry. 'Even with my little knowledge I could see that it was being run in an autocratic and overbearing way. There was very little democracy in the sport and I felt that the nature of that autocracy was coming from Frank. I thought that the power had to be dissolved for the sport to go ahead. That was the main purpose of raising the motion of no confidence,' explains Mr Clare.

With a public report condemning his reign, a split that had taken almost half of his clubs, and open revolt among those who remained, this was an ideal opportunity for Mr Hendry to step down gracefully after 20 years at the top. But stepping down was never the Hendry way, and he mustered his remnant around him for one last stand.

In October 1999, John Clare's motion of no confidence in his rumbustious and illustrious leader is before the Annual General Meeting of the SABA in Edinburgh. The turnout is poor, with only a third of the 77 clubs which Mr Hendry claims to have in his association attending the most important meeting in their history. Tempers are frayed during the five-hour session as Mr Hendry is taken to task for his lack of insurance cover. The leader is under attack from without and within. As the gathering draws to a close the motion of no confidence is presented, debated and balloted. In a staggering last-minute comeback of which any boxer would be proud, Hendry secures the narrowest of points victories – 24 votes to 23 (some clubs having two votes). Later it emerged that he achieved his remarkable win with a sharp spot of gerrymandering.

Hendry is a Dundonian, and the Dundee area has been the hub of his power base. One of the clubs which supported him in the vote of confidence, tipping the balance in his favour, was the Friary Club, also in Dundee. But according to the priest who used to run the Friary, the club no longer exists and should not have a vote. It has no venue, no ring and no boxers. In the words of the priest, Frank Hendry's reign had been protected by the votes of a ghost club. The vote was even cast by a man called Abie Hills, who was a member of the committee at Hendry's own club, St Francis.

While this farce was going on Sportscotland was busy creating the new boxing body to take the sport forward. It was called Amateur Boxing Scotland Ltd (ABS) and its first two appointments were nothing if not bizarre. If Sportscotland was going to restart the funding of Scottish boxing it needed to appoint someone to ensure the money got to the boxers and didn't get caught up in the bitter infighting which persisted. An advert was placed for an administrator, although privately some of the Sportscotland staff had dubbed the post 'The Job From Hell' because of the quarrelling that had taken place over the years.

On The Line learned that of the candidates interviewed for the post, two people stood out above the rest. One was Duncan Forbes, a former senior official with the Prison Service, the other was Ailsa Spindler, who had been running the Scottish Canoe Association. 'I was on the interview panel which took place at the offices of Sportscotland on the outskirts of Edinburgh,' remembers quietly spoken Jimmy Dunn, who had been part of the breakaway SABF. 'I was in favour of Ailsa Spindler because I was very impressed with her presentation and also with the experience that she had. She had worked for the Scottish Canoe Association and secured grants for them of around £43,000 she had also managed the World Ballooning Championships and her general qualifications were second to none.'

Mr Dunn says he and another panel member, Donald Campbell, were strongly in favour of Ms Spindler. Two other panel members, he says, were indifferent between her and Mr Forbes. The delegate from Sportscotland favoured Duncan Forbes. For her part, Ailsa Spindler says she thought the interview went excellently: 'Sometimes you come out of an interview and you know that you've hit all the right buttons and that it has gone really well. I knew I had performed well and thought that I had established a good rapport with the panel. Before the interview I had a look through the job description and knew I had got relevant experience to cover every point. Of course I knew some of the background. You can't have worked in Scottish sport for five years without having seen the boxing officials in meetings having their public squabbles, but I wasn't put off. It was a challenge.'

According to Jimmy Dunn, the interview panel failed to agree on the relative merits of Ailsa Spindler and Duncan Forbes. He says the five members of the panel went home with no decision taken. The next morning, a Saturday, he says he found a message on his answerphone from Sportscotland's Roddy Smith saying that Duncan Forbes had been appointed. Mr Smith rejects the allegation that the appointment was made outside of the interview panel, and his assertion is supported by Dick Rafferty, a Frank Hendry loyalist who was also a member of the panel. Other members insist they went home without a decision, and the appointment was made behind their backs. One of the interviewers went on holiday the day after the panel and didn't discover the result until she returned a fortnight later. Sportscotland had gone against the wishes of two members of the interview board and taken a unilateral decision. It might be argued that, as the body which pays the money, the Sports Council has the right to choose whoever it wants, but then what was the interview process for?

The job went to the eminently capable Mr Forbes, but he shocked his new employers when he resigned after only a few months. His letter of resignation explained how the job was not worth the hassle he was receiving from people who wanted to continue those squabbles which the spurned Ms Spindler had seen so often. But the arguments that drove out Mr Forbes were caused in part by the second of the appointments made for the new boxing board.

Amateur Boxing Scotland, the body formed because Mr Hendry's running of the SABA had been criticized so heavily by McGuigan's independent commission, wanted an international liaison officer. The post wasn't advertised, but instead was handed on a plate to Big Frank himself. Sportscotland's Roddy Smith tried to justify the re-invention of Mr Hendry. 'I think Frank Hendry has been an important fixture in amateur boxing in Scotland for many years, and he is no longer in a decision-making position,' he said defensively. 'He doesn't sit on the council or the board of management and anyway I think it is time to recognize that he has done a lot of positive things for Scottish boxing in the past.'

By inviting Big Frank to hold the post of international liaison officer, ABS and Sportscotland did him a huge favour. They freed him from the hassles of running a national governing body – a role in which he was so heavily criticized – and free to play the airport-hopping role of figurehead, with all of his travel costs eligible for reimbursement from the public purse. ABS could have written to its international parent bodies, AIBA and EABA, and explained that Frank Hendry was no longer mandated to represent Scotland on the international stage, as other countries have done in the past. Instead they chose to endorse his status. Roddy Smith might not think that Mr Hendry remained the ruddy red face of British boxers, but the man himself knows it's true: 'I am representing the boxers,' he brags. 'I am representing the clubs, and all those people who want to criticize me don't know the work that is involved, they're just jealous.'

While Frank Hendry has been sitting on his British boxing throne, none of the constituent nations have been running as they should. In Wales, where the Amateur Boxing Association is led by Frank's old friend and fellow publican Terry Smith, there was a breakaway federation at the same time as the split in Scotland. More than half the clubs left the established body, despite the knowledge that their action would mean expulsion from international competition. Then Stuart Price, the Federation secretary, had a brainwave: he'd make Wales part of England! It was a revolutionary idea that would land him in court.

Mr Price asked the Amateur Boxing Association of England (ABAE) to admit his federation as a newly created Cambrian region. He thought he had secured an agreement and when, following a change of leadership, the ABAE refused to allow his boxers in, the breakaway Welsh Federation took the English to court.

For many years the ABAE had been a steady ship, the white sheep of Britain's boxing family, but this legal attack from Wales could not have come at a worse time.

In September 2000 Sport England (formerly the English Sports Council) insisted that the ABAE chairman postpone his Annual General Meeting while outside auditors scoured the Association's books. Sport England gives more than one million pounds a year to amateur boxing and its officers wanted a clearer picture of where the money was going before they approved the accounts. The ABAE chief executive, Terry Collier, was suspended on full pay, and then quietly allowed to leave without the suspension ever being lifted. The AGM was postponed a further four times, such was the turmoil in England as amateur boxing prepared for its day in court.

Within the oak-panelled walls of the Royal Courts of Justice in London, Frank Hendry was sworn in to testify. Britain's senior amateur boxing official was faced with a choice: he could back the majority of Welsh boxers and allow them to create a new region under the authority of the ABAE, or he could stand by his old friend Terry Smith, from whom the boxers had broken away. Terry and Frank go back a long way, having enjoyed many AIBA conferences together.

Bristling with pugnacious confidence Mr Hendry gave evidence in support of the English refusal to admit the breakaway boxers. He was adamant that the proposed door to recognition for ambitious young Welsh boxers should remain shut.

Judge Justice Garland was clearly impressed by the testimony of Big Frank; he rejected the WABF claim that they had a contract with the ABAE to form a Cambrian Division. On Tuesday 13 March 2001, two weeks after the judgment, a courier weaved through the London traffic to deliver the WABF's appeal against the judge's findings. The case was set to run for months.

In response to a request for an interview from *On The Line*, Frank Hendry arranges for a conference room to be made available in the Dundee Hilton on the banks of the Dee. Resplendent in a striped blazer and a vibrant red and yellow tie he holds out a welcoming hand. Meticulously laid out on the top table are seven piles of documents, including letters of testimony to his sterling work from AIBA and EABA, his letter of appointment as international liaison officer for Scotland and a magazine article describing him, with no hint of irony, as 'A Legend of Scottish Sport' – the case for his defence.

> *OTL*: Alex Arthur says he got 15 minutes' notice
> when he was fighting in Istanbul, that he was in bed
> and was told 15 minutes before an Olympic Qualifier.
> FH: Now I don't know, I can't be responsible for that.
> As far as I am concerned, each boxer should have
> known, should have been told when they were
> boxing. But I certainly wouldn't call the boy a liar. I
> just don't know what went on at that particular tour-

nament, but when it came to Alex Arthur, we tried
our best to get him into all the qualification tournaments, unfortunately the boy was injured but he did
box in one or two and he didn't win.

OTL: And you were unable to get him a wild card?

FH: Yes.

OTL: How much did that disappoint you because you
pride yourself on your influence and it came to
nothing there?

FH: Yeah, I was very disappointed but once again you
can't buck the whole of the world.

OTL: What about the vote of no confidence that you
survived thanks to the votes of a club which didn't
exist, what can you tell us about that?

FH: Oh it did exist.

OTL: It hadn't had any boxers for years, it didn't
have a ring. It was a ghost club.

FH: Once again this is more red herrings. The Friary
Club was in The Friary and they lost the ring because
of some various problems where they trained before.
They came into the St Francis Club which is according to the rules that two clubs could share, providing
that they trained on different nights. They had boxers
in the Scottish Championships with The Friary ABC
on their back so this is another misnomer.

OTL: Well, it's a misnomer that Abie Hills then
boasted about at a council meeting in front of two
witnesses that this had been done for the reason of
getting you back in office.

FH: You'd have to see Abie Hills about that. But again
on the other side of the coin there was actually
people there at the meeting of no confidence that
didn't have a mandate from a club.

OTL: So you were running an organization that had a
vote of no confidence in its senior official and you
didn't even know who was voting?

FH: Yes.

OTL: But you're in charge of this.

FH: I beg your pardon, I'm one person out of eleven. There are eleven members of the council and I'm only one.

OTL: But the buck stops with the head man.

FH: Well, we could see what really happens at the end of the day. I'm quite confident that what I did was correct.

OTL: You were quoted on 6 February 2000 as saying, 'As far as I am concerned the less I have to do with the new body, the better.' And now you're back on the top table as international liaison officer, what changed your mind?

FH: When I thought about the situation and saw what was in front and what was ahead for amateur boxing and I felt that I still had something to offer to make sure that my work in 40 years wasn't in vain.

OTL: Why are so many people keen to bad-mouth Frank Hendry?

FH: Jealousy? I don't know.

OTL: So why do you then want to be involved? You disagree with a lot of the findings of the commission, you clearly don't get on with a number of the people who are in ABS Ltd and yet you want to travel the world representing them. Why is that?

FH: Until such times as I see people coming along that's able to do my job then if I am so minded I will stay.

In June 2001 the executive board of Amateur Boxing Scotland met in Edinburgh and voted by five votes to four to remove Frank Hendry as their International Liason Officer. His positions at British, Commonwealth, Olympic, European and World level had started to be undermined as his tartan power base was finally eroded. After more than 20 years as the king of the scottish ring, Big Frank was beginning to look unsteady.

CHAPTER SIXTEEN

Gone to the Dogs
The Death of Small Greyhound Tracks and What It Means for Dogs

When a greyhound's racing days are over the odds on a happy retirement are shorter than they ought to be. In the past, one lifeline for a dog past its prime has been racing on the independent track scene. In 1998 the prospects for the three dozen such tracks looked grim. But this is a story with a positive ending, thanks in small part, we are told, to the programme we broadcast in November of that year.

Spring 2001
For the first time in years the greyhound industry is looking at a bonanza. For a decade, split from within and attacked from without, by animal charities and others, the big guns of dog racing had been experiencing a bumpy ride and a bad press. But in the middle of a bitter squabble over a fund donated to greyhound racing by the bookies, peace appears to have broken out.

The catalyst for this apparently happy arrangement is a new method of funding agreed between the government, the bookies and the dog and horse racing industries, which in turn was triggered by the alacrity with which the bookmakers have adapted to the opportunities on the internet over the last few years.

The bookmakers had always moaned about the betting tax imposed on them by government. That is the money you pay either when you place a bet or when you collect your winnings. The bookmakers were forced to discharge their duty to support the racing industries by paying over a portion of this levy to the dogs and horses. They recognized the need to support the racing businesses but resented what they saw as an arbitrary and unwieldy tax. However, the government had no reason to give them a choice in the matter – and didn't.

230 BLOWING THE WHISTLE

But the spread of the internet changed the balance of power. As bookmakers moved more of their betting online and more of their revenues offshore, the Treasury foresaw a dramatic slide in income from betting duty, which would not only create a hole in government finance but also lead to a more damaging fall in income to the racing industry, as the value of the levy declined.

In a bid to keep as much as possible of the betting industry cash in Britain, the government is now looking at a radical change to taxing and funding the racing industries. Instead of a tax on stakes or winnings, the new arrangements are to be centred on tax on profits instead. The betting levy, compulsory for the horse-racing industry but voluntary for greyhounds, will also be replaced. Now the regulatory bodies for both horses and dogs will secure better and more predictable revenue by selling their intellectual copyright to the bookies for an annual fee.

This is not only simpler, it will yield much more cash. The easiest way to think of it is in terms of football's Premier League arrangement with TV – with the added dimension of income for the right to broadcast racing information down telephone betting lines, or on the internet.

John Curran, owner of one the best regarded small tracks, is cock-a-hoop and has never felt better about the future. What's more, he blames (at least in part) *On The Line* for his sunny demeanour. 'What that programme did,' he booms down the telephone, 'is that it forced the British Greyhound Racing Board and the National Greyhound Racing Club to take the smaller tracks and independents seriously. We now feel confident that every part of the greyhound industry will benefit in some way from this new money.'

He goes on to explain, 'Before these new arrangements came to light, the big promoters and bigger tracks went their own way and did not listen to anyone else. What that programme did was bring to the attention of the government how the industry was split at the very time the Home Office were looking at overhauling the financial arrangements that supported greyhound racing. It strengthened our hand in calling for the industry to speak with one voice and after the broadcast, the people who had been ignoring us, the bigger operators, actually sat down and started talking to us seriously. The result is there is more unity within the industry than there has ever been and the future has not been brighter for us or the greyhound.'

Curran had long campaigned for an industry in which the interests of the big operators and the small independents could be catered for, where there would be no discrimination between tracks, where the industry could present a united front on issues ranging from greyhound welfare to tax and funding issues. Back in 1998, when he first contacted *On The Line*, it seemed he did not have a prayer of success.

October 1998

It is race night at the small West Yorkshire village of Kinsley. It used to have a mine but that is long gone and today there is not much to it. It is not a particularly cosy or evocative place, as one might expect of a mining village. A dull mixture of Yorkshire yellowstone and 1950s red-brick dwellings hug the B road between Wakefield and Grimethorpe, and that's just about it. Yet for a village denied recognition by all but the most detailed of road maps, Kinsley is a name to be conjured with in the world of greyhound racing.

Reg Bennett has been bringing his dogs racing here since the war. He looks like he was hewn from the stone walls hereabouts. Flat cap and mac. He carefully coaxes the canine cargo from the back of his white Astra van. Vicki's Pride does not look like an athlete as she gazes dolefully around the potholed car park, illuminated only by street lamps some distance away.

But an hour from now she'll be tearing around under the floodlights at the track on the opposite side of the road. You would not imagine that a greyhound stadium lurks behind the low wall opposite. But one does, deceiving the passing motorist because of a sharp dip in the land on the other side.

Reg joins a clump of other racegoers and owners leading their dogs into the Kinsley track. 'As you can see, Kinsley is far better than probably half the London and provincial tracks. They haven't got facilities like these. This is the cream of independent racing,' he says, full of the optimism and expectation typical of owners at this stage in the proceedings.

It certainly seems to fulfil all the requirements for a night at the dogs – a pub, cafe bar, sit-down restaurant, all built around a betting concourse. The track stretches out into the gloom until race time approaches and the floodlights burst out on the track. An observation tower-type structure houses the race commentator and control centre.

On this Tuesday night it is busy enough for the owner John Curran, to be confined to the depths of the kitchens where, wearing his chef's hat literally and metaphorically, he turns out steak, chicken and any bidding of the patrons in the restaurant. There is a community feel about the place, although in fact the race-goers and dog owners have come in from as far afield as York, Manchester and Hull.

One hundred and eighty miles to the south there's another dog track. Even if you have never been, chances are you have an idea about Wimbledon dog track. It is a popular set for a particular type of TV serial or film, of the *Lock, Stock ...* or *Long Good Friday* variety. You could probably fit Kinsley into the plate-glassed grandstand. Behind it on race night there are 3,000 punters scoffing up-market food. As they chomp and swill away, they look out on the panorama of the track. Waiting staff float by offering to place bets on your behalf. It is a great night out.

Wimbledon, owned by the sports entrepreneur Jarvis Astaire, races under National Greyhound Racing Club (NGRC) rules. Independent Kinsley and NGRC Wimbledon represent the two faces of dog racing in the UK and each thinks the other stinks.

John Curran bought Kinsley in 1985 after retiring from the local pit. It is a couple of hundred yards from where he was born and to him it is more than a business. 'I was born into a mining community and basically the track had grown up as part of the mining industry and became part of the culture of an area in which greyhound racing has historically been very popular.'

Less popular of late, though not because of any disenchantment with the dogs, so much as the emasculation of the mining industry that supported the local population. Many people have moved away in search of work and a new life, all of which has left the dog track at Kinsley the second biggest employer in the immediate area – with 64 employees. It runs a programme of 12 races 3 times a week. But you won't find the races listed in the racing press or at the bookies'. Kinsley is avowedly independent. On-course betting is important, but it is not the sole reason for race night.

'The independents are primarily owners that keep their dogs at home,' explains John Curran. 'Some in kennels down the bottom of the garden or on allotments but I have to say many dogs, when they are not racing, are pets and live in the house as part of the family.'

This would never do at an NGRC track – Wimbledon, Walthamstow or Belle Vue – because at an NGRC track the greyhound serves a very different purpose to the predominantly socio-cultural one at an independent. At the NGRC track the dog is there to serve the betting industry.

Indeed, of the 32 NGRC racing circuits, 14 are what are known as BAGS tracks (British Association of Greyhound Stadiums). Most are owned by the bookies direct. The meetings are soulless affairs. They take place largely behind closed doors at places you have heard of, like Wolverhampton, Sheffield or Nottingham, and places you haven't, like Monmore or Crayford. Witnessed only by the CCTV service beamed into the betting shops and a few officials on site, typically the dogs pound round, not to the roar of the punters but the whirr of the hare.

Each year nearly £1.5 billion are wagered on these races, 90 per cent of it direct in the bookies'. With so much money at stake, naturally it is vital that there are strict rules to ensure the integrity of the races. And this is basis of the NGRC system.

The NGRC was formed in 1928 by promoters operating under the auspices of the sports governing body, the British Greyhound Racing Board; its chief executive is Geoffrey Thomas. 'What you get if you go NGRC racing is the dog running in the right name, the form you see is the genuine form, the dog has been checked by a vet beforehand and it will receive treatment by a vet if it is injured. If there is any kind of problem there is a stewards' inquiry and the dogs are regularly tested for drugs. It has integrity and people are coming back to it in droves.'

The implication is that non-NGRC tracks carry the whiff of skulduggery. But for Terry, a regular racer at Kinsley, you can stuff the NGRC. She owns seven dogs and they all live in kennels at the bottom of the garden. She's been racing greyhounds for 20 years: 'I would not go to an NGRC track, never mind race a dog there. You have to bring the dogs in an hour before racing, they get locked up, you have to race them when they want to run them not when you do. I like to take him for a drink of water and wash his feet after the race and then make a fuss of him before putting him in the car and taking him home.'

As Terry indicated, the NGRC experience is very different. Bulk delivered by trainers an hour before the race programme, so they can be identified, tested and checked over by vets, the dogs then stay in a kennel block before being raced. With the race complete, they return to the kennels, where they remain until the trainers pick them up after racing is over.

The two codes may be united by a species but they are clearly separated by a culture. As Geoffrey Thomas would agree, the NGRC it is not for everyone: 'It is not every owner who has a thousand pounds to pay for a dog, then has the money to give it to a professional trainer, whose principal contact with the dog might be walking it on a Sunday and or even just watching it race from a restaurant.' But for a big track, which needs a reliable supply of thousands of quality dogs a year to operate a race programme to the satisfaction of the bookmakers and punters alike, there is little alternative.

This uneasy coexistence might have continued but for two developments. Firstly, in 1992 the then Chancellor, Norman Lamont, prompted the creation of a fund to support the greyhound industry by cutting betting tax and inviting the bookies to contribute to a voluntary fund. Currently, even though not all bookies contribute, it is worth £5 million a year to the grey-hound industry. Secondly, this coincided with a sharp decline in the number of independent tracks. Between 1992 and 1998, 24 tracks went out of business, leaving 32 – the same as operate under NGRC rules. That so many independents went to the wall so quickly was mostly due to a savage economic recession which hit dog-racing communities hard.

John Curran explains, 'With the decline of the traditional industries – mining, steel and various other industries – we have found it harder and harder for owners to keep coming to grey-hound stadiums. Many simply cannot afford to come racing and, more to the point, there was not the money to keep purchasing greyhounds.'

Before the bookies set up their voluntary fund for the industry, it was not worth arguing whether or not the indepen-dents were part of the greyhound industry – but it is now. 'What we have been saying to the BGRB [British Greyhound Racing Board],' explains Curran, 'is that we are part of the greyhound industry, we are enthusiasts of the sport as a whole and we believe that the reduction in the betting levy was brought about by Norman Lamont to help the industry as a whole and not to help a select few.'

Certainly the money pouring into the NGRC from the levy has helped their tracks to refresh their image and not just the neon splendours of Wimbledon, Walthamstow and Belle Vue. The smaller NGRC tracks have spruced themselves up too. But not a penny has trickled down to the independents. John Curran's argument is that with so many independents strug-gling, some of the money should be diverted to them. 'They are spending vast sums of money improving the infrastructures at the NGRC tracks,' Curran complains. 'It is not going back into the grassroots of the industry and that's the people, the owners, the greyhound itself and that is where we are battling with the powers that be.'

But NGRC promoters believe letting the independents share in the fund would hurt them financially by diluting the fund to tracks, they believe, do not deserve any 'industry' support. Jarvis

Astaire is the most powerful promoter in NGRC racing. He says the bookies would never allow their money to go to the independents or, as he calls them, unlicensed tracks.

'There is no way,' complains Jarvis, 'no way at all that they would ever consider contributing money to unlicensed tracks because the bookies won't be party to the kind of racing that takes place there. You cannot trust what's happening, they run under assumed names at various places, there is no form book, no computer form and no one knows what they are betting on. There is no reason why the bookies would refuse bets for any other than a good and valid reason and that good and valid reason is that it is totally unreliable to take a bet at races on those tracks.'

Hinckley in Leicestershire is precisely the kind of track that Mr Astaire has in mind. Tacked onto an industrial estate off the A5, it is not very impressive. A few whitewashed outbuildings butt onto a distinctive grass circuit that has been in Tom Grant's family since 1930.

Tom bridles at the suggestion that his track is disreputable or that the punters don't know what they are betting on. 'It is,' he says, 'a simple affair to identify a racing greyhound. They all have a unique number code tattooed in one of their ears. If the dog has raced under another name here, then it will show up on my computer when I tap in the code from the ear.'

He bashes away on his computer, flicking across his battered desk to the list of dogs down to run on the next race night. 'There you are. Harry's Girl. There is an earmarked tattoo and you can see from this that it ran here last year as Blondie. So on the card we will mark Harry's Girl, ran at Hinckley on such and such a date as Blondie.'

Tom explains, 'The owner is not trying to defraud anyone but what happens is, you might own a dog and call it a name. Race it. Then later on you may decide to get rid and sell it. Someone else buys it, calls it something else and they race it. But Harry's Girl or Blondie, the earmark is the same. That information is marked on the race card. Now this is where they say we defraud the public. It is a load of rubbish.'

Even if we can accept that, in the integrity stakes, NGRC tracks win hands down, it is superfluous to John Curran's case. They know better than most in former mining communities like Kinsley that arguing for special treatment on the grounds of protecting a unique culture or livelihood cuts little ice. Rather, it is the issue of the animals' welfare which the independent tracks say is their strongest card. It is a notion that makes Jarvis Astaire very angry indeed. 'They don't even have vets at the tracks,' he fumes. 'They say they have them on call. Would you like to see an injured animal lying on the ground in front of you while they run around and try and find a vet? We can't run a race without a vet being there. On call is rubbish.'

But the mere fact of having a vet trackside offers no guarantee that the animals' health is of paramount importance. On the edge of the North Yorkshire moors, in the extravagantly named village of Oswaldkirk, lives retired vet Paddy Sweeney. There are few people alive with more experience of treating greyhounds. He is a prolific writer to the racing press and an arch critic of the NGRC and its welfare record.

'The NGRC say, "We employ vets at all our tracks,"' says Paddy, '"and we are particular and concerned about the dogs," but the truth of the matter is that the presence of a vet is largely eyewash. It is hypocrisy to indicate to people that they are concerned about welfare problems and the independent tracks are not. Independent tracks might not have a vet at each race night but they all have arrangements with a local vet to be on call and I think that is sufficient.'

Paddy Sweeney has treated greyhounds to the exclusion of all other animals for more than 30 years and says skulduggery is not confined to one code or the other: 'At an NGRC track the vet is there to make the public believe that the dogs are all fit to run. Several vets over the years have been dismissed by a track for refusing to pass a dog fit, myself included. Those who are doing the job are hoping that, if they do withdraw a dog, the management and trainer will agree that it was unfit to run.'

Jarvis Astaire and the NGRC reject this charge and point out that every race meeting will have reserve dogs available, so there is no need to pass an unfit dog to race. But whatever allegations each side lobs at the other, the central factor that ties the two codes together is the greyhound.

Every year 10,000 new greyhounds are registered to race at NGRC tracks. There is roughly the same number of dogs coming onto the independent scene. But the codes do not compete for the same dogs. Independent racing is a lower grade, as most dogs are past their peak by the time they get to race on them. Many of them are former NGRC animals.

On average a greyhound's lifespan is around 15 years; it is the tragedy of the greyhound that it is past its peak by the time it is 4. It spends over two-thirds of its life retired. But the demand for racing dogs is such that it is one of the most numerous dogs in the UK. The result is there are an awful lot of greyhounds aged three and a half upwards looking for a home. The independent track helps take up some of the slack because the racing is less physically demanding and a dog can keep going until it is six, or in some cases even older. The independent circuits then are essentially second-hand dog markets. Without them thousands more would end up in council pounds or worse.

The NGRC currently spends £150,000 rehoming retired racers but Floyd Hamplet, who edits the *Greyhound Star* magazine, believes that independent tracks deserve to receive some of the fund because of their role in extending a dog's racing life and then the effort put into rehoming after that. 'The independent tracks effectively take away the dogs that are no longer suitable for the NGRC tracks,' explains Hamplet. 'Now ultimately these animals need homes. Presently the people who take these dogs on and race them are given no encouragement whatsoever to keep them when their racing career is finally over.'

While he was more than forthright about the iniquities of the independent scene when it came to the integrity of betting, Jarvis Astaire was less convincing in dismissing the secondary role of the tracks concerning animal welfare, limiting himself to a simple comment: 'I have no evidence of that.'

Astaire, and promoters of his ilk, have no interest in seeing good in the independent scene. To do so would be to admit it has some call on the fund. They genuinely fear that if cash from the fund found its way to the independent tracks it would disappear with little to show in terms of solid improvement to the tracks or for the greyhounds that race there.

Nonetheless, John Curran is clear in his mind what will happen if tracks like his own do not get help and soon. 'We can't survive unless we improve the prize money, unless we can provide help in terms of welfare towards the animals we are retiring. We are going to be slowly starved of owners and ultimately all the tracks will go. The day is coming nearer. It is not a choice I want to make but we may have to join the NGRC system. I would not want to make that choice because I would want dog owners to have the option of which culture they race their dogs.'

Spring 2001
Click on Kinsleydogs.co.uk. Up comes the web page. 'Dog racing for all the family' reads the page banner. The boast, down the side of the location map, reads: 'Kinsley – the newest NGRC track in Britain.' The cream of independent racing no more, John Curran bit the bullet in January 2000. But, he insists, it was no sellout: 'At the end of the day the NGRC is just a club. I was able to negotiate away some of the restrictions that were most offensive to my racers. The dogs need only be locked away for vet and drug checks for 15 minutes after the race, so the owners are still close to them and, I am pleased to say, my regular owners are still bringing their dogs here.'

Treating the independents as part of the same industry has been made a little easier anyway. In the last three years around a dozen 'indies' have closed. The remaining 20 or so, in terms of facilities and patronage, differ little from the smaller NGRC tracks anyway, making crossing the divide less significant.

The chances are, soon there will be no difference between the two. The NGRC and independent are, de facto, likely to be redefined simply as smaller or larger tracks, the key difference being between those tracks that host daytime BAGS meetings and those, like Kinsley, that maintain their traditional thrice-weekly evening meetings. In other words, those that run principally to serve the betting industry, and those that race for the sake of the enthusiast and owner.

One of the strongest arguments for the independents was the secondary welfare role they were perceived to perform by giving private owners an opportunity to race dogs and thus look after them well past their prime. The new funding from rights sales is expected to bring in £38 million instead of just £5 million, as is the current arrangement with the voluntary contribution from the bookies. A million pounds is to be spent homing retired racers. This is a significant increase from the £150,000 the NGRC spent three years ago on dog welfare.

It has been agreed that some of the bookies' fund must find its way to all sectors of the industry and that one way of doing this would be to improve prize money at all tracks. The winner will in future receive a minimum £200 (up from an average of £60), meaning the amateur owner now has a bigger incentive to race and home dogs. All this means that dog racing is likely to become a swisher experience. With this kind of money knocking about we can expect to see an improvement of facilities across the board, also better medical care, more extensive drugs testing and other measures to ensure the integrity of races.

John Curran now has great faith in the proposals which for the moment are contained in a strategy document called the *Future Strategy for Greyhound Racing*. It has yet to be finally ratified by government, the British Greyhound Racing Board and the betting industry. Given the tendency for squabbles to break out wherever there is a large pot of money, one must remain sceptical that the ideal future glimpsed by the likes of John Curran will actually come to pass. We will be watching with interest.

CHAPTER SEVENTEEN

On Your Marks. Get Set. Stay!
The Rule Which Stops Our Promising Athletes Competing Where They Want

Every month ambitious athletes apply to move clubs. But before they can they are forced to apply to a remote body of officials that has the power to ban them from competing for nine months. Who is enforcing this archaic rule? How are they getting away with it? And what is the difference between the terms 'support' and 'not oppose'?

It's not only freezing cold, it's windy, wet and grey – generally not the sort of day to wear very little and run around a muddy park in the middle of Nottinghamshire. The runners here, slowly turning an alarming colour of blue in the sub-zero temperatures, are competing in the National Cross-Country Relay Championships in Mansfield, where glory comes in the form of points for their clubs as opposed to medals, bouquets and fat cheques.

Sensibly wrapped up against the biting wind is Mike Downs, manager of the Bristol Women's team and a 40-year veteran of athletics in Britain. Downs is doing what he does best, busily organizing, counselling and advising the athletes he has brought up from the South-West this morning. He is well known to the rule makers of the sport as well as the letters editors of the athletics press, because in his view the sport is being spoilt by a regulation he thinks should have been scrubbed from the books years ago, and the blazers who enforce it.

'We had one girl who came to us from Peterborough,' he explains. 'She was a cross-country international and for the purposes of loyalty she decided to stay with her own club. But then because her club did not enter the big cross-country and road events, and because of the travelling, she wanted to join Bristol. As a result of this she was actually banned from competing for a total of eight months.'

The object of Mike Downs's ire is an ancient regulation called the First Claims rule. It has been around as long the sport itself and was intended in the sport's history to stop bigger clubs poaching athletes from smaller ones. It is governed by the six regional athletics associations in the United Kingdom: the South, the Midlands and the North in England, plus Wales, Scotland and Northern Ireland. Each has its own Hardship Committee which rules on the individual cases that are put before it. They each have the power, as the Midland committee did in the case of the Bristol runner, to ban an athlete from competing for up to nine months.

In the shadow of the impressive and imposing Dartford Bridge, Steve Clarke lives with his wife, Kerrie. They are both good, keen club runners. In 1999 Steve decided he wanted to leave the club he was with, Dartford, and improve his standard of competition. He joined Belgrave Harriers in south London, one of the best-known clubs in the country. He informed the South of England Hardship Committee as he was required to do by the First Claims rules.

'When I sent up my resignation form,' he says, 'I also sent a detailed letter explaining my reasons, that I hadn't been afforded the opportunities I would have wanted. I then got a letter back telling me I had got a nine-month ban which I challenged immediately. I was aware that the Hardship Committee arbitrate on all moves and that possibly I could get a nine-month ban. But it was a clear cut case: Dartford was happy for me to leave, Belgrave wanted me and I had made an informed decision to move. I wasn't coaxed into the move, it was my own decision and it was a cut-and-dried case. Yet the committee, in their infinite wisdom, decided that the ban, which was of benefit to nobody, was mandatory, and I had to serve it.'

At that time Kerrie had also decided to leave her club, Cambridge Harriers. Unlike Steve, her club had opposed her move, meaning that she should have received a longer ban than Steve; but in a comprehensive defeat for the laws of logic, she only received a three-month ban.

'I wrote Kerrie's application and my own and we received the results on the very same day,' Steve remembers. 'I opened Kerrie's first and saw she had only got three months and I was reasonably satisfied. Then I opened mine and my jaw just hit the ground, I could not believe it. I had written the same letter for both of us!'

The rule which so baffles Mike Downs and Steve Clarke and countless other athletes and coaches is buried as deep in the athletics rule book as it is in history:

Rule 4 paragraph 8: Athletes who resign membership of a club are not eligible to represent their next claim club in any Open Team Competition until the first day of the month preceding the expiration of the nine months from the date of receipt of notice of resignation.

Simply, if you want to run, throw or jump for a new team you can't until we say you can!

The upholders of the First Claims rule meet once a month to consider all applications to move; they then decide on any punishment they see fit. There is very little comeback for an aggrieved athlete apart from an appeal, which many don't bother with. Why would they when it is heard by the same people who handed out the ban in the first place?

The secretary of the South of England Athletics Association (SEAA) committee is Fred Wooding, who has spent 40 years in the sport as competitor, coach and administrator. Naturally, he is a staunch defender of the regulation he and his committee enforce each month. 'People are becoming more fickle daily, they feel that everything should be laid down for them,' he explains in his front room, which doubles up as his office at his house in Bedford. 'It's becoming a very difficult age to live in in many respects, not just in athletics. People feel that today it would be right if they changed clubs immediately without having given any thought to the system. Today they would compete for one club, and if they had it their way tomorrow, or even this afternoon, compete for another club, and tomorrow for yet another club. The complete club system and the league system would all fall down. You must have rules, and every sport has its rules. Our rules may be different to other sports, but nevertheless every sport has its rules as to how and when and how often they can compete.'

Steve Clarke says he agrees that his sport, like any sport, needs rules – just not this particular one: 'I would accept that there has to be a framework of sorts where rules prevent chaos. If you did have the case where athletes can walk away from clubs as they want to, you then have to make sure that people aren't leaving sinking ships to join the clubs who win all the 'in' trophies. There has to be a framework where it's to the mutual benefit of both parties. But they still impose a ban. It is ridiculous and there is no justification of it whatsoever, its an outdated rule book and the people who make the decisions are obviously not informed.'

Clarke was told that along with his letter of resignation he should send the Hardship Committee any supporting material, which he did. 'I sent all the evidence I had to the committee, on the understanding that it would constitute Dartford supporting the move. But the SEAA said, while Dartford didn't oppose the move, it didn't say they automatically supported it. So I then had to go back to Dartford and ask them for a letter of support, which they were only too pleased to give me, but that delayed the process and therefore my ban was delayed.'

This is the crux of the controversy, and gives Mike Downs of Bristol his biggest headache: 'Our biggest beef here in Bristol is that why, if neither club objects to the athlete moving, does it have to go through any committee? Is it really the business of a faceless group of people who sit round a table when really we are talking about a basic human right and a freedom of choice?'

But, as Steve Clarke found out, Dartford only stated they 'didn't oppose' him moving to Belgrave, which isn't good enough for the Hardship Committee. Now, if they had said that they 'supported' his move, that would have been a different matter.

On The Line put Mike Downs's point to SEAA Hardship Committee secretary, Fred Wooding.

FW: The reason for getting involved is the rules, and so we know which athlete is competing for which club.

OTL: But why should you ban them?

FW: Hold on, I didn't say we were going to ban them. If a club in the South of England writes and says, "We support this move, we never ever give a ban of any sort."

OTL: A letter of support is a letter of support, isn't it?

FW: No ... what people may think is a letter of *support* may mean we do not *oppose* the move 'we do not oppose' in this sport is generally believed to mean, say, we have no reason to oppose this change.

OTL: Surely that's good enough?

FW: No, no, no, no, it is not good enough. The rules of the sport say if you have a good reason to change clubs, if you feel that the club does not oppose it, is the club willing to write a letter saying, "we support it," and if the club say 'not oppose' and 'support' mean the same thing, then there is not a problem.

OTL: We are just into semantics here, aren't we?

FW: No, no, no, no! We are not. The whole rule book of athletics is very carefully worded, and 'support' and 'oppose' are not the same. It is the same when you get into the rule book and 'should' and 'must' and 'might' and 'may' are very carefully chosen words and they mean exactly what they say. It isn't semantics at all.

As clear as the mud in Mansfield. It seems that there is an obvious difference in athletics between 'support' and 'not oppose' as there is between 'semantics' and 'carefully chosen words'. Either way, as Steve Clarke pounded the Kent streets on his nightly training run, he knew that whichever phrases were used, he couldn't run competitively for his new club.

'I was simply not prepared to accept that even without a

letter of support and the fact that Dartford were not able to field teams, the Hardship Committee were not prepared to clear me immediately. I rang some other people on the committee and asked them to justify the decision, and it was at this stage that I said that in the absence of any contract between myself and Dartford, you have no legal bind on myself as a human being and who I can and can't run for. I was quite prepared to take legal action, and a series of letters flowed between myself and the committee. About a month later I got the ban halved, so basically I was cleared from immediate effect; but four months had passed which I had lost.'

Before a smattering of rank and file administrators and coaches on a rainy night in Preston, chief executive of UK Athletics, David Moorcroft, sets out his vision for the future of the sport. He says he never suffered at the hands of the Hardship Committee as he stayed with his club, Coventry Godiva, all his career. Part of his vision is that the rule must go: 'It's a rule that had all the right intentions and was put in place a number of years ago when the sport was amateur to protect the smaller clubs from poaching by the bigger clubs and to make it not that easy for people to change clubs at will. I think the principle is still right, that clubs take in people from a young age, free of charge, develop them and put coaching resources in place. It is frustrating for them when a bigger club comes along and pinches athletes. But on the other hand, it is a free world and people are free to choose and people change schools, jobs, universities, and it is no different in sport, and there are ways we can do it and make sure everybody wins.'

Moorcroft has won many admirers for the way he rescued the sport from bankruptcy, and his diplomatic skills have been well used. They will need to be again if everyone is to be kept happy in this case. 'I do think the right way forward is to present a number of possibilities,' he concedes, 'and then debate those fully within the sport and then be brave enough to go with whatever the outcome is. It is just an element of natural justice and fairness and individual choice, and if an individual wants to change club, my personal belief is that they should be able to do that. Not everybody will be pleased but my belief is that if we stay as we are that people will challenge the rule and it will be forced to be changed.'

When David Moorcroft talks of the rule being changed with force, he means, of course, an athlete being hit with a ban for nine months taking it to court, just as Steve Clarke nearly did.

Whether Rule 4 could be challenged like Bosman in football is debatable, but sports lawyer Nick Bitel, who represented Dougie Walker in his drugs case, says that any enterprising athlete who took this to court would have a fair chance of overturning it. 'I think there are enough options and it is just a matter of finding the right case,' he explains. 'Just as Bosman was a very hard set of facts and that led to a change of procedures, you will come up with a very similar case in athletics and this will lead to a challenge.'

UK Athletics is still recovering from the legal bills its predecessor, the British Athletics Federation, was faced with in its case with Diane Modhal. Mindful of this, Bitel, who is also the chief executive of the London Marathon, thinks the sport should be very careful and look to reform the rule book itself: 'The last thing athletics needs is to be saddled with loads of legal bills; that's why it collapsed last time. I would have hoped they would have learned their lesson and they would want to change now without having to pay thousands of pounds in lawyers' fees. This is going to have to come from the grassroots and you do get one or two officials speaking out, and generally this is on its last legs. It's a question of: Are the AAAs going to lead this or be forced into change?'

David Moorcroft agrees: 'I am not too sure what the legal position is but they are amateur athletes and there are no contracts, so there should be no trade element to it. If an individual wants to change club, my personal belief is that they should be able to do that and I think that they should be able to do that once or twice a year and, as I say, try and give them options to try and remain in the club that has nurtured them.'

A transfer window is one option open to the sport. In Mike Downs's eyes, anything, frankly, is better than the status quo. His club, Bristol, also looked at the possibility of a legal challenge, but he hopes that David Moorcroft and the governing body will impose its authority before it gets to that.

'I am very optimistic about UK Athletics,' he admits, 'but there does seem to be a danger in trying to do everything right by everyone and things get delayed. There is a bit of procrastination and they need to be a bit proactive in situations like this. While people are talking about this we know that there are loads of young athletes suffering and having to sit out these bans when they would like to be running for a team. After all, there is a huge drain, every year there are less people competing in athletics – we are losing people partly to other sports, other interests. We can't afford this situation where we are literally discouraging people.'

Bristol comes under the authority of the Midland Counties Athletic Association (MCAA). Of England's three Hardship Committees only the South of England's Fred Wooding agreed to be interviewed. The head of the MCAA didn't even return *On The Line*'s call.

Back in Mansfield, Simon Keen has travelled with his athletes for the cross-country relay championships. He's the manager of Shaftesbury Barnet AC and this weekend he has had to leave one athlete behind, thanks to the First Claims rule. 'We have recently had an experience,' he says, bristling with anger, 'where we had a guy who was second in the English National Cross-Country Championships last year, he has left his home town club which he had stayed loyal to for years. They cannot get teams together, that is the primary reason he has left. He also moved away from Bracknell to Bath. The bad news for him is that he is eligible for us a couple of days after the National Cross-Country and he shouldn't have got any ban at all.'

The athlete, Chris Bolt, heard he had received a ban just a couple of days before the Mansfield event. Inconsistency in the decisions of the Hardship Committee just make matters worse for Keen: 'I am also very upset that another athlete has left us to go to another club and has got no ban at all. Most of the athletes that come to us seem to get nine months, I personally think that we get penalized because we are a bigger club and I think that's wrong. I am extremely angry and I wonder, why do we bother? An athlete leaves us and goes to another club, they don't get a ban, and coming the other way they do get a ban! Maybe we are a better club and maybe that's why we suffer, but it's not fair on the athletes, and at the end of the day the rules are supposed to be there for the athletes, and I personally do not think that it has been done fairly.'

Mike Downs agrees: 'If only they would interpret the rules universally it would really help. We have had so many cases in the last couple of years where we have found out about athletes from other clubs who have had bans of one, two or three months and they are fulfilling the same criteria as us and ours were banned for up to nine months.'

Naturally, Fred Wooding rejects the accusations that he or his fellow committees around the country are inconsistent: 'The logic is what is written on the forms,' he says doggedly. 'If one athlete's form gave a better reason for the person to change clubs then the committee would see it as a better reason and give a ban. If you are suggesting to me that we separate people and have the sheep and the goats or the have and have nots then what I am saying to you is, if two forms arrive saying the same thing, I assure you that they have the same treatment.'

Athletes hate it, coaches hate it, even the national body feels much the same, but it is perpetuated by the middle men. One popular idea would be to cut out the regional bodies altogether, which would cut out a layer of bureaucracy from the sport, and adopt a method of control like the one that Scotland successfully operates unilaterally. This is David Moorcroft's preferred option.

'I wouldn't defend the rule, because it should change. What I would say is that the rule is there for the best possible reasons and it has kept a degree of control as there is a danger that if the rule is scrapped completely there could be chaos, absolute bedlam with people moving regularly for possibly the wrong reasons. But I think there is a way round it: if they choose to remain a member of that club and stay with that club for the rest of their lives and compete for that club in the league, plus they can compete for a national league club so they have two clubs. It's done in Scotland and it's a way of getting the best of both worlds and each club gets the reflected glory when an athlete does well at the Olympic Games or in a national competition.'

All of the six Hardship Committees meet at least once a year to discuss any concerns, including whether there should be any changes to the rules. Fred Wooding claims that he and his fellow members all want the rules brought up to date. Also on that committee is Richard Jenkins of Welsh Athletics. He is surprised, to say the least, to hear that the annual meetings that he attends are hotbeds of athletics radicalism.

'I think the ruling itself isn't beneficial to athletics,' he says, echoing Mike Downs and Simon Keen. 'I have seen too many athletes drop out at a younger age group. If you start putting bans on athletes they are going to turn their back on the sport. It could be that some of the people who rule on First Claims, they have been ... Should I say this?' He pauses, choosing his words carefully, 'They are fossils in a way – they are so long in that position they have lost their view of what the sport is about.'

Jenkins thinks the ruling is too harsh and told the first meeting he attended how it is interpreted in Wales. 'I dropped a bombshell there as we were all asked how we apply the rulings. The Southern Counties said they apply the nine months rigidly, the Midland Counties apply it with discretion and then I come up and say, "Well, the Welsh area has a maximum of three months".' He laughs again, recalling the reaction this received: 'There were a few raised eyebrows. To be honest, some of the aspects of the sport are in the dark ages and we have to drag it through to the twenty-first century and remember that we are here for the benefit of the athletes. And I don't believe the athletes are getting the benefits from the sport they should have.'

Inconsistency across the country blights one Midlands area club in particular. The Harvey Haddon Stadium in the centre of a Nottingham housing estate is home to the Notts Athletics Club. Its chief executive, Ian Jack, reckons his club suffers because it is treated more harshly than some of its near neighbours. 'Each committee is trying to interpret guidelines as best as they can.

Any group of people are going to interpret guidelines differently. Where we suffer is that we are on the Nottinghamshire –Derbyshire border. Derbyshire comes under the North, we come under the Midlands. There are certainly cases where athletes have to try and second-guess what each committee is going to do. They listen to rumours to find out what has been done in the past and try and guess what is better for them, whether it is better to go to a Derbyshire club or Nottinghamshire club. Derby is ten miles up the road from Nottingham but that's far enough to cross the border from the Midlands region to the North and a more lenient application of the rules.

'Athletes moving to the area make their decision based on whether they may get away with a suspension for a month or a full nine months, and at the end of the day, if they are being forced to go to a club that is not really best for them, they may regret it and change again.'

Fred Wooding disagrees that one Hardship Committee is more lenient than another: 'I find it very strange that people should say that the North is liberal and the South is harsh because the North was harsh until very recently and now we work with the same guidelines. I am frequently in touch with the North and we two committees believe that we are working exactly the same. The reason we meet is to try and sing from the same hymn sheet, so we are all trying to do it the same way and if we find we are working differently we try and arrange the most liberal interpretation as to what we should be doing rather than the harshest. Harshness is not in our directory, we are not asked to be harsh, we are always asked to be liberal, but we are asked to maintain the system.'

Inconsistency witnessed by clubs but invisible to Mr Wooding is recognized by David Moorcroft: 'This is one of the most unfair elements of it, and people can quite rightly point to it and if there is a lack of consistency then that cannot be tolerated, hence changing to a more logical way.'

But if David Moorcroft is to drag this rule up to date, the main obstacle he will face could be the structure of the sport itself, and it could be two or more years before it is passed. He outlined the tortuous route it would have to take: 'It will go to congress as an issue, and then be voted on in workshops, and then it will take time to go through a consultation period and that goes on to the Track and Field support team and then the UK board and then a decision will be made. We wouldn't make that decision without massive consultation and the belief that we had got the will of the sport. The rule does not have to be changed overnight, it can be phased in.' But he couldn't make any changes without the support of rank and file members: the old guard from the counties and regions, the fossils that Richard Jenkins refers to.

Fred Wooding refuses to be seen as a fossil. He insists that if there is a campaign for change he and his Hardship Committee comrades will be at the front of it and in his opinion any resistance will come from the athletes: 'I could imagine it might be from those who think the rules are not going soft enough and not being liberal enough. You have to remember there is only a degree of liberality that you can use in it. There must be a system which will work, who you can define who you compete for – and you cannot keep hopping from club to club, I firmly believe. So I believe what I am doing is the best for athletes. I believe that when we ban a person from team competition for nine months it is in the interest of the sport; it may not be in the interest of the individual but the *sport* that there should be such a rule.'

There does seem to be a consensus that the First Claims rule is out of date; it is maintained by well-meaning committees who impose rules on athletes who just want to compete for the club of their choice. Athletics has a new governing body and is moving on, but almost every week in the athletics press the sport is reminded of its history, with the publication of the names of more and more athletes barred from competing by the arbitrary and incongruous rules imposed by the Hardship Committees. Steve Clarke challenged his ban and is now back running for Belgrave Harriers. If there is one good thing to come out of this whole episode for him, it's that he now clearly knows the answer to the question, 'What's the difference between "support" and "not oppose"?'

CHAPTER EIGHTEEN

Fatal Attraction
How Hockey Was Wrong-footed by Its Love Affair With Plastic Grass

Hockey's love affair with artificial pitches destroyed the game's tradi-
tional infrastructure in the 1970s. Now, after 30 years of surviving
plastic, the rulers of one of the more impoverished sports in Britain are
demanding that clubs invest in an even more prohibitively expensive
surface.

Newsagents generally sell the news, they don't make it. But if
rules are there to be broken, Imran Sherwani, a paper seller from
Stoke, did just that with aplomb when he scored twice in Great
Britain's 3–1 gold-medal-winning performance against Germany
at the Seoul Olympics in 1988. For a brief period in the history
of the game, hockey, like Sherwani, became news.

Along with Sherwani were Sean Kerly, Richard Garcia and
Jonathan Potter, names that briefly jostled with Linekar, Carling
or Christie on our back pages. Basking in its newfound glory, the
sport believed the good times had come to stay.

The timing, it seemed, could not have been more fortu-
itous. Hockey's inaugural national league was due to begin weeks
after the Seoul Olympics finished and one could not have asked
for a bigger peg to hang that on than an Olympic gold. There
were other more tangible spin-offs. 'Our international success at
Seoul brought in enough money to help run the league for the
first few years,' remembers Dave Alcock, chairman of the English
National Hockey League.

But the boom did not last, despite the new league and the
gold medal; by the middle of the 1990s the sport could not even
find a sponsor. When the great TV battle for sports rights broke
out in the wake of football's Premier League agreement, hockey

could not get a look-in. Sky TV, with three 24-hour sports channels to fill, preferred to screen truck racing or aerobics 'Australian'
style, rather than hockey. The English Hockey Association (EHA)
on one occasion even offered to pay Sky to televise tournaments.
At the BBC, the sports department, reeling from the loss of
cricket, Grand Prix racing and Premier League football, chose to
go with indoor bowls or darts rather than hockey. Why?

Mike Lewis, sports rights executive at the BBC, when asked
about hockey, sighed and said, 'Hockey is a wonderful sport but
its main trouble is people just do not care, at least not in sufficient numbers, to sit down and watch it on TV. Part of the problem is that players or the teams have no profile, so there is
nothing for the public to latch onto.' The implication is that,
hockey will not be appearing on a TV set near you any time soon.
As you might imagine, the sport does not take kindly to this stun-
ning level of indifference. Hockey folk moan about it and blame
the English Hockey Association. The EHA blames TV for not
seeing the attraction. In reality, hockey probably has no one to
blame but itself for this predicament.

Despite the launch of the new league in the wake of all the
attention surrounding Seoul, the roots of the game were in trouble and had been for some time. In the 1960s there had been
over 4,000 clubs but by 1988 this was down to just over 2,000.
Those clubs that survived typically turned out only two or three
teams on a weekend rather than the half dozen or more that they
used to field.

For a sport that had almost no profile in school, outside the
Grammar and public schools, this was a particular disaster.
Hockey has never had the media coverage of cricket and rugby,
but if nothing else its comprehensive network of clubs ensured
that it was at least a visible sport at grass roots level. Now, however, even though compared to many team sports plenty of
people played it, hockey was disappearing from view in villages
and towns all over the UK. The reason for this vanishing act was
the expensive addiction that the sport first acquired in the 1970s
and that changed everything about hockey and its organization,
both in Britain and abroad – forever.

As the motorway traffic thunders down the M6 from the north, experienced motorists are likely to be contemplating a gamble when they approach junction 12: 'Do I come off and take the A5 to the north and east of Birmingham, or risk the inevitable con-jestion that is a feature of the motorway system through the West Midlands?' What makes this a gamble is that junction 12 is on a bend so you can't actually see if you are looking at an hour's bumper-to-bumper grind through England's second city until you have passed up the A5 option and it is too late.

Frequent travellers in these parts will know this dilemma well. What they might not notice, as they escape the motorway and head towards the first sequence of roundabouts on the A5 to Tamworth and beyond, is a relatively new pitched roof poking above a clump of trees. It is set back from the road on the left, just before you reach the Cannock truck stop. This innocuous looking building is in fact Cannock Hockey clubhouse, the heart of one of Britain's most consistently successful hockey clubs in recent years. So successful that in January 2001 a hockey website posed the question: 'Are Cannock hockey's Manchester United?' It is not just that Cannock have made light work of the fixture list in recent years, they also draw their first XI from all over the country and their facilities are second to none.

Local teacher Paul Singh is club chairman. He wanders around to the back of the clubhouse and looks out onto a well-maintained field: 'That was where our first team pitch used to be. It is the outfield to the cricket square now. As grass pitches went, it was a good one because we had a groundsman that was pre-pared to work at it. But some of the away pitches we played on were terrible.'

It is some years since Cannock played here on the grass. In the warm, convivial atmosphere of the clubhouse bar the TV is tuned to Sky Sports, where excitable presenters and famous former footballers are digesting the scores as the final whistle blows on soccer grounds around the nation. But outside the Cannock clubhouse the action is far from finished. The club's overworked pitch is preparing to stage its fifth match of the day. 'The trouble with grass,' continues Paul Singh, 'was when it was dry you could play reasonable hockey on it but under wet conditions, and particularly if the pitch had not been cared for, it was a great leveller. The quality players found it very difficult.'

But help was at hand. A product, originally developed for the NFL [National Football League] the United States, finally arrived in Britain in the early 1970s. Its impact was to be profound. Although essentially only a plastic carpet, it made junkies out of hockey players. No longer would 'rain stop play', no more would players hack around trying to dig the ball out of a divot hole, there would be no more squelching around in mud and there was less risk of a ball rising up on an uneven surface to smack you in the face or dent your shins. And in addition to this it made you think you were a much better player than you had ever believed!

There was one problem. These plastic pitches were not cheap. At the equivalent of £200,000 each, few hockey clubs could afford one. But such was the draw of playing on so seductive a surface that teams were prepared to abandon their old grass pitches and travel great distances in search of the artificial ones. 'We watched in admiration,' recalls Paul Singh, 'as they went down around the country. We were fortunate in that the local sports centre put one down and so we had access to one nearby.'

But not everyone had one nearby. When Great Britain pulled off its famous victory in Seoul it was a triumph that was just as likely to be the subject of animated discussion on the motorway as in a clubhouse. By 1988 hockey was literally a sport on the move. Clubhouses became little more than meeting points from where teams set off on drives of up to an hour or more, in search of the nearest artificial pitch.

'When we open our doors at midday there are dribs and drabs of people coming in throughout the day,' says the Doncaster club chairman, Dave Miller. 'Gone are the days when at five in the evening the whole place came alive when four teams suddenly appeared with their opposition and crowded out the bar.'

Local authority or university facilities became 'home' to dozens of clubs that for decades previously had been living in and recruiting from their own local communities. Now the first games 'pushed off' mid morning and the clatter of sticks and echoing shouts and screams of players continued until well after dark, typically witnessed only by the next teams to play.

Although almost any hockey player would choose an artificial pitch over a grass one, it did not mean that there were no complaints. The early versions, as anyone who has played football, hockey or any sport on one can testify, left nasty friction burns. Later generations of pitches were set in sand, the so-called sand-based surfaces. These did not burn as badly but they certainly grazed and cut. 'If you play sport on sand it is very abrasive,' explains Graham Griffith, manager of Beeston Hockey Club. 'It cuts you here, there and everywhere. The changing room after a good national league game almost resembles a boxer's dressing room.'

But pure plastic or sand-based, the cost was more or less the same. In 1990, however, just as surviving hockey clubs had acquired a sand-based pitch, had plans for one, or at least relatively easy access to one, up popped technology again. Once more it was a surface that had originated in the United States; once more it was a surface that almost no hockey player could resist. It was the Rolls-Royce of playing surfaces – the water-base pitch. As smooth as snooker cloth to the touch but a little thicker and drenched in water, it hurts no more than falling on any ground would. It does not cut or graze and, importantly, from a hockey player's point of view, the ball rolls true.

Thanks to the lottery, Cannock Hockey Club is in the process of acquiring one. 'The skill level is far better,' says Paul Singh, taking me around a sand-base pitch and enjoying a breather before matches. 'On here you can still get an uneven bounce, you can see places where the sand has gathered; On water-base you don't get any of that, the ball runs true and allows a much more technically advanced game, although I believe any hockey player's game will improve on such a surface.'

As do the International Hockey Federation, who adopted the water-base pitch as its official playing surface in 1990. They declared ten years ago that in the future all major international competition would have to be played on water-base pitches, a move that undoubtedly benefited a few of the richer hockey-playing nations, where the sport was both mature and well supported, but one which was to hit the international ambitions of many third world hockey-playing countries. In the UK it led to a second round of upheaval at club level that could see the sport slip in to long-term decline.

The problem is the same as with the last artificial pitches, only more so. They are very expensive. The average water-base will set you back £500,000 and they only last ten years. So having bought one, a club – which in this country takes very little money at the gate, has little or no sponsorship and no cash from TV rights to distribute – must then set aside £50,000 every year to buy a replacement.

At a time when the last thing hockey in the UK needed was the creation of another pitch elite that is exactly what the English Hockey Association ordered. Days before he left the EHA for a more exalted position in sports administration in Scotland, Nigel Holl was dispatched by the EHA to explain to *On The Line* why it was that from September 2000 all Premier League clubs, must play on water-base pitches. 'It is a challenge, a huge challenge to the game,' said Nigel, spinning for all his worth, 'but it is a challenge to aim for. When we have discussed it with the clubs, that is clearly the direction that they want to go. They can see the benefits in terms of play and in terms of supporting the top level of the game.'

Now, most people would agree that achieving world peace or eradicating hunger are worthy aims, but no government would be foolish enough to put a date on it. It is perhaps an extreme and tasteless analogy but, in hockey terms, the task of converting to water-base inside two and a half years was just as ludicrous an idea.

Out in 'clubland' some viewed the edict with horror. Stourport Hockey Club in the West Midlands had contributed two members to the victorious Seoul squad, but in 1998 they were coming back from a spell in the wilderness and vying for promotion to the national league's first division. 'We have statistics,' said chairman Alistair McIntrye, 'showing that it has taken something like 20 years to shift from grass to synthetic surface. So trying to move from synthetic surfaces to water-base in three years is a silly position to put hockey in.'

When the national league launched in 1988 it was stipulated that league matches had to be played on artificial turf. Stourport did not have this at the time and so on match days, like dozens of other clubs, they picked up their sticks and went on the road. 'We had to travel to Olton, near Birmingham,' recalls Alistair. 'That's about a 50-mile round trip. More recently we made an arrangement with a school the other side of Kidderminster, which is a ten-mile round trip. The rest of the club has travelled out to Reddish or Worcester, so you could say that in the 1990s we were a nomadic club.'

Like dozens of other hockey clubs up and down the land, Stourport longed to return home and put an end to the motorway madness. With the launch of the National Lottery, the means to do so came within their grasp. In all, the National Lottery pumped £58 million into hockey facilities in the first six years of its life, and dozens of clubs, like Stourport, were able to acquire a home-based artificial turf as a result of this windfall. It seemed that all over the UK hockey was finally coming home. But now that the water-base is to be compulsory in the first division, clubs within a shout of top-class hockey have a decision to make.

'We must now consider very seriously if we win promotion whether to refuse it or not,' says Steve Taylor, a club director. 'We have to face facts – it will be years before we could afford a water-base pitch and having finally got ourselves a home base again I am not sure if there will be the appetite to go on the road again.'

Like Stourport, Doncaster Hockey Club have recently taken advantage of lottery funds and laid down an artificial pitch. Unlike Stourport, they would not refuse promotion, but they are as baffled as everyone else by the EHA timetable. Club chairman Dave Miller said: 'This water-base timetable is going to create enormous problems for clubs like Doncaster who are not near a big conurbation, which is where all the water-base pitches are presently. I can't understand the rush.'

The 'rush' is a result of a policy gamble that sprang from a clear view by the EHA that the purpose of hockey in this country is ultimately to serve Great Britain's ambitions on the international scene. Great Britain's women had managed a bronze at Barcelona but the men missed out. In a bid to achieve Olympic glory in Sydney, they recruited two Australians, Chris Spice as performance director and Barry Dancer as national coach.

Both Spice and Dancer came from a culture where elite programmes were mature and based around state academies and so-called 'Super Clubs'. There was no such culture on the UK hockey scene. The strength of the sport in the UK lay in the depth of its club structure. Certainly Chris Spice seemed to have little appreciation of this when he effectively put a half-million-pound entry fee on hockey's top flight by demanding all games be played on the new water-base surface.

The EHA backed this approach because it was their interpretation of the politics of the lottery that international success would be richly rewarded with funds. These in turn could be invested in raising the profile of the sport, speeding up its facilities strategy – and international success would be more likely if our top players were playing regularly on water-base pitches.

'Partly we are in a rush,' explained Nigel Holl, 'because of some of the very challenging targets agreed with the lottery sports fund for our international performance. Let us not pretend otherwise, the lottery money comes in to win medals and we have to win those medals and we have to win them on a timetable that is laid out.'

And what a timetable. In return for lottery cash English hockey pledged to win a medal at Sydney (although they later extended this to Athens 2004) and to remain in the top six in the world. Not even Manchester United with all the dominance they enjoy in domestic football would mortgage their future in such terms.

At the time, the national league's chairman, Dave Alcock, told *On The Line*, 'If we do not win any medals I can see a half-baked strategy with many facilities not built and no money to conclude the development of these strategies and we will be back at square one, having to come up with a new strategy.'

The erratic performance, particularly of the men's team, in the run-up to Sydney was not a good omen. Both the men's and women's campaigns got off to poor starts and did not get much better. Both failed to get through the league stage and were soon out of the medals race – the women finished eighth, the men sixth. With Barry Dancer back in Australia and Chris Spice jumping ship to take up the post of performance director for Rugby Union, it is hard to argue that the sport is in better shape than when they arrived.

The conditions for lottery largesse – Olympic medal and sixth-place world ranking – had been volunteered by the EHA rather than imposed by the Sports Council. Although, as current EHA boss, Mike Hamilton, puts it, 'They have asked some pretty tough questions', there is no chance of the Sports Council pulling the plug on supporting the game, despite talk of world-class support being about 'money for medals'.

However, the sport's facility strategy still finds itself in a bit of a pickle. The dash for water-base was a central element of the strategy presented to the lottery by the EHA. This meant that other hockey clubs up and down the land, that had made lottery applications for artificial turf pitches, found that these were held in abeyance until the EHA application was resolved. It seems that the Sports Council, after taking the EHA to task over the performance at Sydney, has acceded to the request for 20 water-base pitches, although it is unlikely that all will be paid and laid in quite the double-quick time the EHA would like. Eight, at Exeter University, Belle Vue (Manchester), Hightown (near Southport), Beeston (in Nottingham), Cannock, Canterbury and the University of Birmingham (which has plans for two), have the definite go-ahead and should be built soon. But funding for 12 others is pending.

But if the top end of the game will have more water-base pitches to choose from, everyone else, the base upon which the elite rest, is in as much trouble as ever – in fact it is arguably worse off since the 'dash for glory' policies of Chris Spice dominated EHA thinking. The new performance director is Mike Hamilton and he says he is conscious of the need for the EHA to turn its mind to the requirements of the wider hockey family. 'Certainly it is true that the gold medal at Seoul was as a result of a team that sprung from a strong club culture, a culture that existed before the leagues. Perhaps it is time to seek a better balance between the interests of the elite and the more recreationally orientated clubs,' says Hamilton.

Something must be done urgently. Hockey has great difficulty in raising money. By and large it is the players who pay for the game, either by membership subscriptions or by individual sponsorship packages. Many of the people able to donate money to a club are older, probably play for the fifth team or veterans, and joined the game as much for the social aspect as anything else. They do not want to be playing at nine in the morning on a pitch that is miles from home. The fear is that more and more of these players, the bedrock of the game will chuck in their sticks. In the lower reaches it is already happening, much to the alarm of national league chairman, Dave Alcock: 'The social aspect of the game is diminishing and one has to be honest about that. Players are beginning to lose interest in the game. They do not want to have to travel long distances and the emphasis on artificial pitches has added to the drift from our sport.'

Mike McAdam, secretary of the North-West Hockey League, has a story to tell that will be familiar to the hockey-playing community: 'We are losing clubs gradually. A lot of clubs have not got enough players and clubs write to me to say that they can't fulfil their fixtures. Others ask to be relegated so they can avoid travelling. I think it is extremely sad and the EHA should address it very seriously.'

Worse still, at the top of the game a serious geographical divide has appeared. During 2000–01, the very season when Britain was supposed to be basking in another bout of gold-medal glory, there were no teams in the Premier League north of Cannock. If hockey should become a regional sport it would be a disaster from which the game would have difficulty recovering. Perhaps it is too late.

Certainly Dave Alcock offers a bleak analysis: 'Hockey has virtually disappeared from schools in the north of England. As a result, recruiting decent players in the North is very hard indeed. If you aspire to play for Great Britain or England then you want to be playing for one of the top half-dozen teams in the league. With the exception of Cannock in Staffordshire, they are all in the London orbit. Cannock already have a first team with three players who drive down from Merseyside, one from North Wales and one from Chester. I do not think you will see any team in the north of the country in the top league any time soon, if ever.'

National league clubs with water-base pitches provide an irresistable draw to the talented player. This means that local teams will not be able to hold onto squads in sufficient numbers to build themselves up. It is not a level playing field. The introduction of artificial turf sent many clubs to the wall and the advent of water-base has condemned the rest to a second-class experience.

Dave Alcock recalls, 'When Chris Spice first came to the EHA he complained that there was too much bad hockey being played but it is sobering to reflect that the years we think of as the golden age of hockey, the late 1980s, were pre-water-base pitches, pre-multi-million-pound funding from the lottery and pre-national league.'

And this is now hockey's problem. Its principal contribution to culture in this country has been to provide sporting recreation for hundreds of thousands of people week in and week out, yet it has been used as an unsuccessful vehicle to produce a team that competes, unsuccessfully, at world level. Every piece of modern thinking on coaching has been brought to bear in the attempt to bring this about: the best pitches; almost full-time international squads (thanks to the World Class Performance Fund), and a national league with clubs featuring semi-professional players from abroad, usually the southern hemisphere.

Mike Hamilton, it would seem, has inherited a sinking ship. He thinks the sport is a victim of British sporting culture and will probably have difficulty regenerating itself until there is a fundamental overhaul of the way recreational sport is organized in Britain. 'In Holland, Spain or Germany the hockey club is part of a wider sports club to be found in most communities. The cost of laying down an artificial pitch, or indeed any facility, is borne by all sports in the community. Recruitment is easier because multi-sports clubs are well patronized. In Britain there is no way a hockey club with three teams will ever be able to afford a water-base.'

Another difficulty for hockey is that which it craves above all else: recognition in the media. Such recognition is likely to become increasingly elusive the narrower the playing base becomes. One has to consider, had Britain clinched gold in Sydney, the impact given the overall performance of the wider Olympic squad. It would be reasonable to assume that this would have been much less than in Seoul.

Hockey, like all sports, is in a fight for recruits. It has to be able to offer something in this contest and if it cannot offer world domination or TV ratings then it must offer fun. This element has been severely damaged by the artificial pitch, triggering an exodus from the game's roots, taking the clubhouse culture out of the game, thus robbing it of the very reason why many people played hockey in the first place.

Hockey is a wonderful, convivial game played by people of all ages; it has none of the yobbishness or violence associated with football, or the boorishness and aggression sometimes found in rugby. It is simply a great game, fun to play, not so great to watch. Perhaps those who champion amateur sport should champion hockey, and hockey should look to protect and develop what it has rather than focusing on what it has not.

INDEX

Kalmykia 74–6
Kamsky, Gata 83
Karpov, Anatoly 83
Kasparov, Gary 80
Keen, Simon 248
King, Don 18, 21, 25
Kinsley dog track 231–2, 233,
   234, 237, 239
Kirby, Emma 181
Knight, Elizabeth 196
kong sau 161
Krovatin, Gerald 22–3, 24–5
Kushner, Cedric 23, 24, 26

Lamont, Norman 234
Lancashire cricket club 71, 72,
   115
lasix 29, 30, 31, 33, 35, 36
Law Commission 170
Lee, Martin 191
Lee, Robert W. Junior 11, 12, 14,
   22, 26
Lee, Robert W. Senior 11, 12,
   13, 15, 16, 21
   secret recordings of 16–20, 25
   trial 22–6
Leng, Caroline 190
Lewis, Butch 15–16, 25
Lewis, Lennox 20, 21
Lewis, Mike 254
Lewis, Peter 161
limited-rules fighting 160–72
Littleborough, road running
   129, 130
London Knights 106, 107
lottery money 8, 44, 60
   British Academy of Sport 42,
      46, 48, 53, 57
   chess 86, 87, 88
   hockey 257, 259, 260
   World Class Performance
      Fund 55

Luther King III, Rev. Martin 24

McAdam, Mike 262
McGuigan, Barry 220–1
McLaurin, Lord 48, 52, 55
McLeod, Mike 121–2, 128–9
McNeil, Colin 217, 218
McNeil, Ian 143, 144
McSorley, Marty 104, 107
mafia, US 12
Major, John 42, 43, 48, 192
Manchester, bowling clubs
   175–6
Marcelle, Clint 112–14
Marlin, David 31, 32, 37
martial arts 160–72
Matthews, Jabez 210–11, 212
Megson, Gary 113, 114
Members Courses, golf 151
Meyrowitz, Bob 162–3, 164,
   165, 171, 172
Middlesborough football club
   110
Midland Counties Athletic
Association (MCAA) 248
Milton Keynes Council 168
Mitchell, Dennis 101
mixed martial arts training 167
Modhal, Diane 91, 99–100, 101,
   102
Monsall, Ray 140
Moorcroft, David 246–7,
   249–50, 251
Moorer, Michael 14
Morgan, Ivor 195, 198
Morgan, Joanna 38, 39
Morris, Estelle 198
Morton Hooper, Tony 96–7, 101–2
Moss Side Stables 28
Mowlam, Mo 110
Muhammad Ali Boxing Reform
   Act 27

272